OFFGRID PRESENTS

OVERLAND

PROJECT GUIDE TO OFFROAD, BUG OUT & OVERLANDING VEHICLES

Copyright ©2023 Caribou Media Group, LLC

All rights reserved. No portion of this publication may be reproduced or transmitted in any form or by any means, electronic or mechanical, including photocopy, recording, or any information storage and retrieval system, without permission in writing from the publisher, except by a reviewer who may quote brief passages in a critical article or review to be printed in a magazine or newspaper, or electronically transmitted on radio, television, or the Internet.

Published by

Recoil Offgrid Books, an imprint of Caribou Media Group, LLC
5583 W. Waterford Ln. Suite D, Appleton, WI, 54913
offgridweb.com | gundigest.com

To order books or other products call 920.471.4522 ext.104
or visit us online at gundigeststore.com

DISCLAIMER: Prices and details for items featured in RECOIL are set by the manufacturers and retailers, and are subject to change without notice. Please read all local and federal laws carefully before attempting to purchase any products shown in this guide or building your own firearms. Laws change frequently and, although our text was accurate at the time it was originally published, it may have changed between then and what's currently legal.

ISBN-13: 978-1-959265-10-8

Edited and designed by Recoil Offgrid Staff

Printed in China

ScoutAutomatedPrintCode

TABLE OF CONTENTS

SECTION 1
Trucks
Mid-size or full-size, ½-ton or ¾-ton, gas or diesel — pickup trucks are the classic platform for an overland vehicle build.

P. 6

SECTION 2
Jeeps
Perhaps the most popular off-road vehicle of all time, the venerable Jeep deserves its own section.

P. 110

SECTION 3
SUVs
With room for passengers and secure storage for cargo, 4x4 SUVs are ideal for adventuring with the whole family.

P. 140

SECTION 4
Motorcycles & UTVs
These compact vehicles are light, fast, and nimble enough to go where full-size rigs can't.

P. 204

SECTION 5
Extreme
From a 5-ton military truck to an armored personnel carrier, these vehicles are truly unconventional.

P. 246

Introduction

*"Do not follow where the path may lead.
Go instead where there is no path and leave a trail."*

– Ralph Waldo Emerson

Mobility is a central aspect of independence. As children, we go through phases of increased mobility — crawling, walking, running, riding a bike, and eventually driving a car. With each stage of life, we gain the ability to venture further from the nest, reaching outside our comfort zone and accepting the risks that come with it. Make no mistake, there are *always* risks. If you expect to avoid danger, you can stay on your couch and experience the world through your TV, computer, or smartphone screen... but we can all agree that's not a life well-lived.

Statistically, driving a vehicle is the most dangerous activity we do on a daily basis. Road traffic crashes are one of the top ten causes of death for Americans under the age of 55, and more than 1.5 million injuries are reported as a result of crashes every year. So how do we balance these inherent risks with the many rewards of the open road? At OFFGRID magazine, we believe the answer is simple: preparedness.

Each time you get behind the wheel, you prepare for unexpected and dangerous situations, even if you do so subconsciously. The simple act of putting on a seatbelt is a step towards emergency preparedness — you're not hoping a crash occurs, but rather taking a preventative measure to enhance your safety if it does. The same can be said for placing a flashlight in the center console, a first aid kit in the glovebox, or jumper cables in the trunk. These are some of the simplest vehicle preparedness items that every car should have.

For those of us who venture off the beaten path — off-roaders, campers, hikers, hunters, fishermen, cross-country adventurers, and so on — preparedness is substantially more important than it is to the average motorist. A breakdown on the side of the interstate is a minor inconvenience; that same breakdown on a desolate mountain trail outside the reach of cell towers is much more challenging. Add severe weather to the mix, and it can escalate into a life-threatening situation. This fact has led many of us to take extra steps to make our vehicles more self-sufficient and secure for long journeys through remote areas. This is the principal tenet of building an overland vehicle.

Overland vehicles run the gamut from mild to extreme, and they can have two wheels, four wheels, or even no wheels at all. This book contains examples of all of the above. Some are ordinary trucks outfitted with all-terrain tires, a few pieces of recovery gear, basic hand tools, and emergency communications equipment. Knowledge and experience are more important than any piece of gear, so it's not necessary to break the bank to improve your vehicle's preparedness. But on the other end of the spectrum, you'll find high-dollar, custom-built rigs that incorporate long-travel suspension systems, heavily-upgraded drivetrains, advanced electronics, full sleeping quarters, and enough storage space to sustain an entire family for weeks. Some have mounted guns and armor for use on battlefields overseas, or for truly apocalyptic situations. There are even a few decommissioned military vehicles, including a tank, which push the limits of what an overland vehicle might be.

The articles we've assembled in this book come from the pages of OFFGRID magazine as well as our sister publications RECOIL and CARNIVORE. We've separated them into five categories: Trucks, Jeeps, SUVs, Motorcycles & UTVs, and Extreme vehicles. Whether your overland vehicle of choice has two wheels and a two-stroke engine, four wheels and a V6, or six wheels and an industrial-grade, turbo-diesel V8, we're certain you'll find something of interest here. And while we don't expect you to mimic any of these builds entirely, we hope you'll find some elements of inspiration for your own overland vehicle project. Stay safe, enjoy the drive, and blaze new trails with self-sufficient confidence.

— *Patrick McCarthy*
Editor, RECOIL OFFGRID

Trucks

War Wagon
Inside Wilco Products' Urban Attack Tundra
By C.D.

he problem with bug-out vehicles is that they are, as the name implies, reserved for bugging out — retreating. There's no shame in having this as your main strategy, but we all know that the need to remain flexible during a critical event is as important as getting your hits and keeping your gun running. In an EOTWAWKI scenario, your so-called bug-out vehicle could be called upon to conduct a frontal assault, support an ambush, evacuate casualties, set up a roadblock, or serve as a V-8-powered battering ram.

The ever-flexible staff at Wilco Products realized this, and it didn't take long for them to convince us that they could build a full-on urban attack truck that was capable of so much more than being loaded up with MOLLE gear and high-tailing it to the hills. With the help of a former U.S. Navy SEAL Ground Mobility program manager, the project quickly took shape and the Toyota "War Wagon" was born.

Roger Wilco
Wilco's experience is widespread, but the company's passion for Baja-style desert racing certainly played a huge part in the project, as did its ability to consider the high level of versatility required of a

modern pickup truck turned do-it-all vehicle. After careful consideration, the project managers decided to focus on three key areas: increased protection, efficient gear integration, and better off-road capabilities. But before even a single welding torch was sparked, a suitable platform for the build needed to be found.

Normally dealing with the storied Ford Raptor line, Wilco decided to go a different route and instead employed a Toyota for this build. A strong stock truck with a solid engine, the modern Tundras are also wickedly capable in the dirt. There was no debate about the drive system; four-wheel-drive would be essential to meet the demands of the unknown. It was also determined that a Double Cab configuration with a 6½-foot bed provided the best balance between interior and exterior room. With the objectives made clear and the proper truck in place, the work started.

Under the watchful eyes of their former SEAL advisor, the Wilco crew began by designing an integrated bedrail system that would be the backbone of the build. Much like a rail setup for a rifle, the bedrails provided a place for Wilco to attach various pieces of furniture that could be modified and moved around. Ammo cans were outfitted with rail mounts, while a Powertank mount was constructed to

1 TIREGATE

With 2-inch diameter by 0.95- to 0.120-inch-thick wall tubing — powder-coated in semi-gloss black — the VTXL TireGate is stylish enough for the streets, yet tough enough for hard use. The rear-facing spare tire doubles as a push bar in the event that the Tundra needs a boost.

MAKE:
Wilco Products

MODEL:
VTXL TireGate

MSRP:
$949

URL:
www.tiregate.com

2 REAR BUMPER

Even with the TireGate in place, Wilco stressed the need for maximum protection on the rear of the Tundra. This rear guard emulates the stock bumper's shape, but provides 100 times the strength.

MAKE:
Wilco Products

MODEL:
Custom Rear Bumper (steel production model available by year's end)

MSRP:
Contact for pricing

URL:
www.tiregate.com

3 ALUMINUM FRONT BUMPER

Custom built from 6061 T6 aluminum, this bumper was designed to be able to handle a large frontal impact. Ramming speed!

MAKE:
Wilco Products

MODEL:
Custom Front Bumper

MSRP:
Contact for pricing

URL:
www.tiregate.com

4 PRIMARY LIGHT

Providing incredible output in a relatively small and extremely durable package, the main OnX LED light bar utilizes off-road racing technology for extremely bright night driving capabilities.

MAKE:
Baja Designs

MODEL:
OnX Two-Cell 15-inch LED Light Bar

MSRP:
$695 (plus $75 wiring harness and $58 switch kit)

URL:
www.bajadesigns.com

5 BEDRAILS

Along with the roof rack and modular mounts, this test version of Wilco's bedrail system adds integrity and makes for simple storage that doesn't clutter the back of the truck. Pre-production versions will be released at the SEMA show at the end of the year.

MAKE:
Wilco Products

MODEL:
Custom Bedrails

MSRP:
Contact for pricing

URL:
www.tiregate.com

6 AMMO CAN MOUNTS

To help aid easy access to vital supplies (tools, tire chains and ammunition), a series of modular ammo cans can be mounted anywhere along the bedrail system. Bolts can be swapped for quick-pins in areas where thieves are punished by lead.

MAKE:
Wilco Products

MODEL:
Custom Ammo Can Mounts

MSRP:
Contact for pricing

URL:
www.tiregate.com

1 POWERTANK WITH MOUNT

This portable air tank makes on-the-fly tire inflations a snap, and can even run pneumatic power tools (such as an angle grinder for slicing through locks).

MAKE: Powertank
MODEL: 15-Pound Off-Road Series
MSRP: $687 (Power Tank); contact Wilco for pricing (Mount)
URL: www.powertank.com

2 ADJUSTABLE SUSPENSION

Height adjustable, spring seat monotube shocks that feature Pro Comp's exclusive Vehicle Specific Ride Tuning (VSRT) create the ultimate in adjustability and handling performance in nasty terrain.

MAKE: Pro Comp
MODEL: Pro Runner SS Shocks
MSRP: Contact for pricing
URL: www.procompusa.com

3 ROOF RACK

Maximizing storage space and adding a mounting point for additional lights, the Tundra's roof rack can support a spare tire, although this negatively affects the truck's center of gravity. We drove the Toyota hard off-road with more than 200 pounds on top and the well-made roof rack didn't so much as budge.

MAKE: Wilco Products
MODEL: Custom Roof Rack
MSRP: Contact for pricing
URL: www.tiregate.com

4 LT295/65R18 TIRES

Rock rejection ribs, a two-step tread block design and reinforced tri-ply construction helps to minimize flats and enhance stability, precision and durability.

MAKE: Pro Comp
MODEL: XTREME MT2 Radial Tires
MSRP: $400 each
URL: www.procompusa.com

5 18-INCH WHEELS

A durable flat-black powdercoat and sculpted eight-spoke design ensure that this wheel can stand up to any demands encountered on an excursion.

MAKE: Pro Comp
MODEL: Series 7033 Wheels
MSRP: $167 each
URL: www.procompusa.com

6 CERTIFIED SERVICE

(Not pictured)
When it comes to installing and tuning a full-size truck's suspension, consulting the experts is key; 4 Wheel Parts made sure that the Tundra was 100 percent squared away.

MAKE: 4 Wheel Parts
MSRP: Contact for pricing
URL: www.4wheelparts.com

1 SECONDARY DRIVING LIGHTS

With illumination out to 300 meters, each 4,300-lumen Squadron light packs four CREE XM-L2 LEDs into a super-rugged, aircraft-grade aluminum housing. Wilco tucked them away for maximum protection.

MAKE:
Baja Designs

MODEL:
Squadron LED 3-inch Driving Light

MSRP:
$300 each (plus $20 wiring harness)

URL:
www.bajadesigns.com

2 PISTOL LOCK BOX

Made from 14-guage, heavy-duty steel and bolted securely into the truck, the removable Smittybilt Lock Box offers excellent secure storage space for a secondary weapon and extra mags.

MAKE:
Smittybilt

MODEL:
Secure Lock Box with Mounting Sleeve

MSRP:
$70

URL:
www.smittybilt.com

3 SIDE SPOT LIGHTS

Literally the brightest LED lights ounce for ounce on the market, these lightweight accessory lights crank out over 1,800 lumens while drawing less than 22 watts.

MAKE:
Baja Designs

MODEL:
SII LED 3-Inch Flood/Work Lights

MSRP:
$175 each (plus $14 wiring harness)

URL:
www.bajadesigns.com

4 MOLLE-COMPATIBLE SEAT COVERS

With an integrated MOLLE platform and six standard pouches, Coverking's Tactical Seat Covers allow for uncluttered storage of gear and components.

MAKE:
Coverking

MODEL:
Tactical Custom Seat Covers

MSRP:
$230

URL:
www.coverking.com

5 .50-CALIBER M2HB MACHINEGUN

What truck owner doesn't want a heavy machinegun in the bed of his vehicle?

PROVIDED BY:
Independent Studio Services

URL:
www.issprops.com

6 CUSTOM FABRICATED LIGHT MOUNTS/ WIRING

(Not pictured)

As an authorized Baja Designs dealer, SoCal SuperTrucks made sure that the lights were wired and mounted correctly for minimal battery drain and maximum illumination. They were also able to tie in an aftermarket infrared backup camera to the factory monitor/head unit.

MAKE:
SoCal SuperTrucks

MSRP:
Contact for pricing

URL:
www.socalsupertrucks.com

provide easy and quick roadside air access in the event of a flat tire. They soon decided to integrate a roof rack into this configuration. Despite the fact that Toyotas are notorious for bed/cab flex, a free-floating system was designed to keep the weight off of the actual roof of the cab. Many off-roaders opt to place a spare on the roof, but Wilco's Baja experience has proven that a 140-pound spare on the top of the vehicle does not lend itself to better handling — or ease of use, especially when alone or under fire.

Once the bedrail system was dialed in, Wilco removed the stock tailgate and installed the crown jewel of its off-road collection: the VTXL TireGate. Proven to be both durable and functional, the TireGate places the spare in a much more practical location (in terms of both weight bias and access) and adds a bit of room to the bed without compromising performance. Two quick-pins and a pivot allow the TireGate to be opened in a hurry, and the large spare acts as a makeshift push bar in case the Tundra needs to be pushed to safety by a supporting vehicle. The next step for Wilco was to fabricate a durable rear bumper guard that would function as a step into the bed; in conjunction with the TireGate, these mods effectively turned the rear end of the Toyota into a fortress of clean lines and steel tubing.

Forward Facing

The next step for the build was the topic of much debate: What to do with the front end of the truck. The Wilco team knew that the end result needed to be strong enough to blast through a barrier, but weight can add up quickly and the front end of the truck is not where you want additional pounds. The solution, they determined, was a matter of materials: Wilco opted for an aluminum bumper/grille guard. As the part began to take shape, mounts were installed to accommodate what Wilco considered to be one of the most important aspects of the project build: the lights.

Baja Designs has made a name in off-road night racing for a reason, and the company's LED technology is second to none. Consulting with the Wilco crew, Baja Designs suggested that a primary OnX two-cell 15-inch driving light be mounted atop the bumper guard to provide the majority of nighttime needs. Additionally, two forward-facing Squadron 3-inch LEDs would be tucked inside of the grille guard to provide auxiliary illumination while staying completely out of the way. All three lights were mounted and tested in order to find the best throw at high speeds. Lastly, Baja Designs opted to mount two SII 3-inch sidelights to the roof rack. These super-bright spots can be activated both to the sides and the rear of the vehicle, creating an *I Am Legend* functionality that can turn a dark city

street or back road into a safe avenue of approach. SoCal SuperTrucks took care of all wiring and made sure that the waterproof connectors were tucked out of the way and integrated into the various rail systems of the truck.

With all of the armor and lighting in place, Wilco handed the truck off to the team at 4 Wheel Parts to install a multitude of Pro Comp components aimed at transforming the mild stock Toyota chassis into an off-road race-ready platform. Various lift kits were considered before Pro Comp's exclusive Vehicle Specific Ride Tuning (VSRT) suspension came up as the perfect solution for this project. With several inches of adjustability, the suspension keeps the Toyota at a reasonable height and doesn't murder the fuel mileage, while also giving the truck a much more race-inspired stance. Although the stock wheels are strong, Pro Comp's Series 7033 wheels were put in place for even more resistance against warping and damage over hard hits. For an aggressive pattern that could still be ripped down a city street, Pro Comp's XTREME MT2 tires gave the Tundra the footing it needed for both on- and off-road performance.

Firepower

Finally, Coverking's MOLLE-compatible seat covers were placed inside, and a Smittybilt pistol lock box was bolted to the floor of the cab. But the best modification was still to come.

With so much bed space available, Wilco chose to employ a tripod-mounted, belt-fed .50-caliber M2HB machinegun in the center of the bed. With shooters in the passenger and back seats able to cover the front and sides of the vehicle, the .50-cal is able to rain down deadly fire on pursuers, evaders, and everyone in between. Of course, we'll keep this mod tucked away in a safe place until the SHTF, but we're confident that if and when things get nasty, the incredible firepower provided by the 50 will make the already-menacing Tundra a force to be reckoned with.

In the end, the crew at Wilco did precisely what they set out to do: apply carefully considered modifications to an already-capable stock platform in order to create a versatile and tough vehicle. Although this truck can be driven around a city without drawing too much attention, it can easily transition to rugged off-road use, and the pre-existing mounting points for heavy weapons give it the potential to become a force multiplier in the truest sense of the term.

Whatever the end purpose it serves, Wilco Products' Toyota Tundra is certainly more than a bug-out vehicle — this truck is able to bug out, in, over, around, and through whatever is in its path, depending on what the mission dictates.

MAKE: Toyota
MODEL: Tundra Limited Edition Double Cab
YEAR: 2011
ENGINE: 5.7L V-8
DRIVETRAIN: 4WD/ Six-Speed Automatic

Dillon Defender

This Land Rover Has Everything You Need for a Trip to the Mall. Assuming the Mall is in Mogadishu.

By Iain Harrison
Photography by Henry Z. De Kuyper

This might just be the most formidable vehicle we've ever featured in our magazine. Why? There are many reasons, but we'll start with three. The kinder, gentler end of the force continuum is handled by a pair of 240 Bravos. But when things get a little hairy, the crew has the option to employ the persuasive power of 3,000 rounds of 7.62mm, courtesy of an M134D minigun.

1 OPTICS

Mounted to the rear bumper is a telescopic mast holding a FLIR TacFLIR 230 RSTA system with both visible and IR stabilized cameras. Vehicle commander can control the ball from his station and has a color monitor which can provide 360 degree views while the Defender is hull down behind cover. Exoskeleton folds down to the rear and provides rollover protection to crew. FLIR system cost: $165,000.

2 LIGHTS
Infra red driving lights provide illumination for driver and commander while running in darkness under NODs. Bull bar has plenty of tie-down points for camo nets and personal kit.

Conceived as a complete bolt-on kit, the Dillon Defender package allows a standard Land Rover GS 110 to transform into a gun truck, requiring only basic handtools and an afternoon's worth of spannering to complete the job. According to Mike Leavitt, a former Marine and Baja racer who is Dillon Aero's brains behind the project, Special Forces teams had been using local talent and materials while downrange to fashion gun mounts on whatever vehicles they happened to be using.

With the almost universal availability of the Land Rover, it was a natural choice as the basis for the Dillon Defender, creating a dedicated fire support vehicle that could overwhelm any enemy with a devastating volume of accurate fire. "Because of our relationship with a lot of those guys, they asked us for a palletized kit that would allow conversion without a whole lot of modifications to the vehicle," Leavitt says. "We came up with a sectionalized system that breaks down into a 4x4-foot cube, and with it, there's no drilling or welding needed, just basic handtools."

The DD's beefy bumpers bolt up to the stock frame mounts and, once in place, serve as the foundation for the rest of the system. Originally, the rollcage and ring mount were supported by a framework of one-piece vertical members, but that got refined further once word got around the SF community. According to Leavitt, "Some guys from Fort Bragg came forth with the requirement for a vehicle that would be ready to fight within 60 seconds of being deployed from a Chinook."

As it stood, the original Dillon Defender was too tall to fit inside the cargo bay, so a system of locking hinges was incorporated into the rollcage to allow it to fold backward. Obviously, with 500 pounds of ammo in the ready-use racks plus the weight of the gun and batteries, standing the assembly back up is no easy task. "During demonstrations, we cheat a little by running the winch cable over the hood and attaching it to the rollcage," Leavitt says. "As the driver backs out of the Chinook, he bumps the winch button and up she goes." Spring-loaded locking pins within the hinges deploy automatically, ensuring a solid joint.

Because of the minigun's appetite for delicious, wholesome, and linked 4B1T (pronounced "four-bit" and meaning "four ball rounds and one tracer"), the Defender is strewn with quick-detach mounting points for ammo cans and cargo bins. These were adapted from aircraft seat tracks, allowing for secure, yet quickly released containers to be snapped into place. Think Picatinny rails, but for trucks.

IR floodlights provide illumination for driving under goggles, while a winch bumper offers plenty of tie-down and recovery points. In order to handle the extra weight, ASFIR springs and shocks can be incorporated into the kit, depending on the wishes of the user. One item that is very rarely touched, however, is the

1 WINCH
Substantial winch bumper has aircraft seat track at strategic points for QD storage containers.

2 TAIL GUN
Tail gunner provides rear protection with M240B while M134D can rotate 360 degrees. Ring mount has its own power supply, so there's nothing to restrict its swing.

3 AIR TANK
Air tank provides power for telescopic mast, tools and tires.

4 MOTOR
The inline-four stock Land Rover engine is utterly reliable and long lived, even in extremely dusty desert conditions.

engine. Although the 2.5L naturally aspirated diesel lump produces barely enough horsepower to get out of its own way, it's bulletproof and will run on marginal fuel in any environment. "I don't need it to sound cool. I don't need it to go fast. I just need it to get from point A to point B every single time I turn the key," says Leavitt. And really, who's going to have the balls to challenge you at a stoplight when you're rocking a minigun up top?

Although the Land Rover was the first and obvious choice as a base vehicle, others are undergoing fitment, including Mercedes G wagons, Toyota HiLux trucks, and several UTVs. So, next time you see a Polaris RZR at your local big-box sporting goods store, think how cool it would look with an M134 on the roof.

Battering Ram

Spike's Tactical's Contemporary Take on a Classic Dodge

By John Schwartze
Photography by Q Concepts

2013 DODGE
3500
6.7L CUMMINS DIESEL
SIX-SPEED AUTOMATIC

Having a vehicle to promote your business is never a bad idea. However, it seems that most promotional cars or trucks are all show and no business. Typically they're nothing more than some blinged-out, lifted pickup with wild graphics and tinted windows that the owner uses to drive to nightclubs so he can get out and high-five his "yes" crowd. In other words, they proudly represent their company by driving something that looks like Pimp My Ride threw up on it.

For those of you familiar with Spike's Tactical and its products, you'll know the company is a no-nonsense brand with a fighting spirit and Second Amendment verbiage pumping through its veins. So when Spike himself was going to invest in a truck to tout his namesake business, we knew that any pretentious B.S. would take a backseat to practicality and style...literally. After all, how many trucks do you see out there with the bed removed for a 360-degree ring-mounted minigun? We thought so.

So how did all this come to pass? Rob Fife of Gunner Fabrications had become friends with Spike Register (owner of Spike's Tactical) not only through being a customer, but also a fellow gearhead and gun enthusiast. After bumping into each other at SEMA and the SHOT Show, Rob continually hit up Spike about creating a promotional truck for him that'd do his company's mission statement justice on four wheels. Rob sold Spike on the idea of doing a modern interpretation of the old Dodge Power Wagons and Carryalls popular in the '40s and '50s. If you're unfamiliar with what these look like, take some time

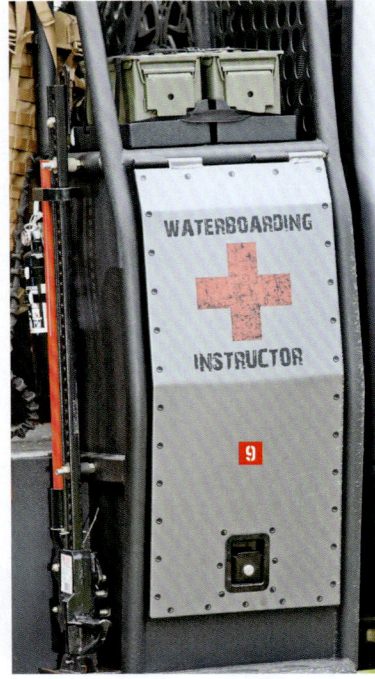

1 EXO-SKELETON
MAKE: Custom
URL: www.gunnerfabrication.com

2 TOP LIGHT BAR
MAKE: Rigid Industries
MODEL: 50-inch
URL: www.rigidindustries.com

3 CENTER LIGHT BAR
MAKE: Rigid Industries
MODEL: 20-inch
URL: www.rigidindustries.com

4 LOWER LIGHTS
MAKE: Rigid Industries
MODEL: 12-inch dual-stack
URL: www.rigidindustries.com

5 HEADLIGHTS
MAKE: Recon Accessories
MODEL: Smoked Projector Headlights
URL: www.gorecon.com

6 WINCH
MAKE: Smittybilt
MODEL: XRC12 10,000-lb
URL: www.smittybilt.com

7 WHEELS
MAKE: Stazworks
MODEL: Cheyenne w/double bead lock
URL: www.stazworks.com

8 TIRES
MAKE: Toyo
MODEL: MT 40/15.5R20
URL: www.toyotires.com

9 STORAGE COMPARTMENTS
MAKE: Custom
URL: www.gunnerfabrication.com

to Google them. They're definitely fierce-looking trucks and way more off-road capable than their Ford and Chevy counterparts of the day.

The platform they ultimately agreed on was a Cummins-diesel-powered 2013 Dodge 3500. Spike bought the truck new and had it delivered to a dealership in Texas near Rob's shop and off they went. Spike essentially gave Rob carte blanche on the theme for it. Other than knowing he wanted a machinegun on the back and some Rigid lights, it was essentially a blank canvas to strike a balance between cool and killer. Since Spike's Tactical offers a lower called the Hellbreaker with engraving reminiscent of the A10 nose art — and Rob is also a fan of the aircraft — it was a natural choice to go with a Thunderbolt-themed truck.

Spike wanted a 40-inch tire, and Rob likes to keep things low-slung, so it was tricky to find a way to incorporate both. A 3.5-inch long-arm Icon Suspension coilover replacement up front helps stabilize things, given the increased wheel size. Rob cut about 6 inches out of where the fenders were and added flares back on. The corners of the cab were also sliced into and replated to help with clearance issues. The tubing on the front was all custom made to protect the engine, and also folds down to be able to access it or serve as a nifty cowcatcher (or insurgent plow).

The truck was vinyl-wrapped in red, gray, and black to give it some distinctive menace instead of going with a predictable olive drab green paintjob. Rigid lights adorn the front and sides and a siren also provides some additional "out of the way, dumbass" decibels. Custom lockers were built into the sides and back to house some ARs and other goodies. The ring mount for the Vietnam-era minigun is an M66 unit off a 5-ton military truck, circa 1986.

The original 52-gallon gas tank was exchanged for a smaller 32-gallon cell in the rear to accommodate the platform that sits where the bed once was. It's all protected by a custom-made ¼-inch skidplate. Running boards were added to the back and flushed out with rear hangers. The hitch assembly was moved to the outside so it can haul a fifth wheel and the bed could serve as a platform for a side-by-side if need be. Stainless hardware and aluminum on the deck plates helps keep everything corrosion resistant.

Inside this beast, things continue to get interesting. An A10 control stick operates the airhorn, forward-facing lights, and siren — and Spike can even toggle through the gears with it since the shift linkage was moved from the column to the center. A FLIR thermal camera system sits on top of the cab and complements the night vision accouterments Spike has inside the truck. Mastercraft Baja RS seats reside in place of the originals and straddle the custom switch panel for the lights. A GPS monitor and FLIR monitor sit in front of the passenger, and everyone, including the gunner, can communicate via a Rugged Radios RRP660 intercom with Vox operations and iPhone quick-connect.

This truck has already been on some long treks, and we think it's a pretty healthy interpretation of a vintage battlefield hauler. Oh, and you may also see it sporting a paddleboard on the custom-made roof rack. After all, warfare often calls for watersports intermissions. Don't laugh — Robert Duvall showed us this is in fact a practical activity to celebrate successful strafing runs. ✶

1 RING MOUNT
MAKE:
U.S. Military M66

2 MINIGUN
MAKE:
General Electric
MODEL:
24-volt .308 caliber

3 WEAPON LIGHT
MAKE:
Surefire
MODEL:
Hellfire
URL:
www.surefire.com

4 THERMAL IMAGING
MAKE:
FLIR
URL:
www.flir.com

5 SEATS
MAKE:
Mastercraft
MODEL:
Baja RS
URL:
www.mastercraftsafety.com

6 SWITCH CONSOLE
MAKE:
Custom
URL:
www.gunnerfabrication.com

7 SHIFTER/CONTROLLER
MAKE:
A10 Thunderbolt

8 RIFLE
MAKE:
Spike's Tactical
MODEL:
ST Compressor SBR - 300BLK w/ MRS-2 Suppressor, Spike's Tactical billet micro sights, and Black Spider M0129 micro red dot
URL:
www.spikestactical.com

You Are What You Drive

John Wayne Walding's F-250 "Super Duty" is a Vehicular Metaphor for His Life's Mantra

By John Schwartze
Photos by Q Concepts

2011 FORD F-250 SUPER DUTY
6.7L DIESEL V-8
6R140 AUTOMATIC
WWW.STOESCUSTOM.COM, WWW.ROADARMOR.COM,
WWW.STARWOODMOTORS.COM

In RECOIL Issue 19, we profiled John Wayne Walding, a decorated Green Beret nearly killed in the Battle of Shok Valley who also became the first amputee to complete Special Forces sniper school. While his commitment to his country and the Army speaks for itself, honoring an individual like Walding with a vehicle to commemorate his service and approach to life is no easy feat. First, you need the right concept. Second, you need the right materials. And last but not least, you need the right builders to combine all these elements into something practical, personal, and robust enough to make other Special Forces operators say, "Hey, I'd drive that."

Mark Hanson, CEO of Road Armor, first began conceptualizing a truck along those lines with his friend, the legendary SEAL sniper Chris Kyle. The reason being, when special operation forces (SOF) personnel retire after getting to use some of the most sophisticated technology on the planet, buying an off-the-lot car or truck isn't exactly a lateral move. Since so many in the SOF community continue work in a similar arena after their military service, it only makes sense that their means of transportation speaks to that lifestyle. Initially, Kyle's Ford longbed F-350 was to serve as the platform for this brainchild…then the unimaginable happened.

Kyle's sudden death put the brakes on the project, but Hanson didn't give up hope. Walding was also a friend of Kyle, had a similar truck that Hanson knew about, and felt he'd be someone Kyle would've wanted to see this

1 IR LIGHTS
MAKE:
Rigid Industries
MODEL:
4-inch IR LED Lights
URL:
www.rigidindustries.com

2 WINCH
MAKE:
Warn
MODEL:
16.5ti
URL:
www.warn.com

3 BUMPER
MAKE:
Road Armor
MODEL:
Ford Super Duty Front Stealth Winch Bumper With Pre-Runner Guard
URL:
www.roadarmor.com

4 LOWER LIGHT BAR
MAKE:
Rigid Industries
MODEL:
20-inch Single-Row LED Light
URL:
www.rigidindustries.com

5 GRILLE
MAKE:
Rigid Industries
MODEL:
Super Duty LED Grille
URL:
www.rigidindustries.com

6 BUMPER LIGHTS
MAKE:
Rigid Industries
MODEL:
D-Series LED Lights
URL:
www.rigidindustries.com

7 TIRES
MAKE:
Toyo
MODEL:
Open Country 35x12.5xR20
URL:
www.toyotires.com

8 WHEELS
MAKE:
BMF
MODEL:
Novakane
URL:
www.bmfwheels.com

9 FENDER FLARES
MAKE:
Bushwacker
MODEL:
Pocket-Style Fender Flare
URL:
www.bushwacker.com

10 UPHOLSTERY
MAKE:
Ferrari
MODEL:
458 leather with custom stitching
URL:
www.starwoodmotors.com

project come to life with. It was only a matter of time before Walding and Hanson teamed up to turn his 2011 F-250 Super Duty into what he'd previously envisioned. "He carries stuff in his truck that's part of his daily life," Hanson says. "Anything you'd need at the range can be put in that truck."

Aesthetically the truck is pretty inconspicuous from afar, but that's pretty apropos for the quiet professional who drives it. The entire body has been coated in a Kevlar-based lining by Starwood Motors. It can spend a day at the range getting filthy and all it needs is a good pressure wash. No fading, no waxing necessary, and it's lifetime guaranteed. The Road Armor custom bumpers and fender flares were Kryptek coated, a pattern popular with operators. In the back you'll find an ARB air compressor and Gun Vault for Walding to store his gear. The DiamondBack truck cover keeps everything sealed up and is strong enough to support the weight of two quads.

The 6.7L diesel has been upgraded with a Spartan tuner, Airaid intake, AirDog fuel system, and exhales through a large-diameter Magnaflow exhaust. A 4-inch Pro Comp lift accommodates the large BMF Novakane wheels and Toyo meats. Up front you'll find a variety of Rigid Industries LED and IR lights as well as a Rigid custom grille and Warn 16.5ti winch.

Starwood Motors used Ferrari 458 leather on the seats, the headrests of which are embroidered with Walding's company logo on one side — 5 Toes Custom — and the Green Beret insignia on the other. And since duty is nothing without honor, the center armrest has also been stitched with names of the fallen soldiers Walding served with. "These guys made an impact on John to live his life better," Hanson says. "I owe it to the fallen to live well; to be a father, but a good father. To be a husband, but a good husband," Walding says. A Gunner Fab pistol mount resides on the

1 RIFLE
MAKE: 5 Toes Custom
MODEL: 5.56 16-inch with 1-8.5x34mm Bushnell Elite optic, AR Gold trigger
URL:
www.5toescustom.com
www.bushnell.com
www.americantrigger.com

2 RIFLE
MAKE: 5 Toes Custom
MODEL: 5TC .308 LRPR (long-range precision rifle) Remington 700 trued; Proof Research carbon-fiber barrel; Remington RACS chassis; Jewell trigger
URL:
www.5toescustom.com
www.proofresearch.com
www.remington.com
www.brownells.com

3 RIFLE
MAKE: 5 Toes Custom
MODEL: .308 Come and Take It; 5TC D.O.L. Action; Obermeyer barrel; Manners T6A stock; Jewell trigger
URL:
www.5toescustom.com
www.obermeyerbarrels.com
www.mannersstocks.com
www.brownells.com

4 RIFLE
MAKE: Daniel Defense
MODEL: M4 16-inch with Trijicon ACOG optic; Bravo Company OSS Bannar brake; AR Gold trigger
URL:
www.danieldefense.com
www.trijicon.com
www.bravocompanyusa.com
www.americantrigger.com

5 RIFLE
MAKE: 5 Toes Custom
MODEL: .308 with 16-inch Proof Research carbon-fiber barrel; Bravo Company OSS Bannar brake; AR Gold trigger
URL:
www.5toescustom.com
www.proofresearch.com
www.bravocompanyusa.com
www.americantrigger.com

6 RIFLE
MAKE: 5 Toes Custom
MODEL: 5.56 16-inch with Vortex 1-6x optic, CMC trigger
URL:
www.5toescustom.com
www.vortexoptics.com
www.cmctriggers.com

7 STORAGE
MAKE: Truck Vault
MODEL: Custom
URL:
www.truckvault.com

8 PISTOL
MAKE: Kimber
MODEL: Custom 1911 Desert Warrior .45
URL:
www.kimberamerica.com

9 HOLSTER
MAKE: Gunner Fab
MODEL: Pistol Clamp Mount CO-CLMP
URL:
www.conditionzeromounts.com

driver side door — carjackers, you've been warned.

Delivery of the finished product to Walding was carried out by Hanson and Chris Kyle's brother Jeff. The official send-off was caught on camera, and was an emotional affair on many levels. "It gave me some closure about Chris," Hanson says. "We were about to start on Chris' truck when he was killed. We got to finish with someone who Chris knew and would have approved of. John was one of Chris' heroes."

"To me it represents what the special operators stand for; everything worth doing is worth overdoing," Walding says. "There were times in my life I've protected the American dream, but wasn't living it. I could never afford a truck like this and it's a way of receiving thanks. You never realize how much it means when people say thanks to a veteran."

War-X-Four

A Marine Infantryman's Take on the Ideal Truck

By John Schwartze
Photos by Joseph Dowling

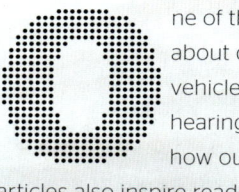ne of the fun things about covering vehicles like this is hearing stories of how our Transport articles also inspire readers to start their own build. In this case, Chris Pate of San Antonio, Texas, befriended an individual whose Tundra had appeared in our Issue 12 of RECOIL, and it got him thinking about what his dream vehicle would be. Having served 10 years in the Marine Corps, much of which was as an infantry squad leader in Iraq and Afghanistan, and participated in MMA, Chris wasn't about to spend his deployment pay on some latte-sipping hybrid.

He wanted to create the biggest, baddest Tacoma out there. Why a Tacoma? He'd previously owned one and knew that it could not only take a beating, but could hold its own next to Tundras and Jeeps. So he got to calling dealerships until he found one two hours away that had the platform he wanted — double cab, TRD package, four-wheel drive, and it had to come in black.

Now that the he had the base, next came getting endorsements from companies that made the products he believed in. The goal? To take his truck all way to SEMA, one of the world's biggest automobile aftermarket conventions. And after coordinating with sponsors while he was deployed, in 2015 he got a chance to do just that. They knew he was serious, and backed his play. So let's see all the cool gear that made its way into the mix.

2011 TOYOTA TACOMA TRD SPORT 4X4 4L V-6 AUTOMATIC

1 LIGHT
MAKE: Golight
MODEL: Stryker HID
URL: www.golight.com

2 LIGHT
MAKE: Pro Comp
MODEL: Pro Comp 7-inch HID
URL: www.procompusa.com

3 LIGHTBAR
MAKE: Zero Dark Lighting
MODEL: 20-inch LED lightbar
URL: www.zerodarklighting.com

4 LIGHT
MAKE: Zero Dark Lighting
MODEL: 3D Rocket Pod
URL: www.zerodarklighting.com

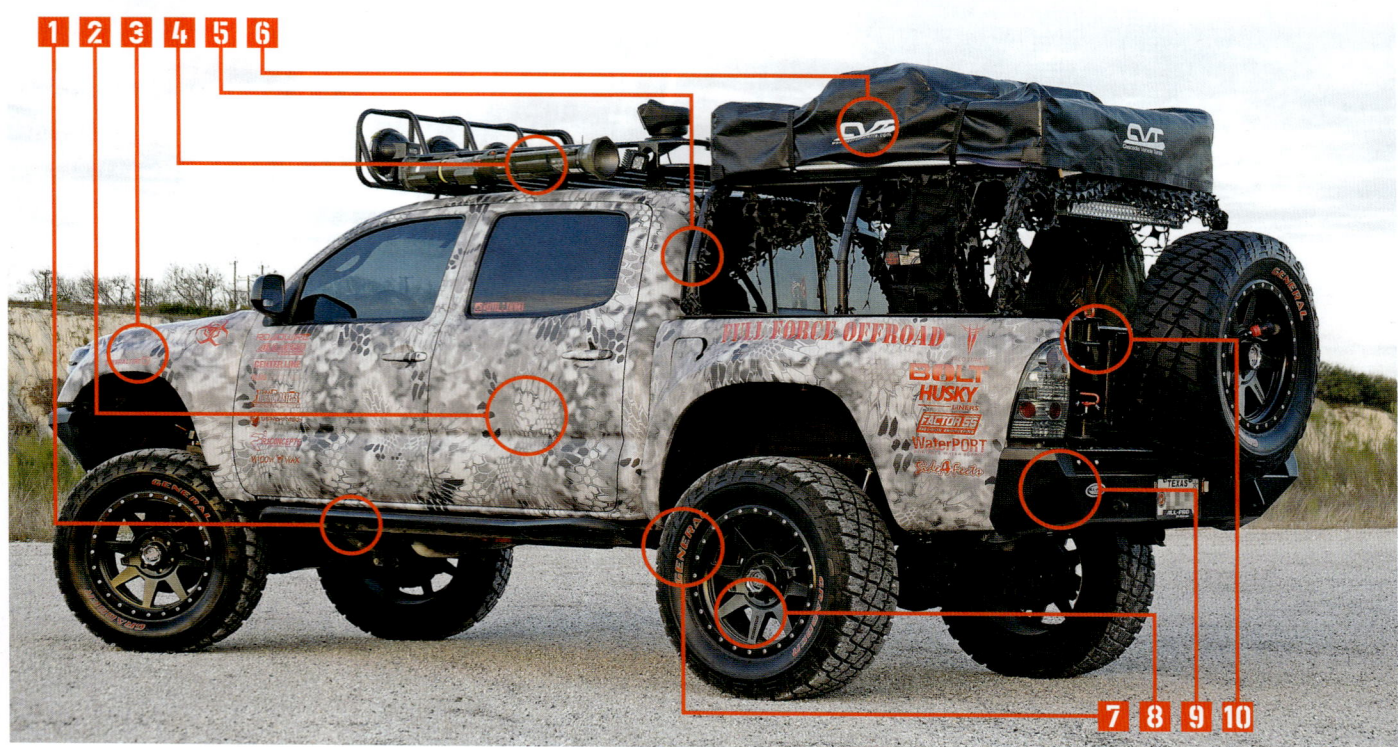

1 ROCK SLIDERS
MAKE:
All Pro Offroad
MODEL:
Extreme-Duty APEX Series Rock Sliders
URL:
www.allprooffroad.com

2 KRYPTEK RAID WRAP
MATERIALS/PATTERN:
www.usnightvision.com
INSTALLATION:
www.sideafects.com

3 FENDERS
MAKE:
Glassworks Unlimited
MODEL:
4-inch front, 4.5-inch rear
URL:
www.glassworksunlimited.com

4 ROCKET LAUNCHER
MAKE:
Saab Bofors Dynamics
MODEL:
AT4

5 ROOF RACK
MAKE:
Smittybilt
MODEL:
Defender
URL:
www.smittybilt.com

6 TENT
MAKE:
Cascadia Vehicle Roof Top Tents
MODEL:
CVT Mt. Shasta
URL:
www.cascadiatents.com

7 TIRES
MAKE:
General Tire
MODEL:
35-inch Grabber MT
URL:
www.generaltire.com

8 WHEELS
MAKE:
Center Line
MODEL:
20-inch RT-2
URL:
www.centerlinewheels.com

9 REAR BUMPER
MAKE:
All Pro Offroad
MODEL:
High clearance rear bumper
URL:
www.allprooffroad.com

10 TIRE MOUNT
MAKE:
Wilco Offroad
MODEL:
Tiregate Vertical Mount
URL:
www.wilcooffroad.com

11 RIFLE

DWS AR-15 Alpha Shooting Sports stainless steal fluted heavy 16-inch barrel and lower parts kit, DWS titanium nitride/ZrN-coated BCG with Strike Indusitres MegaFins-XL M-LOK handguard, Strike Industries M-LOK Covers V2, Strike Industries Hex Selector Switches with 60/90 Combo Shaft 3-in-1, BCM grip, Magpul pro sights, Hexmag magazine, Mission First minimalist stock, Strike Industries Triple Crown-Comp with Ferfrans concussion reduction device
URL:
www.facebook.com/TomorrowsAdvancedGunfighters

The V-6 motor was upgraded with a Volant cold air intake and ram scoop, along with straight pipe exhaust. The four-wheel-drive system was re-geared for the larger Center Line wheels and 35-inch General Tires by Nitro Gear & Axle. Those huge meats are brought to a stop with the help of R1 Concepts E-Line series rotors. A 6-inch Fabtech high-performance lift with Dirt Logic shocks, Icon Vehicle Dynamics Uniball upper control arms, and powdercoated coilovers round out the suspension accouterments.

Bodywork consists of a 2014 front end, custom mesh grille, All Pro Offroad rock sliders, single hoop Apex front bumper with a Warn winch, and All Pro Offroad metal rear bumper. Lights abound with ProComp 7-inch HID lights (two spot and two flood) lights. Police Strobes and LED lights in the grille, two

5 PISTOLS

(Top) Glock 17 Gen 4 with DWS EXO slide packages and RMR slidecut package with Trijicon Suppressor Night Sights. Trijicon RMR with custom stippling, frame reduction and undercuts. Cerakoted graphite black with DWS trigger job, threaded and fluted S3fsolutions black nitride barrel with S3f ext base pad.

(Middle) DWS Glock 17 Gen 3 with MRK II Destroyer slide package hand-polished and coated titanium nitride. Slide also has RMR cut and plate cover package. ALG Defense 6-Second Mount and Aimpoint T2 optic. Also a S3fsolutions black nitride fluted barrel. Custom stippling and frame reduction with undercuts.

(Bottom) DWS M&P 9mm with enhanced EDC slide package with black multicam cerakote. Match grade Storm Lake threaded barrel. Trijicon HD Night Sights and Salient Arms trigger with Apex duty carry kit. Inforce APL light with 10-8 Performance magwell. DWS ext base plate.

URL:
www.facebook.com/
TomorrowsAdvancedGunfighters

Golight HID Stryker Searchlights operated by an interior joystick, and various other LEDs reside in the hoodscoop and license plate. IPCW Bermuda black LED taillights, and custom headlights with HIDs, red and white halos, and red LEDs round out the package. Glassworks front and rear flared fenders allow space for some dips and jumps when this thing hits the dirt. A full Kryptek Typhon wrap adds a bit of camo effect to the overall aesthetic.

All Pro Offroad storage sits in the bed for some of Chris' Dynamic Weapons Solutions firearms. A Defender roof rack, CVT Mt. Shasta three-person tent, and WaterPORT portable water supply help keep supplies stacked up and off-road trips a bit more practical when not in the comforts of custom leather seats. Two Optima batteries help keep juice flowing to the Uniden Bearcat CB Radio, Pioneer head unit, and custom stereo that are situated in a carbon-fiber dash with a custom console. Oh, a police siren and a HornBlaster's Conductors Special train horn kit will ensure a path is cleared, even for the hearing impaired who will probably feel the sound on their teeth.

Although Chris plans on selling this beauty, he's already eyeballing a new project. Thanks for your service to our country. We're glad you can enjoy the fruits of your labor in one badass truck.

1 FRONT BUMPER
MAKE: All Pro Offroad
MODEL: Apex
URL: allprooffroad.com

2 WINCH
MAKE: Warn
MODEL: ZEON 8
URL: warn.com

3 SEATS
MAKE: Roadwire
MODEL: Leather
URL: roadwire.com

4 MACHETE
MAKE: Gerber Gear
MODEL: Gator
URL: gerbergear.com

Miami Vice

Perhaps Crockett and Tubbs Should Trade the Ferrari in for a Devolro Diablo

By John Schwartze
Photos by Q Concepts

DEVOLRO DIABLO
CURRENT MODEL TOYOTA
TUNDRA
5.7L SUPERCHARGED
iFORCE V-8
4WD SIX-SPEED AUTOMATIC
WWW.DEVOLRO.COM

hile perusing a random web search for "bug-out vehicles" one day, we came across an image of this truck. That alone was enough to warrant further investigation of the website. What we found was a company in Miami called Devolro that began around 2000 after founder Ed Orlov received offers to buy a truck he'd bought and modified for hunting expeditions. Then, he decided to see if he could generate the same interest by making more. And he did.

What does Devolro mean? It's actually Orlov Ed spelled backward. The company offers several models of trucks built on the most recent Toyota Tundra platforms since they felt it offered the best quality to carry the company's name, although plans to include Dodge, Jeep, and Chevy in their fleet are in the pipeline, says Devolro Manager Kiril Kalan. If you own a truck and want some of the same modifications made to it, bring it in and Devolro can give it the same proverbial Q Branch treatment.

The Diablo is Devolro's flagship vehicle, which, going over the list of options, is definitely not just some tacticool,

TRUCKS • MIAMI VICE | 81

trust-fund-baby truck that's all show and no go. Want a supercharged motor? Check. Ballistic armoring? Done. Weapons storage? You got it. Mobile office? You can have that too. Total build time, depending on your options, is approximately four to six weeks. So let's delve deeper in into Devolro's trappings.

A 7-inch lift includes BDS components and control arms with Icon Vehicle Dynamics Stage 5 shocks and coilovers. The particular model pictured here had 22-inch Fuel Wheels and Falken run-flat rubber. Brembo six-piston breaks bring this hulking giant to a stop. How hulking? Fully loaded, a Diablo tips the scales around 7,000 pounds — that's pretty good considering the GVWR is about the same as a factory Tundra.

Powering the Diablo is a supercharged 5.7L iForce V-8 with an upgraded transmission and ECU to handle the additional torque and horsepower, make that 525 hp and 500 lb-ft of torque. A 46-gallon tank replaces the factory version, which Kalan tells us gives a fully loaded Diablo a range of approximately 500 miles. Owners can choose from one or two batteries that can be switched between main and auxiliary power for optional Warn winches or inverter switches that may be located in the cab or bed for any accessories you want to bring along. A towing capacity of 10,000 pounds means your bug-out boat or ATVs can come along without a problem.

The entire body is coated in Line-X for durability and can be tinted to any standard vehicle color. Clients can also choose proprietary armor paneling from B6 to B7 level. Areas of protection include the body, roof, floor, frame, battery, rear door, fuel tank, engine, exhaust, and door supports. Ballistic glass and a 42mm composite windshield rated at NIJ III-A standards are other options. Devolro claims a full dose of B7 and special glass only adds 750 pounds and is rated to withstand 7.62x51mm rounds.

Clients can select built-in enclosures for weapons storage in the

1 ROOF LIGHTBAR
MAKE: Rigid
MODEL: 50-inch LED
URL: www.rigidindustries.com

2 SIDE LIGHTBAR
MAKE: Rigid
MODEL: 20-inch LED
URL: www.rigidindustries.com

3 BODY ARMOR
MAKE: Devolro
MODEL: B6 or B7
URL: www.devolro.com

4 BODY COATING
MAKE: Line-X
COLOR: Black (other colors available)
URL: www.linex.com

5 BRAKES
MAKE: Brembo
MODEL: Six-piston big brake kit
URL: www.brembo.com

6 WHEELS
MAKE: Fuel Off-Road Wheels
MODEL: R22 five-piece
URL: www.fueloffroad.com

7 FRONT LIGHTS
MAKE: ARB
MODEL: LED 7-inch foglights
URL: www.arbusa.com

8 WINCH
MAKE: Warn
MODEL: 9.5cti
URL: www.warn.com

9 SUSPENSION
MAKE: BDS Suspension
MODEL: 7-inch lift
URL: www.bds-suspension.com

10 TIRES
MAKE: Falken
MODEL: Wildpeak A/T-01
URL: www.falkentire.com

1 REAR LIGHTBAR
MAKE:
Xtreme LED Lights
MODEL:
60-inch Scanning Amber, White, and Red Lightbar
URL:
www.xtremeledlights.com

bed for long guns and a biometric lock box in the cab for handguns. An in-house upholstery team can create any design combo using Italian leather and Alcantara or exotic materials like gator and ostrich. Enhanced sound system and multimedia options consist of a laptop, tablet, hotspot, portable printer, and sat phone.

You'll find yourself approximately $100,000 to $200,000 lighter in the billfold if you'd like one of these built-to-order badass trucks. Compared to what DIYers have told us they've got sunk in their personal survivalist rides, this seems pretty comparable.

We've really only scratched the surface with the amount of options you can get, so we suggest you check them out online or request a spec sheet to get the full whack of accoutrements to choose from. Owners have a hand in selecting all the options that go into the ride so they're heavily involved in the build decisions.

While it might be out of your price range, at least you know a company is out there creating what is, by all appearances, a serious truck for the survivalist with plenty of discretionary income. Even if it doesn't suit your particular needs we'd have to say it'd be in the top 10 purchases we'd probably make after getting six out of six on the lotto.

Garrison Ford

Watch What Happens When an F-150 Gets a Special Forces Makeover

By John Schwartze
Photos by Q Concepts

When you hear the term "technical" as it relates to trucks used by third-world militants, you probably envision a dirty Toyota Hilux packed with guys holding AKs and a Dushka mounted to a jury-rigged tube cage. But have you ever wondered what an American version of a technical would look like if it were done right? However, we think that term might be a bit insulting when describing the Operator F-150 — it's not just a technical, it's a technical knockout! That's what happens when the garrison fills out a vehicular wish list.

TRUCKS • GARRISON FORD | 35

After the success of the Green Beret Jeep featured in RECOIL Issue 21, the guys at Road Armor teamed up again with Scott Neil of Operator to create something representing the kinds of trucks that Special Forces personnel would commandeer or build while deployed. But rather than using only what they had at their disposal, this time they got carte blanche on build decisions, checking off everything needed to make a light-strike vehicle they'd be willing to go to battle with. From tip to tail, it doesn't look like they left anything out, whether stateside or in combat.

A '15 F-150 4x4 was selected as the platform, but rather than just packing it with some loose gear and calling it a day, the intention was to make it faster, tougher, and more modular. The Whipple Twin Screw supercharger ensures speed won't be a problem, cranking out over 500 hp. A custom MagnaFlow stainless cat-back exhaust keeps the engine exhaling without a problem. Of course, crawling over rough terrain is a must, so the addition of a BDS 4-inch lift, Air Lift RideControl, BMF wheels, and Toyo Open Country tires certainly help this thing kick sand in the face of its enemies.

The Road Armor Stealth winch bumpers will clear a path, surely as cowcatchers on locomotives did. The assault rack was custom made by Road Armor, in particular to avoid having to add front supports. A host of Rigid Industries lightbars, both standard and infrared, are operated via an sPOD control panel. Condition Zero mounts for pistols and rifles on the interior are plentiful, and seats were given extra pouches for storage. A generous coating of DuPont

Kevlar-impregnated coating help keep the body protected.

As you can see, the exterior is outfitted with tons of accessories. Everything from a Hi-Lift jack, Pull-Pal winch anchor, shovel, CO_2 tanks for air tools, and Rotopax for fuel and water have their place on the cage. And those who aren't wise enough to move out of the way will

1 LIGHTBAR
MAKE: Rigid Industries
MODEL: E2 30-inch Combo
URL: rigidindustries.com

2 MACHINE GUN
MAKE: Executive Armament LLC
MODEL: .50 Cal
URL: n/a

3 CAGE
MAKE: Road Armor
MODEL: custom
URL: www.roadarmor.com

4 FUEL CANS
MAKE: Rotopax
MODEL: 4-gallon
URL: www.rotopax.com

5 BUMPERS
MAKE: Road Armor
MODEL: Stealth Winch w/Lonestar Guard
URL: www.roadarmor.com

6 BODY
MAKE: DuPont
MODEL: Kevlar coating
URL: starwoodmotors.com

7 WINCH
MAKE: Warn
MODEL: Zeon 12K, front; M8000, rear
URL: www.warn.com

8 WHEELS
MAKE: BMF
MODEL: 20-inch
URL: www.bmfwheels.com

9 TIRES
MAKE: Toyo
MODEL: 35x12.50R20 Open Country MT
URL: www.toyotires.com

1 JACK
MAKE: Hi-Lift Jacks
MODEL: All-Cast
URL: www.hi-lift.com

2 GUN STORAGE
MAKE: TruckVault
MODEL: F-150
URL: www.truckvault.com

3 AIR TANKS
MAKE: Smittybilt
MODEL: Compact Air System
URL: www.smittybilt.com

4 SUPERCHARGER
MAKE: Whipple Superchargers
MODEL: Twin Screw
URL: www.whipplesuperchargers.com

5 UPHOLSTERY
MAKE: CamoLiner
MODEL: Custom Leather
URL: www.camoliner.com

be greeted by a .50-caliber machine gun on a Dillon Aero mount. A Truck Vault also keeps plenty of spare rifles on hand. We're not sure we could've asked for anything that wasn't already included, except maybe a date with Abigail Ratchford.

So there you have it. Instead of being limited by what you can source while in a combat theater, the minds at Road Armor and some of our nation's most elite military groups have created one killer 4x4 that not only redefines the term "tactical vehicle" but is also a nod to all those who serve in the Special Forces. We look forward to seeing more of what their brainstorming can come up with in the future.

OPERATOR & OPERATOR CUSTOM WORKS

Operator provides best-in-class service, support, products, and consulting to customers globally, with the motto, "Fear None." The company's event arm, "Operator Challenge," hosts a unique series of demanding challenges that test competitors' shooting, outdoor skill sets, and physical and mental prowess skill sets. Operator also provides consumers with a test and evaluation program, called "Mission Ready," on products that meet the level of quality an operator utilizes on the battlefield. Operator is owned by former operators and always ensures portions of the company's profits benefit special operations' charities across all branches of military service. ➔ www.usoperator.com

Operator Custom Works is a service disabled veteran-owned company run by former special operators who have a passion for hot rods, 4x4s, and guns. OCW is fully stocked with the latest tools and automotive fabrication equipment needed for modifications, new parts, installations, or complete builds.
➔ www.operatorcustomworks.com

Spare No Expense

How Does One Back Up Their Vehicular Backup Plan? Get One for Every Occasion

By John Schwartze
Photos by Mark Saint

SURVIVOR TRUCK 3
2014 RAM 1500 4X4 CREW CAB
5.7L HEMI
EIGHT-SPEED ELECTRONIC
WWW.SURVIVORTRUCK.COM
WWW.ONESTOPSURVIVAL.COM

If we could indulge our vehicular interests in the same manner we do our firearms, then it wouldn't take long to amass a fleet that'd rival our childhood Hot Wheels collection. With our daily drivers, though, we can usually only afford to buy one that can accomplish a variety of tasks. With each survival-oriented vehicle we cover in this publication, the point is to give you, dear reader, some inspiration to start thinking about what would best suit your individual needs and budget if you could only pick one. Some people, however, aren't limited to just one.

You'll probably recall the name Survivor Truck if you're a regular reader of RECOIL. We previously covered owner Jim DeLozier's first two iterations of said vehicle in Issues 8 and 22. The first one being an '80 Chevy C70 that'd damn near rival an MRAP; the second being a Cummins-diesel-powered Ford Excursion. Each has its own unique story and purpose. Jim's created yet another that now encompasses all three major U.S. automakers. Why? What could he possibly do with all these trucks? We asked Jim the same questions, to which he answered, "Whatever I want."

Let's back up a little and revisit Jim's initial intentions. While living in California, Jim couldn't help but cogitate on what sort of vehicle would enable him to go a long distance with a lot of gear if SHTF. There was no way to do that with what he had at the time. So if he

TRUCKS • SPARE NO EXPENSE | 39

had to get 500 miles away from the Golden State with family and supplies, Survivor Truck 1 became the solution to that problem.

Now that he no longer resides in the land of background checks to buy ammo, the next obstacle was how to make the first version smaller and still get a safe distance with enough people and gear to make escape practical. Survivor Truck 2 took care of just that. Now, the question became, what could he drive on a daily basis instead of just having a vehicle for an emergency and also be a bit more mainstream for his clients? Answer — a kitted-out '14 Ram.

Yes, it's a Dodge, but Fiat Chrysler Automobiles changed the truck line name to Ram as of 2010. "I was looking at new trucks and wanted something I could drive everyday that was light, small, and efficient," DeLozier says. "The Ram was the best value. A Ford or Chevy with the same payload would've cost me $10K more, and $15K more for a Toyota. The Ram came with a bumper-to-bumper lifetime warranty for an extra $2,400, an eight-speed electronic HD transmission, and a 5.7L Hemi. Before it's loaded down I can get 22 mpg highway, and around 17 to 18 around town."

1 WHEELS
MAKE: RBP
MODEL: 94 R Black, 17x9
URL: rollingbigpower.com

2 TIRES
MAKE: Cooper
MODEL: Discoverer STT Pro, 33-inch
URL: us.coopertire.com

3 BUMPERS
MAKE: Iron Cross Automotive
MODEL: Ram 1500
URL: www.ironcrossautomotive.com

4 ACCESSORY LIGHTS
MAKE: Golight
MODEL: 3x4
URL: golight.com

5 LIGHTBAR (BOTTOM)
MAKE: Rigid Industries
MODEL: RDS
URL: rigidindustries.com

6 ACCESSORY LIGHTS
MAKE: Rigid Industries
MODEL: 2x2
URL: rigidindustries.com

7 LIGHTBAR (TOP)
MAKE: Fenix
MODEL: 52-inch AI-5217 speed-sensing adjustable beam (spot/flood) with strobe and manual controls
URL: www.fenixlight.com

Being as hard on trucks as he is, Jim felt the performance combined with the warranty was nothing to sneeze at. Next came the ancillaries. Jim added a Rancho Shocks leveling kit in front with stiffer shocks in the rear, as well as Hellwig self-leveling airbags and antisway bar, and a VIAIR tank and compressors. Then came the need

1 SAW
MAKE:
Broco
MODEL:
Mini Breaching Saw
URL:
www.broco-rankin.com

2 BACKPACK
MAKE:
5.11 Tactical
MODEL:
Rush72
URL:
www.511tactical.com

3 EXTRICATION KIT
MAKE:
One Stop Survival
MODEL:
Extreme Rescue and Extrication Kit
URL:
www.onestopsurvival.com

4 ONBOARD AIR SYSTEM
MAKE:
VIAIR
MODEL:
Dual 444C OBA
URL:
www.viaircorp.com

1 RIFLE
MAKE:
Springfield Armory
MODEL:
M1A in Sage EBR chassis
URL:
www.springfield-armory.com

2 RIFLE
MAKE:
Remington
MODEL:
700 / McRee chassis
URL:
www.remington.com

3 PISTOL
MAKE:
Heckler & Koch
MODEL:
VP9 Tactical
URL:
www.hk-usa.com

4 MISC. DRAWER CONTENTS
Three custom AR-15s, Haley Stretegic Disruptive Environments chest rigs, Watershed Bags, Chinook Medical EPMK 1 medical kit, Strider Knives machete, three Glock 41s, Kestrel Ballistic Weather Meter and DROP unit, Leupold LTO Tracker handheld thermal tool

5 SHOTGUN
MAKE:
Remington
MODEL:
VangComp Custom 870
URL:
www.remington.com

6 STORAGE
MAKE:
Decked
MODEL:
Dodge Ram 1500
URL:
www.decked.com

7 SPARE TIRE CARRIER
MAKE:
Wilco Offroad
MODEL:
Hitchgate
URL:
www.wilcooffroad.com

8 SEAT COVER
MAKE:
Wet Okole
MODEL:
Dodge Ram
URL:
www.wetokole.com

to outfit the bed to hold more gear. Jim reached out to Steve Ellis at Urban Garage and gave him a rough sketch of what he was looking for. Ellis welded up a bed rack to support the Cascadia Vehicle Tents Mt. Rainier 3+ person tent. Jim then designed mounts for lights, cameras, RotopaX fuel cans, fire extinguisher, and GoLights.

The fuel can mounts wrap vertically around the cans, making them very secure and completely supporting the weight, providing a platform for a 360-degree pan/tilt GoLight searchlights on each side that are controlled by two joysticks. Jim also added a beveled scene light on each side and created recessed areas for bed lighting, both provided by Whelen. The rear lighting, flood lighting, and RDS lightbar in the front were provided by Rigid Industries and the emergency lighting and adjustable-beam lightbar are from Fenix and are controlled by two Switch Pros eight-switch control modules.

The bumpers come from Iron Cross Automotive with LED bumper lights and a Warn Winch, shackles, and Spydura synthetic cable. The truck's exterior was shod in LineX for durability. For electronics, three Odyssey Extreme AGM batteries are charged and controlled through a Blue Sea ML Remote Battery Switch automatic charge relay and 200-amp circuit breaker for each feed, with fuses and relays on each appliance for total protection of the system.

The C4ISR (Command, Control, Communications, Computers, Intelligence, Surveillance, and Reconnaissance) system consists of a Panasonic VG-Z1 Toughpad

mounted in a Havis docking station and four full-time cameras (IR, thermal, PTZ) in BASH (Ballistic Anti-Shock Housings) from Dotworkz. Cameras and monitor by VDO are powered through a solid-state computer, MoFi 4G/LTE router MobileMark antenna. All of this is integrated with his other vehicles via a Silvus Technologies tactical mesh network configured by Brent Kinnaman at K-Tac Communications in San Diego. There is also a Cobra Electronics CB radio and 2,400-watt power inverter, two-way radio hard mount, and portable HAM radio.

We think it's safe to say Jim isn't building mall crawlers and has something that'll enable him to face sh*t head on if things get hairy. If you're in the market to create your own survival vehicle, feel free to reach out to Jim via his websites for consultation. At this point he's on track to be the Q Branch of tactical trucks, so there's a good chance he can point you in the right direction if you're not sure where to start and want to turn your daily into a bug-out vehicle. It's probably only a matter of time before we're reporting on yet another addition to his armada of vehicles. Anyone want to take bets on an Aston Martin with revolving plates? We're not ruling it out.

TRUCKS • SPARE NO EXPENSE | 43

Fighting Chance

Mil-Spec Automotive Has Transformed the Hummer H1 into What it Should've Been All Along — an Uncompromising, Purpose-Built Vehicle

By John Schwartze
Photos by Robert McGaffin

MIL-SPEC AUTOMOTIVE
HUMMER H1
6.6L LBZ DURAMAX
ALLISON 1000 TRANSMISSION
WWW.MILSPECAUTO.COM

Think about the various flare-ups in the automotive industry you've lived through. Many vehicles debut to great fanfare, but their flame is often extinguished just as quickly as it began. Outfits independent of the Big Three like DeLorean, Vector, Tucker, and Fisker certainly burst upon the scene to tremendous optimism. Unfortunately, they found themselves added to a growing list of names that automotive enthusiasts wax philosophically about what could've been. The public is also left to wonder if anyone's got the cojones to resurrect the brand and improve where others fell short. The tale of Hummer also falls into this category of missed opportunities, but perhaps now the elements have aligned for it to finally reach its intended potential.

Let's face it, there's a certain exaggerated charm the Hummer H1 has. It's like a real-life version of the AA-powered Stompers many of us had as kids. It originally started as a military vehicle known as the High Mobility Multipurpose Wheeled Vehicle (HMMWV or "Humvee") in the 1980s and garnered the attention of some high-profile people who wanted to own one. Schwarzenegger played a key role in developing a civilian version with AM General, and soon enough demand was cultivated to justify making them available to the general public.

It was hastily given some upgrades like a vac-formed plastic interior and other creature comforts not found in the military version to make it more consumer-friendly, but still wasn't engineered with as much attention to detail as it should've been for a daily driver. Eventually, GM acquired the brand, made some other alterations, and added models to the fleet that weren't really true to the original DNA. Design problems and a number of other factors continued to plague the brand until it was discontinued about a decade ago.

So what happened? Hummer seemed to have all the ingredients to be successful, but perhaps it was just never given

a chance to truly show off what it was capable of. Mil-Spec Automotive (MSA) wondered the same thing and contemplated what it'd look like today if the bugs had been worked out and better technology had been integrated. The company started restoring and flipping surplus Humvees in a garage and recognized there really wasn't anyone out there giving the brand any love in the resto-mod space. Now they're efforts have expanded to a full production facility in Michigan, so they've clearly found others who share their interest in seeing the continuation of this comeback story.

Although GM slapped the Hummer name on the H2 and H3, MSA's focus is improving the civilian H1 because of its military pedigree and the fact that it has a VIN, which makes registration a non-issue. A few small differences aside, basically the civilian H1 is identical to the military version anyway. The company sources their own vehicles to begin the rebuilding process, but also offers a program for those who want their personal H1 to be gussied up with the same enhancements. "It's really a remanufacturing process, not a restoration," says Ian Broekman, MSA chief innovation officer. Each vehicle takes about three to five months to build.

As you'd expect, the platform of the truck was robust to begin with, but never optimized for the general public and came from the factory with various imperfections that need to be ironed out. MSA tears the vehicle down to its body and frame, which are the only parts of the truck they retain — everything else is new old stock, fabricated, or produced in-house by the company. For instance, the trucks rolled off the line with about a 1-inch margin on the frame. Flaws like that are corrected, the frame is boxed, and components are individually powdercoated and reassembled with improved hardware. The aluminum bodies are inspected, any oxidation is repaired, and an impressive three-stage insulation process is applied to reduce the noisiness Hummers had a reputation for.

Among one of the benefits Hummers were known for having was a chassis focused purely on performing off-road, so you have great ground clearance with portal axles. Although it's a bit challenging to access and wrench on, their front mid-engine layout gives them a near 50/50 weight distribution. However, the H1's original drivetrain became notorious for being inefficient, poorly cooled, and about as powerful as a flabby balloon. Thankfully, the original setup has been ditched in favor of a powertrain MSA hand-builds with enough suds to power a platform this big.

Owners can now look forward to a balanced and blueprinted LBZ 6.6L Duramax paired to an Allison six-speed transmission with part-time 4WD, and a manual transfer case with 4H, 2H, and 4L. Now you're looking at nearly 500 hp with about 1,000 lb-ft of torque, giving you about 20 mpg freeway and 13 to 15 mpg city. At the moment, MSA isn't offering gas engines. An upgraded cooling setup is incorporated in the front, along with a transmission cooling system in the rear.

Since the H1s rolled off the same assembly line as the military versions, the spring rates were identical, which meant the civilian version had the same stiffly sprung suspension as one intended to be armored. MSA redesigns the suspension geometry for equal travel and a more comfort-

Although the front mid-engine layout is a bitch to get to, it's now powered by an efficiently cooled diesel 6.6L Duramax.

From left to right, the MSA impresarios: Chris Van Scyoc (president), Adam Mitchell (CEO/owner), Ian Broekman (CIO).

able ride. Stopping power comes by way of a new braking setup from Wilwood. It's all sitting on 20-inch LRG wheels with Nitto meats.

The interiors have been heavily revamped to get away from the cheapo, compartmentalized original versions. They're luxurious, yes, but not so much that it clashes with the ballsy character of the vehicle. GPS analog gauges give classic aesthetics with contemporary technology as well as a JL audio system with Bluetooth and Sirius XM. Extensive mods were made to mount seats for more legroom. Hand-stitched marine-grade leather, brushed aluminum accents, three-point seatbelts, MOMO steering wheel, improved HVAC setup, backup cameras, and interior storage are just some of the revised appointments to look forward to. Someone finally thought it through this time.

Since you're looking at what's basically a hand-built vehicle, prices hover just north of $200K and go

up from there for versions that are fully spec'd out. MSA is also scoping out some other vehicles with a military history that they can offer to the public with their own unique approach to revitalization. We anxiously await they're next endeavor, and if they give it the same meticulous rebirth that they've brought to the Hummer, we may have to start buying more Powerball tickets so we can add one to our driveway. It's nice to see that guys with a passion for their craft gave a sh*t enough about this heavyweight to bring it out of retirement and put it back in the fight.

To Hellwig and Gone

Trailers? Where We're Going We Don't Need Trailers

By John Schwartze
Photos by RECOIL Staff and Courtesy Hellwig Products

OPERATOR
2017 FORD F-350 4WD LARIAT
2018 TEXTRON WILDCAT X UTV
6.7L DIESEL V-8
SIX-SPEED AUTOMATIC
WWW.HELLWIGPRODUCTS.COM

It's easy to wander around automotive events like SEMA seeing products that are really nothing more than booth bling and will probably never actually get much practical application. But like marrying a Playboy Bunny and getting separate beds, you can't really resist asking yourself what the point is if it's solely for appearances. When we saw the Hellwig Operator for the first time, we couldn't help but be impressed. It looked like an overlanding version of a 747 with the space shuttle mounted on top. From stem to stern, to say it's meant for off-roading wouldn't do it justice. After all, how many other trucks can you think of that successfully piggybacked a 1,200-pound Textron Wildcat onto the back?

First, a little bit about Hellwig Products. The company's heritage actually dates back to post World War II when founder Rudy Hellwig noticed vehicles consistently sagging in the rear when hauling heavy loads. Necessity being the mother of all invention led Rudy to create the Hellwig Helper Spring. He sold the product door to door in Southern California upon seeing cars or trucks suffering from this affliction and made the repair right there in the driveway for $7. Hellwig's been a fixture in the automotive industry ever since, known especially for its 4140 hot-form-forged chromoly steel sway bars and other load-support and sway-control equipment.

Fast-forward to 2017 and this imposing 4x4 known as the Operator was conceived. The Hellwig Operator was a Ford Project Vehicle Program — a program Ford set up to give aftermarket manufacturers a chance to modify a Blue Oval vehicle and then buy it for a nominal amount. A Ford F-350 long-bed crew-cab was chosen because of its versatility and the sheer amount of accesso-

ries it can hold. Hellwig submitted a very thorough proposal, detailing the build concept, what gear would be installed and, most importantly, the Hellwig products being developed for this new project.

Hellwig wanted a platform to show the capabilities of their products and needed a unique vehicle to do so. Being an avid supporter of our military, the die was cast on the overall theme. Since the company's also known for its side-by-side gear, the question then became how to integrate everything into one package. Then, the ball was rolling to get other companies involved who shared their vision. The end result is nothing short of a truck guy's shopping spree of dream parts.

So, how'd they get that UTV mounted? It's a rather interesting piece of engineering. Sherptek pitched in with a custom-made Dragon Bak Dek designed to hold a SxS, rooftop tent, or anything else that could fit. Interestingly enough this deck also has amenities for bed mounted fuel tanks for both the SxS or the F-350 and uses "infinite" tie-down/attachment points on the deck and sides for securing gear, allowing an awning, Hi-Lift jack, shovel, and Daystar liquid cans to be mounted. All loaded up, it weighs about 2,300 pounds over factory GVWR and stands 11 feet, 9 inches tall.

The deck itself is built on skids, so it doesn't ride on or touch the bedrails of the truck. It actually has its own stands that match the bed's profile, and sandwich the bed to the frame. The weight of the UTV and rack is supported by Hellwig's Big Wig air springs, while the high center of gravity is kept in check by the addition of front and rear sway bars, a Viair compressor, and a 4.5-inch Icon Vehicle Dynamics suspension system with dual front reservoirs.

Theresa Contreras and her team at LGE-CTS Motorsports laid on the hand-painted digi-cam exterior, often mistaken for a vinyl wrap. They also reengineered the Fab Fours bumpers in the front to accommodate a Warn winch. The powerplant is a stock 6.7L diesel V-8 with the six-speed trans, upgraded with Magna-Flow Pro DPF performance exhaust.

Since it already makes about 1,000 lb-ft of torque, it's got plenty of lead in its pencil, but a Pedal Commander module was added to make the throttle a bit more responsive. The exterior is also decked out with Bushwacker fender flares, an ARB rooftop tent and awning, McLean Metalworks hitch hammock, and Rigid Industries lightbars, all operated by a Whelen controller, just to scratch the surface.

The interior was redone with 5.11 Tactical pants material as well as MOLLE webbing installed on the underside and backs of the seats to hold various packs for first-aid, communications, and recovery gear. Rugged Radios headsets and Whelen PA system and lightbar also adorn the interior, while 17-inch Method Race Wheels beadlocks and 37-inch Falken Wild Peak M/Ts round out the rolling stock.

The RECOIL team had a chance to get behind the wheel of the Operator on a trip up steep mountain mining roads from Phoenix on into Prescott, Arizona, through low-hanging brush, dried-out desert washes, and slushy snow-covered mountains. In some areas the trails were barely wider than the truck. Although the Empire didn't have Wookiees in mind when they designed these roads back in the 1800s for horses and buggies, for such a large vehicle we admired how well it performed and had a blast driving it.

By the numbers, this truck probably has around $180,000 in it. Check out the sidebar for the full litany of products. Unlike some that are all show and no go, we can attest it was built with one purpose in mind, an all-in-one way of getting out in the dirt and having fun … without having to tow your toys behind it.

Hellwig Products Operator Build Sheet	
Company Name	Product
Icon Vehicle Dynamics	4.5" Suspension System Stage 5
MagnaFlow	PRO DPF Performance Exhaust
Method	17" NV HD Set of 5
Falken	37" Wild Peak M/T Off Road Tires (Set of 5)
AMP Research	XL Retracting Side Steps and Bed Step
AVS	Aeroskin II, Window Trim, Headlight Covers
T-Rex Grilles	X-Metal Grille
Daystar	Liquid Cans (4)
Mag-Hytec	Diff Covers and Transmission Pan
Fab Fours	Vengeance Front and Rear Bumpers
Warn Industries	16.5TI-S Winch
Warn Industries	Hub Ford O5SD Blk
Warn Industries	Pro Vantage 2500 (Deck Winch to Pull SxS)
Bolt	Receiver Lock and Misc. Locks
Rigid Industries	Lights (Adapt, 2x2" Corner Lights 4 of Them, 2-6x1" Reverse Lights, Rock Lights Set of 4)
Wilco	Pre Runner Tail Gate
Bushwacker	Pocket Style Fender Flares and Trail Armor Rocker/Sill Covers
Viair	Compressor and Air Tank
Sherptek	Dragon Bak Toy Dek
Hellwig Products	Front Sway Bar
Hellwig Products	Rear Sway Bar
Hellwig Products	Big Wig Air Springs
Hellwig Products	Auto Leveling Air System
Hi Lift Jack	Jack, Mounts and Accessories
Krazy Beaver	Shovel
Optima Batteries	Batteries
5.11 Tactical	Material for Interior, Including Numerous Bags
Whelen	Light Bar and PA System
Billet Badges	Custom Hellwig Side Vents
Mac's Custom Tie Downs	Wheel Straps and Motorcycle Tie-Downs
Rugged Radios	Radio in Truck, Radio and Headsets in SXS, 2 Handheld Radios
R-M	Paint
Textron	Wild Cat X
SSV Works	Head Unit and Speakers for SXS
Trigger	Wireless Switch Solution (SXS)
Buggy Whips	Whips for Truck and SXS (1-2 ft., 1-6 ft.)
Assault	Detachable Steering Wheel/Side Mirrors
Expeditions Essentials	Stove/Kitchen
ARB	Roof Top Tent and Awning
McLean Metalworks	Hitch Hammock

TRUCKS • TO HELLWIG AND GONE

Himalaya is Giving Land Rover Defenders a Contemporary American Makeover

By John Schwartze
Photos by Himalaya

Cool Britannia

HIMALAYA SPECTRE
GM LS3
6L80E SIX-SPEED AUTOMATIC
WWW.DRIVEHIMALAYA.COM

Aston Martin was nearing bankruptcy before an increasingly popular movie franchise put a certain MI6 agent behind the wheel of a tricked-out DB5. Although it was a fairly new concept at the time, it showed the power of product placement. Nowadays, cinema and corporate marketing go together like lawyers and tasseled loafers. If you're a fan of the Bond movies, you've probably felt the urge to go buy something its star was wearing, drinking, or driving. Now's your chance.

Recently there's been a rise in boutique companies taking older platforms and giving them modern enhancements. Whether it's Singer's pulse-pounding take on vintage 911 Porsches or our recent look at Mil-Spec Automotive's revamped Hummers in Issue 44, the level of artistry and upgraded engineering are enough to make discerning car buffs like Jay Leno take notice. They saved the best aspects of the old, worked out the kinks in the original design, and infused it all with the best technology on the market. Himalaya is just such a company applying this approach to Land Rover Defenders.

The original Defender line was part of Land Rover's fleet from the '80s up until it ceased production in 2016. Part of this model's appeal was the consistency of the iconic body. For instance, you could take the doors off a 2015 model and bolt them onto a 1988. However, since the Defender was utilitarian in nature, its fit and finish wasn't what you'd see (or expect) in current SUVs. If you've ever driven an original Defender then you know they're loud, hot, and clanky. That is, until Himalaya gets a hold of them.

The company gives customers three tiers of options. If original is your thing, they offer Defenders by Himalaya, which are essentially resto-mods. Refinements at this level include new body panels, better insulation, larger brake packages, tighter panel fitment, improved engine gearing, modern audio systems, and custom interiors, just to name a few. Even if you want a total stock-spec restoration, Himalaya offers that option as well. According to company president Greg Shondel, the company has the largest supply of new takeoff parts in North America from sets of doors to bonnets to full bodies.

The mid-level tier takes that classic build and upgrades it to a modern drivetrain with custom brakes and suspension, among other updates. On the top end is the true Himalaya, which is a limited yearly production. Himalaya's flagship model is a reimagined Defender 110 called the Spectre and named after the Land Rover Defender SVX seen in the previous Bond flick of the same name. Himalaya didn't build the one in the movie, but its vehicular tribute is one we'd

Himalaya's flagship model is the Spectre, a handmade, crew-cab-style Defender.

The Spectre's slant-back exterior features a Safety Devices exo-cage and Front Runner Vehicle Outfitters roof rack.

The Spectre's suspension includes 4 inches of ride height to clear the 37-inch tires. Custom coil springs are inserted, and extended-length control arms are built in-house with articulating Johnny Joints from Currie Enterprises. Ride is controlled by Fox Racing remote-reservoir shocks.

gladly survive on Cup O'Noodles long enough to be able to buy.

Since GM has practically cornered the market on gas crate engines, drivetrains have been punched up with a 525-horsepower LS3 with an optional Whipple supercharger or a Cummins R2.8 turbodiesel. The motor is tied to a six-speed automatic and all-wheel-drive transfer case. Dynatrac axles, 37-inch Toyo tires, and Brembo brakes occupy a custom-designed coilover suspension setup and Richards frame that's been fully welded, boxed, and hot-dip galvanized. The only thing that's "Land Rover" on the vehicle are the new body panels themselves.

Touches like billet adornments where plastic resided on the originals, a rear tire carrier, a slant-back Safety Devices cage, and crew-cab-style body give them a well-balanced practicality beyond the factory pedigree. On the inside, you'll be treated to Ruskin leather, heated Recaro seats, Dakota Digital gauges, Momo steering wheel, Alcantara headliner, Exmoor LED lighting, Kenwood head unit, and JL Audio speakers. And yes, the list goes on.

This year, Himalaya plans on building a proving grounds-type facility in Wyoming, as testing its builds thoroughly enough to identify weaknesses is a big part of their playbook. Whether it's pinpointing areas that need improvement while sitting in traffic or trying to break something off-road, they want customers to feel like they got it right and work with them to select the build that's conducive to their lifestyle. One-off custom builds are something they're constantly taking orders for.

"When you pull up in Spectre, in a lot of ways it seems like you're invading wherever you're pulling up," Shondel says. That's the kind of first impression we'd enjoy far more than whatever arriving in a Maserati Levante might evoke. Chances are that'd cause assumptions that you smell like Drakkar and still listen to Coldplay.

We're impressed with Himalaya's ability to combine sophistication, aggressive looks, and functional architecture. Expect to spend $115,000 to $250,000, depending on your preferences. As far as a martini shaker, Omega watch, and white dinner jacket, you'll have to spring for those on your own. Oddly enough, Land Rover has reintroduced the Defender for 2020, and you'll be seeing it in the 25th Bond movie if you haven't already.

If you own a stock Defender and want a ground-up restoration, Himalaya can bring it back to all its original glory.

Himalaya can work with customers on creating custom one-off builds that make sense for their unique needs.

Surplus Spending

An Impulsive Auction Bid Led Jason Squires to Dive Headfirst into the Challenges of Owning a Military Surplus Humvee

By Patrick McCarthy

Even if you consider yourself a paragon of fiscal responsibility and level-headed decision-making, you've probably made at least a few impulse buys throughout your life. These might've been inexpensive items, such as a candy bar from the grocery store checkout line, or more substantial expenditures, such as a new gun you just couldn't resist. For Jason Squires, a spontaneous purchase led to a sudden feeling of buyer's remorse and an especially awkward conversation with his wife. "I said, 'I think I purchased a 1991 M998 HMMWV.' She thought I had a stroke."

Squires, who you may recognize from his written contributions to RECOIL and its sister publications, is a lawyer by trade. Several years ago, he was speaking with a close friend who was going through law school, and who had previously deployed on combat tours to Iraq and Afghanistan. Squires recalls, "He bragged about the Humvee (HMMWV in official parlance) and said if I ever get the opportunity to purchase one, do it." This idea took hold, and he began casually browsing online listings, but was initially discouraged by the abundance of half-baked project vehicles on the secondhand market. "Most of the military Humvees for sale were obvious wrecks. Buyers would pick these trucks up at military salvage sales and then attempt to perform simple restorations before selling them."

1991 AM General M998 HMMWV

ENGINE: GM 6.5L diesel V-8 (originally built with a 6.2L V-8; records indicate the engine was replaced by the Army in 2003)

TRANSMISSION: Three-speed automatic

DRIVELINE: Full-time four-wheel-drive with two-speed locking transfer case and geared hubs

TIRES: 37x12.5x16.5 Goodyear Wrangler MT

EXTERIOR DIMENSIONS: 15 feet long, 7 feet wide, 6 feet tall

GROUND CLEARANCE: 16 inches

TOP SPEED: 55 mph (safe)/70 mph (at redline)

A .30-caliber machine gun attaches to a swingarm mount on the left corner of the bed. This weapon is fully functional.

After purchasing the Humvee, Squires modified it based on USSOCOM GMV specs. This meant installing a .50-caliber gun turret on the roof with an integrated ballistic shield. The gun in this photo is an inert replica, but Squires owns a real one as well.

Swinging aside the spare tire and folding down the tailgate reveals a wide, flat cargo area with plenty of room for fuel, water, food, and other gear.

Under the forward-opening hood, you'll find a General Motors 6.5L diesel engine. This naturally aspirated V-8 produces 160 horsepower and 290 ft-lb of torque — not exactly a recipe for speed, but it pairs well with the Humvee's low gearing to overcome difficult terrain.

Eventually, Squires came across GovPlanet, a website that auctions off military vehicles and other surplus equipment. Browsing these listings became a cathartic experience, especially during hard days in the courtroom. "I was representing a man on a complex felony trial, and I was really stressed out. My client was so guilty he fled the jurisdiction before trial. I had to sit there next to an empty chair and attempt to create reasonable doubt for the jury. I pictured myself in the Humvee having fun in the desert, not sitting in a courtroom. This fantasy created an impulsivity where I placed a $6,100 bid on a HM-MVW in Yermo, California. At the 2:15 break, I checked my emails, and saw 'You won the auction!' I was shocked."

After sheepishly explaining the situation to his wife, Squires wired the money, filled out the requisite paperwork, and awaited its delivery with nervous excitement. "The auctions have dozens of pictures from all angles, and a video starting the vehicle. I knew it started and ran, but it's a static inspection and I didn't know if it even rolled." Five months later, it arrived on a flatbed trailer, and he soon realized he was in over his head. "I didn't even know how to start the thing. There are no keys on military Humvees. You simply turn the switch, wait for the glow plugs, and then it fires right up." However, this revealed yet another problem. "I was concerned about my new baby being stolen. I removed the batteries every night, which was a total pain. They're under the passenger seat. I didn't know any of this." Later, he'd install a kill switch with a proximity transponder to prevent unauthorized joyrides.

First-time ownership of a military surplus vehicle came with many other challenges. "Licensing the truck was tricky. The paperwork that comes with it is just an invoice, really. I remember the GovPlanet rep saying, 'The title costs an extra $125.' Instead, they should've said, 'Do you want to drive the truck on real roads? If so, buy the title.' I did not take the vehicle with me to register it. I simply handed [the Motor Vehicle Division] the documents and demanded a title. Gutsy, but it paid off. I didn't want some MVD tire-kicker asking about a rearview mirror and airbags."

With the new registration and license plate in hand, Squires began driving the Humvee to the gun range, his kids' school, and most frequently, gas stations. "A Humvee has you at the gas station quite often. Mine gets 10 miles to the gallon." Despite its 55-mile-per-hour effective top speed, roaring mud tires, and lack of doors, he says he has taken it on several 600-mile road trips. He even drives it to court sometimes. "I don't go to trial; I go to war! You want an attorney saving you who drives a Humvee or a Prius? These are my jokes when I'm asked why the hell I'm in a military vehicle wearing a suit and tie."

Of all the hurdles Squires faced with the Humvee, maintaining it was the most formidable. Unlike the U.S. Department of Defense, he didn't have warehouses full of spare parts and fleet maintenance techs on retainer. "From very early on, I knew I needed a mechanic. I would talk to any Army guy who would listen. I got a lot of 'Hell yeah! I rocked a Humvee all the way across Iraq.' I would say, 'Great, what oil do you put in the gearbox?' Every single time, they would look at me quizzically and respond, 'Oh, I didn't mess with that stuff.'" Eventually, he found a qualified Army light-wheel mechanic, and began learning from the veteran's 17 years of experience wrenching on Humvees. "I was able to take apart every single thing and slowly rebuild or replace anything that needed servicing. That process took months, but I loved every second of it. I would come home, take off my suit, and dive in."

In addition to the basic maintenance, Squires also sourced some rare parts to convert his Humvee to Ground Mobility Vehicle (GMV) specifications. The GMV was a USSOCOM program that modified Humvees to meet the needs of U.S. Special-Operations Forces; upgrades included additional armor plating and a top-mounted gun turret with ballistic "chicken shield." Although the .50-caliber belt-fed in these photos is an inert replica, Squires also owns the real deal, which he mounts at the range for some full-auto fun. Another mount on the rear quarter panel holds a .30-caliber machine gun.

Squires says this vehicle has led to some unusual interactions. One person veered close enough to high-five him while cruising on the highway. A concerned neighbor came by and asked if he was joining a militia. His most memorable experience was with an agent at a U.S.

With two mounted machine guns, zero doors, and a payload of diesel fuel and survival gear, Jason Squires' HMMWV is anything but subtle.

Border Patrol checkpoint in southern Arizona. "I look like a military truck, but I'm clearly not military. He's looking at me the way the warden looked at Paul Newman in *Cool Hand Luke*, mirrored sunglasses and a what-in-the-hell-do-we-have-here look on his face. I'm slowly moving, clunking over these little speed bumps at 2 miles per hour, waiting for him to grab me and yank me out of the truck. As I passed him, he yelled 'Stop!' He walked around the vehicle looking at each thing and approached the driver's side, then said 'Go in style, brother. Go in style.'"

Function Over Fashion

The Dos & Don'ts of Overland Truck Modification

By Chris Denison

any hunters and recreational shooters (two groups that spend a ton of time outdoors) have successfully used functional, camping-related modifications to turn their personal vehicles into mobile base camps. What started out as simply sleeping in your truck has turned into "overlanding," an entire industry centered on self-reliant adventures in kitted-out rigs.

However, much like the well-meaning firearm enthusiasts who head straight for the fancy bolt-ons without first doping in their iron sights, so too do countless aspiring overlanders begin by adding hundreds of pounds of furniture to their trucks or SUVs without ever addressing the performance ramifications — wasting wads of money in the process.

In this article, we'll walk you through RECOIL's top five areas of consideration for overland vehicle modifications. Using our 2011 Toyota Tundra project truck as an example, we'll share key recommendations to consider and pitfalls to avoid, plus one huge money-saving tip.

Suspension & Handling

DO: Consider upgrading the suspension.
DON'T: Screw up the stock geometry!

We see far too many decked-out overland rigs that are precariously perched upon stock suspension, the four-wheeled equivalent of putting a $3,000 rifle scope on a $30 mount. Worse yet, many of these trucks have been lifted to the moon, which creates a wealth of problems if done incorrectly. You see, when a vehicle like this Toyota is lifted (with either a spacer lift or aftermarket shock), the suspension is slightly extended and will no longer be aligned to factory specifications. Driving with this stock geometry out of whack typically leads to handling issues and premature tire wear. Not only that, but a spacer lift makes it impossible for the stock bumpstops to contact the frame when bottoming out, meaning that the suspension cannot properly disperse the bottoming force as it was originally designed. This can permanently damage your vehicle, including the frame.

The Total Chaos Fabrication Upper Control Arms and Elka suspension components are the heart and soul of this build, providing a solid platform to begin adding weight.

Wilco Offroad's ADV Chase Rack 2.0 allowed us to mount the KC Hilites light bar, C2 work lights, Pelican iM3200 case, and Tred GT Recovery Boards. Notice the lack of tent.

We knew that for serious off-road use, our project Tundra would require aftermarket coilover suspension that was designed with the correct collapsed and extended measurements to optimize the truck's performance, particularly with added weight on board. Step one of our build was to link up with Total Chaos, a California-based fabrication shop that handles everything from Baja race vehicles to top-secret military contracts. We opted to go with Elka's 2.5 DC reservoir front and rear shock kit for the truck, using Total Chaos' aftermarket upper control arms (UCAs) to make all necessary geometry changes so that the Toyota would be aligned back to factory specifications.

Along with correcting the geometry, the powdercoated Total Chaos UCAs replace the stock rubber bushings with polyurethane to reduce suspension flex under braking and articulation. Swapping the stock ball joint out with a 100-percent stainless steel, 1-inch uniball not only gave us something that was far stronger than the stock joint, but also allowed for more suspension travel — a big plus in rough terrain. To round things out, we chose to install new LT285/65R18 Toyo Open Country A/T II tires all around — a super grippy tread pattern that's also incredibly durable on- and off-road, along with some Bushwacker pocket-style fender flares, which help minimize the amount of excess roost that flies off the tires in nasty terrain.

The first phase of work on the rig was done at Toytec Lifts, a company in Denver that specializes in overland projects. When the Tundra rolled out of Toytec's service bay with the upgraded suspension, components, and tires, the vehicle looked somewhat unassuming compared to the excessively outfitted #overlandtundras you see on social media. However, we now

had a ready-to-modify platform that was so functional, it could've easily pounded sand whoops down the Baja Peninsula. Given the performance gains that we'd earned by preserving the factory handling ability, this massive first step was well worth the effort.

Armor & Racks

DO: Protect your investment with quality components.
DON'T: Sacrifice practicality for trendiness. The final build needs to be usable for you.

Before you spend a dime on armor or racks, make a list. Like, literally, sit down with a pen and paper, and identify what you're trying to achieve from the start. In this case, the vehicle's owner routinely hauls motorcycles in the bed, so a topper or bed-mounted rack was a non-starter. Protection also ranked high as a "need," as did easy access to the spare tire. As such, we installed a TireGate Racerunner and ADV Chase Rack 2.0 roof rack from Wilco Performance.

Relocating the spare adds a bit of clearance underneath and makes the tire ultra-easy to get to on the trail. Up top, the ADV Chase Rack allows for numerous options for hauling gear when the bed is full of motorcycles. You really must see this rack in person to appreciate the ingenuity behind the design; everything is super-reinforced, but also adjustable. Depending on the terrain, the rack is designed to handle between 150 and 300 pounds of gear. A fabricator friend whipped up the custom front bumper and rear bumper guards to protect both ends of the truck from major impacts.

Possibly the toughest mod added to this whole truck are the White Knuckle rock sliders. These puppies protect the actual body and frame of the vehicle from rocks, and the crazy-solid mounting means that you can also put a jack under the sliders to get a wheel or two off the ground. Not to mention, they make a nice step bar for use when entering and exiting the truck.

At the gun range, the bed of your pickup truck is a valuable workspace, yet many of us put up with the stock, plastic bedliners for way longer than we should. A quality spray-on bedliner is a luxurious upgrade

The KC Hilites Pro6 LED light bar: 13,800 raw lumens of UFO-level illumination.

that'll protect your bed, while wildly increasing grip. We opted to go with Bullet Liner, the most durable and UV-resistant spray-on bedliner that we could find. Bullet Liner by Tuff Skin in Orange County, California, did an immaculate job spraying down the bed and while they were at it, we had them coat the Tundra's front grille and mirror caps as well. Both were suffering from a bit of normal wear and tear, and the Bullet Liner finish ended up looking awesome.

Lights
DO: Illuminate in all directions, not just out front.
DON'T: Be fooled by cheap, unreliable knockoffs.

Although many aftermarket lights aren't suitable for street use, the benefits off-road are huge. Lights with powerful throw can make traveling at high speeds a vastly safer affair, while well-positioned ditch and work lights can make low-speed crawling or even hanging out in camp immensely more enjoyable. After much research, we approached KC Hilites and explained that this Tundra would be used for year-round forays into the high desert and mountains to access remote, private shooting ranges and off-road trail systems. These adventures rarely conclude before sundown. The KC Hilites crew immediately threw a slew of recommendations our way.

The first light to go on was a 39-inch Gravity LED Pro6 light bar, which is insane for high-speed dirt roads and dusty conditions. This roof-mounted illumination was augmented by a 10-inch FLEX LED center lightbar and a pair of G4 LED fog lights, that offer low, ultra-wide illumination that's also street legal. For low-speed scenarios, a pair of KC FLEX LED two-light systems, mounted roughly 25 degrees off to each side, serve as ditch lights with a nice spread pattern. Out back, we fabbed up some custom mounts for the 2-inch C-series C2 work lights, which can illuminate the truck bed or light up beside the vehicle for gun or game cleaning. This was all topped off by a series of three 2-inch Cyclone lights mounted on each side of the tire carrier that we linked to the turn signals, backup, and brake lights, respectively; these little guys are mild enough to not be a hazard to other drivers yet are universal and compact, making them a popular choice for all things overland.

Of course, all the added lighting needed to be driven by a power distribution system. Our choice was an American-made sPOD SourceLT — basically a small, solid-state six-circuit control system that offers a super clean way to power and control all the lights. There's only a single cable that goes into the cab, and everything is controlled via a mini six-switch panel that we mounted just in front of the shifter. The SourceLT units are wicked cool, and they can be set up to operate lights, radios, snowplows, fans — pretty much anything that originates from the battery. There's even an app which allows you to dim, flash, and link the lights via Bluetooth!

Now, a word to the wise: Good lights can be pricey, but just like the optics on your rifle, you get what you pay for. We've seen numerous truck and Jeep owners outfit their vehicles with cheap, foreign-made copies of popular lights, only to have them burn out or fail altogether within weeks of installation. Don't be fooled; these knockoffs are a massive waste of cash and can potentially fry critical components on your truck if you're not careful.

Interior
DO: Reduce clutter and plan for big messes.
DON'T: Overcomplicate things. It's not a helicopter!

Most shooters hold these truths to be self-evident: that following a weekend of camping and shooting/hunting, your vehicle's interior will look like a bomb went off inside, and your seats are going to need some serious cleaning. The antidote is as simple as adding a little organization and finding durable seat covers.

On the organization side of the house, we can't say enough good things about Greyman Tactical's seatback organizers and rifle racks. Essentially a mounting place for all things MOLLE, these rigid panels can be removed from your seat in seconds, yet they firmly hold ridiculous amounts of weight and clutter (including long-guns) keeping your cab infinitely better organized than if you just stack stuff on the floor. In the case of this Tundra, we found

Finding tidy places to stash loose bits of kit can keep clutter-related cursing to a minimum.

TRUCKS • FUNCTION OVER FASHION | **65**

that we'd travel to the back country with our rifles in locked cases, and then transfer one of them to the seatback for quick access while traversing through the boonies.

The question of seat covers had us somewhat stumped until we discovered Wet Okole, a company out of Los Angeles that makes crazy-durable covers out of wetsuit-like materials; that is, nylon-laminated neoprene. We've chucked everything from wet dogs to filthy snow gear onto these covers, and they clean up laughably well no matter what the mess. While seat covers aren't the sexiest of overland modifications, you'll be super glad that you went with a quality choice here.

Beyond the organization and the protection sits a bit of a rabbit hole, if you aren't careful: additional pouches, radios, tablet cradles, drink holders, and electronic accessories can amount to maddening clutter when met with a standard camping load-out. Keep your interior simple and clean, and you'll avoid the frustration of having all your crap go flying the first time you barrel through a ditch too fast.

Accessories
DO: Remember, ounces equal pounds.
DON'T: Waste your money!

In keeping with the theme of performance, this Tundra sports a minimalistic spat of bolt-ons: first, there's the Pelican iM3200 Storm rifle case, which we hard-mounted to the roof rack. Yes, rifle cases scream "GUN!" and sure, if a thief wants this badly enough, they're going to get it. But considering this offers weatherproof long-gun storage on the exterior of the vehicle, we had to include it. Truth be told, if there's a rifle inside, the truck won't be left unattended, and if the case is empty then it's going to remain unlocked (to show would-be thieves that the juice isn't worth the squeeze of removing an empty case). For camping trips, this

The sPOD mini six-switch panel and SourceLT power and control the array of lights.

In all conditions, the Bullet Liner by Tuff Skin helps keep loose items from shifting around in the bed.

By keeping the accessories to a minimum, the Tundra's handling isn't the least bit negatively affected by excess weight.

is an excellent place to toss loose gear that'd otherwise roll around in the bed of the truck.

Next, we went with two overland-specific accessories: a Krazy Beaver shovel and a pair of Tred GT Recovery Boards. The shovel is a great all-around tool that's lightweight and works awesome; as for the boards, these are invaluable when stuck in deep sand or snow, and we've found them to be a Godsend on vehicles that don't have winches. And these, ladies and gentlemen, are the extent of the trendy overland accessories that we included on this truck.

At this point, we can feel the scorn welling up inside a few of you. "Where's the Hi-Lift jack?" you ask. Much like firearms, Hi-Lifts are useful tools that can be deadly if used incorrectly. Plus, they're heavy. If you choose to include one on your vehicle, good for you — just make sure you know exactly how to operate it, otherwise you're merely hauling a 30-pound accessory. "OK," you say, "but what about the utility can racks? The portable shower? The folding table?" These things and accessories like them, in our humble opinion, belong in the bed of the truck; they need not be permanently affixed to the vehicle. Every bit of weight you add will affect the handling of the truck in some way, and it's our belief that going slick is vastly preferable to overdoing it.

Which brings us to our final point, the money-saving tip that we teased earlier: There's a lot of buzz surrounding roof-top mounted tents within the overland space, making this one of the first accessories that new overlanders gravitate toward. Our advice? Don't do it. Even with hardy aftermarket suspension, adding that much weight to the top of the vehicle results in body roll and wallowing. Plus, rooftop tents catch a ton of wind and usually cause your fuel efficiency to plummet. Many rooftop tents run upward of $2,000, while a quality six-man, four-season tent can be found for under $400, and you can set it up anywhere — not just where you park.

As a bonus, if someone in your group badly cuts themselves chopping firewood, you don't need to first wrap up your tent before hauling butt to the nearest urgent care for stitches. Yes, we realize that speaking out against rooftop tents is sacrilege in the overland world. But unless you routinely camp in swamps, you use a tent more than 200 nights a year, or you've just got money to burn, a rooftop tent is probably not the best solution, even though they look cool.

Aftermath

Whether you have a 10-year-old truck or a brand-new vehicle, we hope you'll use the above information to help guide your overland modification decisions in the future. This Tundra's configuration is by no means the definitive overland rig; it's merely an example of one of the countless ways you can set up a truck. Yes, we dedicated a ton of space to the handling and suspension — because it's that important. No, this truck doesn't look half as Gucci as the decked-out rigs you can find on Instagram. But when it comes to pure function and performance, this vehicle and those that have been modified in a similar fashion will provide a high degree of usability to the outdoor-hungry end user.

PARTS LIST

COMPANY	PRODUCT	PRICE	CONTACT
Total Chaos Fabrication	2nd Gen Tundra Upper Control Arms; 1-inch Stainless Steel Uniball Replacement Kit; Polyurethane Bushing Kit	$918 (UCAs) $198 (Uniball) $60 (Bushings)	www.chaosfab.com
Elka Suspension	2.5 DC Reservoir Front and Rear Shock Kit	$3,400	www.elkasuspension.com
Toyo Tire	Open Country A/T II	Contact Your Local Dealer	www.toyotires.com
ToyTec Lifts	Labor	Contact For Pricing	www.toyteclifts.com
Wilco Offroad	ADV Chase Rack 2.0; TireGate RaceRunner; Quick Fist Mounting Brackets	$1,350 (rack) $1,664 (TireGate) $52 (Quick Fists)	www.wilcooffroad.com
White Knuckle Offroad	Rock Sliders	$920	www.white-knuckleoffroad.com
KC Hilites	Gravity LED Pro6 LED Light Bar; KC Flex LED 10-inch Light Bar; KC Flex LED Ditch Mount 2-Light System — Spread Beam; Gravity LED G4 LED Fog Light Pair; 2-inch C-Series C2 LEDs; 2-inch Cyclone LED Lights (Clear/Amber/Red)	$1,300 (Pro6) $495 (10-inch Flex) $606 (Ditch Lights) $310 (Fogs) $132 (C2 Lights) $174 (Cyclones)	www.kchilites.com
sPOD	SourceLT with Mini6 Switch Panel	$580	www.4x4spod.com
High County Performance 4X4	Light Wiring	Contact For Pricing	www.hcp4x4.com
Bullet Liner by Tuff Skin	Spray Bed Liner	Contact For Pricing	www.bulletlinerbytuffskin.com
Bushwacker	Pocket Style Fender Flares	$499	www.bushwacker.com
Pelican	iM3200 Storm Long Case	$274	www.pelican.com
Tred	GT Recovery Boards	$200	www.arbusa.com
Krazy Beaver	Shovel	$85	www.krazybeavertools.com
Greyman Tactical	Vehicle Rifle Rack — Rubber Clamps + 15.25 x 25 RMP	$250	www.greymantactical.com
Wet Okole	Seat Covers	$544	www.wetokole.com

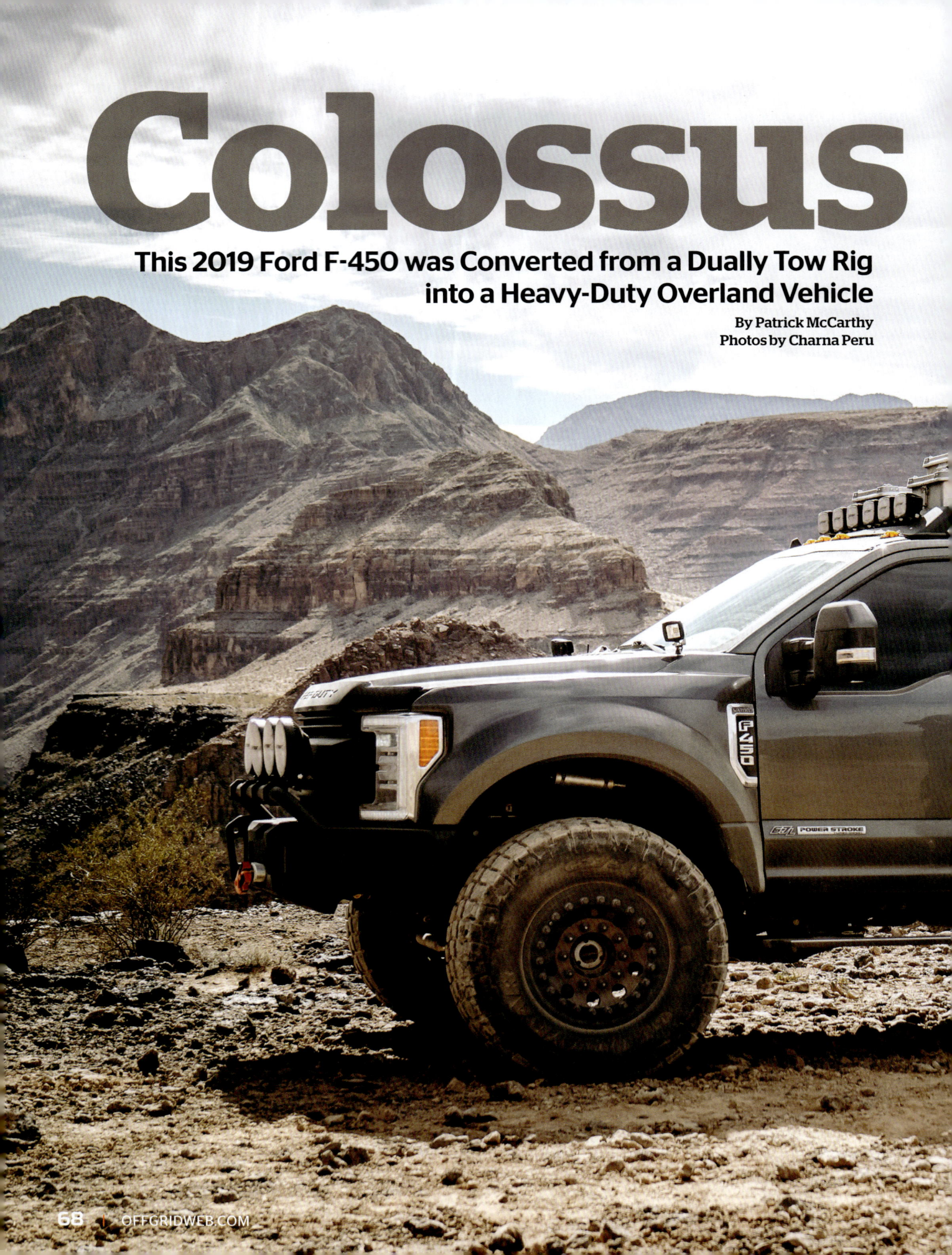

Colossus

This 2019 Ford F-450 was Converted from a Dually Tow Rig into a Heavy-Duty Overland Vehicle

By Patrick McCarthy
Photos by Charna Peru

With an 8,600-pound curb weight — roughly equivalent to three Toyota Corollas — and 35,000-pound maximum towing capacity, this Ford F-450 is about as much truck as you can get before graduating to a commercial-grade model. Unlike its F-250 and F-350 Super Duty siblings, the 2019 F-450 was only available with a 6.7L turbo-diesel V-8 that produces 450 horsepower and 935 pound-feet of torque, and only offered in dual-rear-wheel (aka "dually") configuration. It's perfectly suited to driving coast-to-coast with a massive trailer in tow but might be considered overkill for an overland vehicle build — that is, unless you're the Peru family.

Justice Peru writes, "What you see today definitely wasn't our Plan A or even our Plan B. If I had to guess, I'd say we are on Plan E or F at this point." In 2019, he was spending about 85 percent of the year traveling for work. "I was missing my son's milestones and being omitted from family memories. I told my wife [Charna] that she and our son should join me on the road." Charna was hesitant to spend most of the year bouncing between hotels and airports, so the two settled on the idea of creating a tiny home on wheels. Unlike a cumbersome RV that would be relegated to highways and truck stops, the Peru family wanted a truck that was ready for any adventure, on-road or off-road.

The first version of this project was inspired by Earthroamer, a company that builds custom, turnkey overland rigs on the Ford F-550 4x4 chassis. However, prices for those trucks start at $665,000 and can easily surpass $800,000. The Peru family wanted to spend far less than that, yet retain most of the capabilities. It wouldn't be easy.

After leaving the dealership in their new F-450, the first step was to switch the towing-oriented dually setup to an off-road-friendly single rear wheel and widen the front track width to match. "I spent a lot of time researching the components for the super single conversion. This wasn't a catalog build by any means. More times than not, we had to go with the only option rather than what we'd prefer," Justice recalls. A local diesel mechanic — 321 Auto in Merritt Island, Florida — installed the Carli suspension, wider McNeil Racing front fenders, 20x10-inch Stazworks wheels, and 41-inch Goodyear tires. The front bumper contains a Smittybilt XRC Gen2 12,000-pound winch. The rear bumper features containers for water and fuel, as well as a prototype reinforced tire carrier that was needed to support the hefty 206-pound full-size spare tire.

Initially, the truck was configured with an aluminum camper in the bed, but limited capabilities and structural issues led the Perus to ditch that setup after a few months. Now, the truck is configured to tow a Black Series HQ17 off-road camper. That left the bed open for a prototype Mule Expedition Equipment rack, which offers adjustable height to clear dirt bikes and other tall cargo. The rack supports a 23Zero Kabari roof-top tent and two Peregrine 180 awnings, so the Peru family can still have a comfortable place to sleep when they're not towing the camper. A second Mule rack was added to the truck's roof, and carries four AluBoxes loaded with gear, plus a 23Zero Peregrine shower enclosure.

The F-450 rides on a Carli 4.5-inch Pintop suspension kit with King 2.5-inch shocks up front and Carli heavy-duty leaf springs with 3-inch lift blocks in the rear. Since the new camper weighs up to 9,000 pounds loaded, Air Lift Load Lifter airbags were also installed, along with Daystar airbag cradles that are detached to maximize off-road suspension travel when they're not in use.

To illuminate the highways, trails, and campsites where this truck resides, Justice added an array of LightForce products. These include four HTX2s and two Strikers on the front bumper, six more Strikers on the roof rack, four Nightfall ROK 40s on the rear bumper and ditch brackets, and a handful of ROK 20 and ROK 9 utility lights all around the

When the F-450 isn't towing a trailer or weighed down with cargo, the Air Lift airbags and Daystar cradles can be disconnected from the axle to allow full suspension articulation.

To switch from a dually rear end to a "super single" setup with square track width, Justice added custom Stazworks forged aluminum wheels and wider McNeil Racing front fenders.

The F-450's gargantuan spare tire weighs 206 pounds, and most swing-away carriers aren't built to handle that kind of weight. So, ExpeditionOne used the truck as a test bed for a new beefed-up prototype Dual Swing rear bumper (available by special order).

bed rack. An RCR-Force-12 control unit from Switch Pros toggles all the lighting on and off.

Inside the cab, two-thirds of the Lariat trim rear bench seat have been removed to make room for a DIY platform that contains toolboxes, a storage cubby, a Goal Zero 500X portable power station, and a Dometic CFX3 35 fridge. A smaller Dometic CCF-T fridge was installed in the center console to keep drinks and snacks cool. There's still enough room in the back of the cab for the Perus' dog and one passenger. Up front, 67 Designs phone mounts make it convenient to check downloaded OnX Maps for off-grid navigation, and a RAM floor mount holds an iPad that monitors the F-450's vitals through the EZ LYNK Auto Agent app. Handheld Rugged Radios allow communication with spotters on difficult trails.

Justice writes, "Our truck is our only vehicle. With about 100,000 miles in 2.5 years, it has made multiple cross-country trips transitioning from pavement to dirt with just a change in tire pressure." He and Charna — who took all the photos seen in this article — have bombed through trails in Baja, crossed Imogene Pass in Colorado, and even completed the famous Top of the World trail near Moab, Utah. "Due to our longer wheelbase and the lines being more for Jeeps, my wife had to walk most of the trail just to spot me on the technical parts. Slowly but surely, we made it to the top just before sunset. If you've ever been, you know that view is absolutely worth it."

2019 "TINY HOME TOY HAULER" FORD F-450 4X4 LARIAT

DRIVETRAIN: 6.7L Power Stroke turbo-diesel V-8 with S&B Filters intake, intercooler pipe, MAP sensor spacer, and 68-gallon fuel tank; TorqShift 6R140 automatic transmission with Proven Diesel tune; PMF Dana 60 front axle truss and front diff cover

SUSPENSION: Carli 4.5-inch Pintop front suspension kit with torsion sway bar, radius arms, and King 2.5-inch remote reservoir shocks; Carli Deaver HD rear leveling leaf springs on 3-inch lift blocks, Air Lift Load Lifter 5,000 airbags, Daystar airbag cradles (all components from CJC Off Road)

WHEELS & TIRES: 20x10 Stazworks 3-Piece Forged Super Single wheels with G275 335/80R20 Goodyear tires

BODY MODIFICATIONS: McNeil Racing 6-inch bulge front fenders, ExpeditionOne Ultra HD front bumper (modified to fit wide fenders) and prototype reinforced Dual Swing rear bumper, Ford OEM upgraded LED headlights and black XL grille, Mule Expedition Equipment roof rack and customized 8-foot bed rack, Icky Concepts bulkhead MOLLE panel

LIGHTING & ACCESSORIES: 23Zero tent, awnings, and shower enclosure; LightForce LED lights with Switch Pros control unit, Smittybilt winch with Custom Splice 3/8-inch Diamondback Mainline rope and Factor 55 UltraHook, dual Extreme Outback Magnum air compressors, Equipt1 AluBox cases, Dometic refrigerator, Goal Zero Yeti 500X power station, iPad in RAM Mount

URL: tinyhometoyhauler.com
IG: @tinyhometoyhauler

Technical K.O.

Dillon Aero's Minigun-Equipped Ford Ranger Isn't Your Typical Pickup with a Machine Gun Bolted to the Bed

By Patrick McCarthy

The term "technical" is often used to describe a civilian vehicle — usually a 4x4 pickup like the venerable Toyota Hilux — that has been modified to carry an onboard weapon system such as a heavy machine gun, anti-aircraft cannon, or anti-tank rocket launcher. The underlying light, mobile weapon concept dates back far beyond the automobile to horse-drawn tachanka carts of the First World War and carroballistas (essentially huge crossbows mounted on carriages) of the Roman Empire. However, according to the book Technicals: Non-Standard Tactical Vehicles from the Great War to Modern Special Forces by Leigh Neville, this descriptor originated during the Somali Civil War in the early 1990s, where NGOs hired local gunmen in "Mad Max-style armed pickup trucks" for protection under the guise of being "technical advisers."

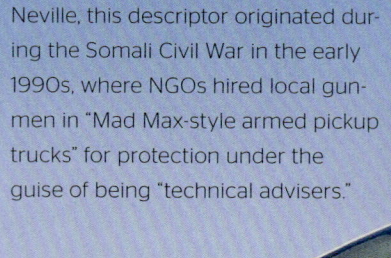

The bed cage was designed to accommodate overland accessories such as these Rotopax fuel canisters.

Fox coilovers with remote-reservoir shocks allow this Ranger to handle washboard desert roads smoothly at speed.

This high-clearance Coastal Offroad rear bumper includes a swing-out with a full-size spare tire, trash bag, and antenna mount.

A Mil-spec PRC-113 radio adds communication capabilities to this truck. To save space on the dash, its bulky amplifier was relocated to the floor behind the center console.

As with other weapon concepts that have persisted through history, technicals still appear in nearly every modern conflict because they're extremely effective. Unlike purpose-built military vehicles that require specialized, expensive parts and complex maintenance routines, technicals are based on vehicles that can be purchased locally and serviced at any Jiffy Lube (or its third-world equivalent). Their weapon components are bolted or welded in place, so they can just as easily be removed and exchanged. And if the vehicle is damaged in combat, repairing or replacing it is a matter of tens of thousands of dollars, not hundreds of thousands.

Arizona-based weapon manufacturer Dillon Aero recognized the merits of the technical formula, but wanted to put its own spin on it — literally. The Dillon team purchased this 2021 Ford Ranger and equipped it with the company's Multi-Mission Capable (MMC) system, which is a modular, power-operated turret that can accept a wide variety of weapons. The compatibility list includes M240 and M60 medium machine guns, M2 .50-caliber heavy machine gun, MK19/MK47/H&K GMG automatic grenade launchers, the Russian PKM, and many others. But this truck features the cream of the crop — Dillon Aero's M134D minigun, which doles out a staggering 3,000 rounds of 7.62 NATO per minute. That's 50 rounds per second, or about four times the rate of fire of an M240. While taking photos for this article, we had the opportunity to send some rounds downrange with the M134D in the MMC turret, and we can only describe it is as a firehose of hot

lead. If you can use one without grinning ear-to-ear, we can't be friends.

As cool as the minigun is, there's more to this truck than its armament. A representative told us, "The Dillon Aero Ford Ranger goes a step further with the engineering effort to mount field-deployable communication systems that allow for ground control of military and civilian aircraft. We also implemented overland features that allow for extended capability in various mission settings." The most noticeable upgrade is a one-of-a-kind custom bed cage that supports the MMC system; Dillon engineers designed and prototyped it using CAD files provided by Ford. The truck also features Coastal Offroad front and rear bumper sheetmetal kits, which were welded and finished in-house. The front bumper contains four Baja Designs LED lights and a Warn winch; the rear bumper has a swing-out spare tire carrier and antenna mount. That antenna is connected to a Mil-spec PRC-113 VHF/UHF radio that sits atop the truck's dash.

For improved off-road capability, the Ranger was equipped with ShrockWorks rock sliders, a Coastal Off-road skid plate, Fox remote-reservoir shocks, 17-inch Fifteen52 wheels, and 33-inch BFGoodrich all-terrain tires. Additionally, a Roam Adventure Co. awning was bolted onto the Prinsu roof rack, and Rotopax fuel canisters were installed on the bed cage.

Although technicals are typically the work of "austere" mechanics and fabricators in war-torn countries, it's not hard to see why mainstream manufacturers like Dillon Aero (and Global Military Products, distributors of the Scorpion mortar truck we featured in Issue 61) are getting on board with the idea. It's much easier and more cost-effective to install a

The Dillon Aero MMC turret system built into this custom bed cage helps the operator maintain control of the M134D as it spews a near-continuous beam of rounds downrange. This weapon produces a considerable pile of spent brass and belt links after a few short bursts.

The MMC turret accepts a variety of weapons, including heavy machine guns and grenade launchers, but this Ranger is equipped with Dillon's own M134D Minigun. We're told they also have plans to try it with the .50-caliber 503D Gatling gun in the near future.

weapon system on a locally sourced civilian truck than it is to send a custom-built military vehicle halfway across the globe and keep it running. Kyle Goodale of Dillon's Special Projects skunkworks explained, "We've had many vehicle platforms come into the shop, usually built for one purpose or another … The Ranger represents the first project of its type for Dillon Aero, where the Special Projects division was given a blank slate to build upon. We look forward to implementing it in our testing processes for various weapon systems such as the 503D (.50-caliber Gatling gun) platform and having a good time with it as well."

2021 FORD RANGER XLT SUPERCREW 4X4

DRIVETRAIN: 2.3L EcoBoost 4-cylinder with 10-speed automatic transmission

SUSPENSION: Fox Performance Elite Series 2.5 remote reservoir coilover shocks

ARMAMENT: Dillon Aero MMC turret system equipped with Dillon Aero M134D Minigun and Trijicon MGRS sight

WHEELS & TIRES: 17-inch Fifteen52 Turbomac HD wheels, 285/70R17 BFGoodrich All-Terrain T/A KO2 tires

BODY MODIFICATIONS: Dillon Aero custom bed cage, Coastal Offroad front/rear bumpers and skid plate, ShrockWorks rock sliders, Prinsu roof rack, Roam Adventure Co. awning, Rotopax fuel containers

ELECTRONICS: Baja Designs Squadron Pro bumper lights and S2 Pro A-pillar lights on SDHQ brackets, sPOD HD light/accessory controller, PRC-113 radio with VRC-83 amplifier and bumper-mounted antenna, Warn winch

OWNER & BUILDER: Dillon Aero Inc. Scottsdale, Arizona

WEB: dillonaero.com

SPECIAL THANKS: Foothills Fabrication, ShrockWorks, Coastal Offroad, SDHQ Motorsports

A New Path

This Custom Super Duty Was Built to Meet the Needs of a Triple-Amputee U.S. Navy EOD Veteran

By Patrick McCarthy
Photos by Iain Harrison

Andrew Bottrell's life changed instantly on October 1, 2011. Less than four months earlier, he deployed to Afghanistan as a U.S. Navy Explosive Ordnance Disposal (EOD) tech attached to SEAL Team 10. On that fateful day, the vehicle Bottrell was riding in was struck by a roadside IED. In the wake of the explosion, he realized he had sustained severe injuries to his left arm and both legs — this would result in the amputation of all three limbs. As he spent the following months enduring painful physical therapy and learning to use his new prosthetics, he maintained a strong sense of determination. "Always dominate your life — do not let your life dictate what you do or how you live. If you do not like your situation, change it. Do not blame somebody else for it and do not wait for somebody else to do something about it."

In 2018, Richard Harrison (aka The Old Man) of the famous TV series *Pawn Stars* passed away. He was a Navy veteran and loved vehicles, so his son Rick Harrison decided to give a custom truck to a wounded Navy vet in his father's memory. Rick teamed up with Wounded Warriors Family Support (WWFS) to accomplish this goal; Bottrell was nominated by the EOD Warrior Foundation and eventually chosen.

WWFS had built custom trucks for other wounded veterans in the past, so they approached Bottrell and offered him a new 2019 Ford F-250

Hunting is one of Bottrell's favorite hobbies, so he enjoys having a truck that serves as a comfortable base of operations in remote areas. Adding a Skin It Rite gambrel to the crane allows him to skin game easily.

One Nut Shell container houses a battery monitor, circuit breaker, and master power switch for the four onboard LiFePO4 batteries. Those batteries are hidden between the outer walls of the TruckVault drawer system and the inner walls of the truck bed.

The power-operated SpitzLift crane swings out and extends up to 4 feet, helping Andrew Bottrell hoist coolers and other heavy items into the bed or the TruckVault drawers. With a mast extension, it can also lift the rooftop tent off the top of the rack.

Super Duty with hand controls, an automatic wheelchair lift, and any other modifications to make his life easier. Bottrell explained that he doesn't own a wheelchair, and they replied, "Well, what would you like to have added to your truck?" After he put together a wish list, WWFS started on the build.

First, Bottrell's F-250 was sent to Kelderman in Iowa to receive a variety of the company's air suspension upgrades. The front suspension was replaced with a Kelderman 2-stage stock height kit, and the rear suspension was swapped out for a stock height 4-link system. An Air Lift control system was also installed, along with dual compressors in a weather-resistant box, two 3-gallon air tanks, sensors, wiring, and more. Bottrell says, "It's like riding on a cloud — it's so smooth."

The next stop was at Nuthouse Industries in Ohio, where it received a Tech 3 Series Expedition Bed Rack equipped with numerous accessories. One side of the rack features two Rotopax diesel containers and a water container; the other side carries another water container plus two 18-inch Nut Shell modular storage boxes. The first box contains the brain of the Super Duty's auxiliary power system, a Xantrex charger/inverter, which is linked to the truck's alternator and four Dragonfly Energy LiFePO4 batteries in the bed. This system provides 400 amp-hours of power, which is accessible from a power strip inside the second Nut Shell box.

This electricity can be used to power a SpitzLift DC-powered crane in the bed, allowing Bottrell to lift heavy gear in and out of the truck,

Each side of the Nuthouse Industries bed rack is equipped with storage for fuel or water tanks and other gear. It's also equipped with area lighting for nighttime activities.

or even suspend a deer for gutting and skinning after a hunt. The batteries also power the deluxe lighting package Nuthouse Industries installed on its rack, a Dometic CFX100 fridge-freezer for camping trips, and various other small electronics. The fridge typically sits alongside a Canyon Coolers Navigator on a Cargoglide sliding platform, which is bolted to the top of the TruckVault locking drawer system. Nuthouse also installed Fab Fours bumpers, Warn winch, Rigid Industries LED lights, and even ported air from the Kelderman tanks so Bottrell can re-inflate his truck's tires on the trail. In case of emergencies in remote locations, a WeBoost cell phone network extender and a Garmin InReach satellite communicator ensure he can always call for help.

Finally, Bottrell had an iKamper rooftop tent and a Bush Company 270-degree awning attached to the top of the rack, making the truck a comfortable base camp for multi-day outings. But even without the spacious tent, Bottrell pointed out one upside to having detachable limbs: "I disassemble, so I can stretch out on the back seat to sleep."

With all these upgrades, Bottrell's F-250 is equipped with everything he needs for an active lifestyle off the grid — spare fuel, shelter, water, cold food and drinks, lighting, and more than enough juice to run power tools and other electronics. So far, he has used it to hunt wild pigs with his dad in central California, hunt elk in Montana, and hunt Nilgai antelope in Texas, as well as for several cross-country road trips.

Although losing three limbs wasn't the path Bottrell anticipated taking

The Kelderman adjustable air suspension allows this F-250 to ride smoothly, both on and off road, regardless of how much weight is loaded into the bed.

2019 FORD F-250 LARIAT SPORT 4X4

DRIVETRAIN: 6.7L Power Stroke turbo-diesel V-8 with hand controls and a Titan 55-gallon fuel tank

SUSPENSION: Kelderman 2-Stage front and 4-link rear air suspension, Air Lift 3H Electronic Air Control System, dual air compressors, dual 3-gallon air tanks

WHEELS & TIRES: Stock 20-inch wheels with 285/65R20 BFGoodrich KO2 tires

BODY MODIFICATIONS: Nuthouse Industries Tech 3 Series Expedition Bed Rack with Nut Shell storage boxes, Rotopax plates, and Maxtrax mounts; TruckVault Field Ranger bed drawer system, CargoGlide CG1000XL bed slide, Fab Fours Matrix front bumper and Vengeance rear bumper, iKamper xCover rooftop tent, Bush Company 270 XT awning

ELECTRONICS: Four 100-amp-hour Dragonfly Energy heated 12-volt LiFePO4 batteries with Xantrex Freedom XC 2000-watt inverter/charger and custom power box containing a Victron Energy battery monitor, Blue Sea Systems circuit breakers, and a power strip; SpitzLift LTD-4QRT 4-foot DC-powered crane, Rigid Industries bumper lights, Nuthouse Industries deluxe bed rack lighting package, Dometic CFX100 fridge/freezer, Warn Zeon 12-S Platinum winch

INTERIOR UPGRADES: Console Vault center console safe, Greyman Tactical seat back MOLLE panels, Garmin Navigator tablet on a Ram Mount, WeBoost cell phone network extender

OWNER: Andrew Bottrell, San Diego, CA

SPECIAL THANKS: Wounded Warriors Family Support, Rick Harrison from Pawn Stars, Nuthouse Industries, and Dragonfly Energy

in life, he hasn't let that stop him or even slow him down. He's thankful for the new truck that has made it easier for him to enjoy adventures with his family and friends.

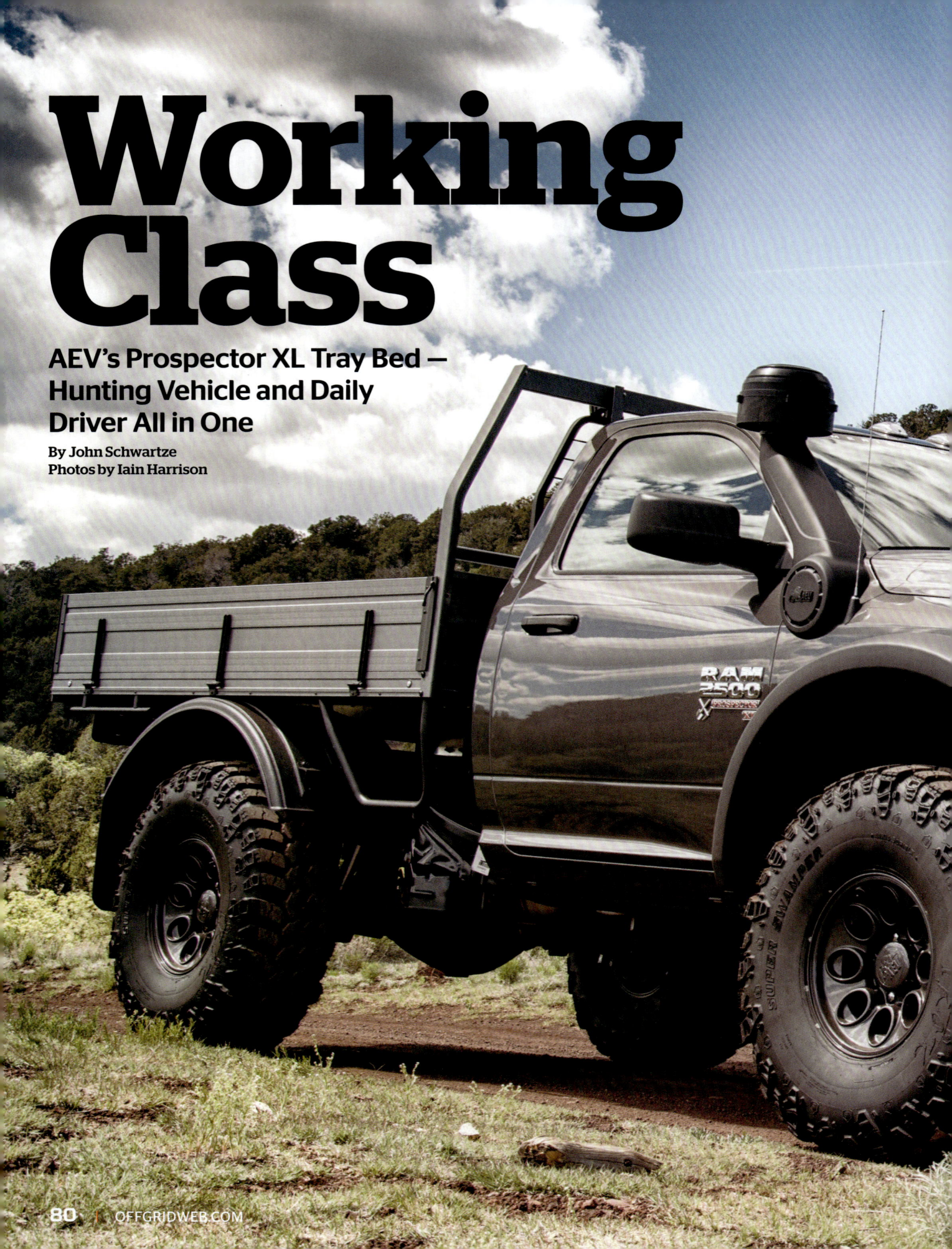

Working Class

AEV's Prospector XL Tray Bed —
Hunting Vehicle and Daily
Driver All in One

By John Schwartze
Photos by Iain Harrison

Have you ever been to a restaurant where the menu is the culinary version of *War and Peace*? When your options become too abundant, it's easy to suffer from paralysis by analysis. So what exactly does one need in a vehicle that'll serve as both your daily driver as well as withstand the rigors of an off-road hunting trip? Let's face it, most of us aren't trust-fund babies, so we need a multipurpose vehicle. After all, we just spent X amount of dollars on a rifle, optic, clothing, license, tags … you get the picture. If we want to avoid buying another vehicle used solely for hunting (and a subsequent divorce) then let's deconstruct what's really important.

AEV PROSPECTOR XL TRAY BED
MAKE: Ram
URL: www.aev-conversions.com

TRUCKS • WORKING CLASS | **81**

Top: With only a 3-inch lift, the Prospector XL Tray Bed is proportionally well balanced. You might not realize it's sitting on a set of 17x10 AEV Katla wheels.

Middle: Retractable side steps are a nice touch and tuck up out of the way when you're ascending some jagged terrain.

Bottom: Onboard air connections are a part of the ARB front and rear air lockers to help keep power to the wheels and put the "limited" back in limited slip.

Stop for a second and imagine you're back in the 1950s on a hunting trip. You don't have ATVs, UTVs, side-by-sides and all these vehicles that have become the new normal of off-road transportation, but did that ruin one's ability to have a successful outing? Nope. You just needed something that'd haul people, supplies, and game; work in a variety of settings; and be robust enough to take a beating. So fast-forward to present day. While a vintage Chevy Thriftmaster may no longer be the best option, a vehicle that checks off the aforementioned prerequisites with some modern conveniences is definitely worth a look.

If you haven't heard of American Expeditions Vehicles, or AEV for short, it was born out of owner Dave Harriton's firsthand experience in learning what off-road vehicles really needed to endure the brutal conditions of Montana. His need to improve upon his own personal YJ Jeep with a stretched wheelbase and add other custom touches didn't go unnoticed, and he soon found himself taking orders when people caught on to his eye for engineering. From there the company snowballed into not only aftermarket parts, but also offers turnkey custom vehicles for sale.

The issue with most custom vehicles (and even firearms) is that you're combining a bunch of parts from different companies who are operating in a vacuum about their product's compatibility with other aftermarket offerings. People often discover when they're thousands of dollars into a build that many parts just don't play well together. That creates not only lots of experimentation and additional costs, but you end up sacrificing reliability and comfort. In order to avoid the "truckenstein" situation, AEV manufactures its parts to work together and virtually all are made right here in the U.S. to ensure quality control and unified function.

AEV's latest creation is the Prospector XL Tray Bed. Ram has been churning out some of the best trucks on the market in recent years, and the addition of rear coil springs offers a variety of spring rate options for your overall package. The goal at AEV was not to deviate from the stock steering geometry and ride quality, which is the usual can of worms opened with larger tires, shocks, and other typical off-road add-ons. The focus is to retain the Dodge DNA in terms of appearance and parts versatility, but make it perform like it's competing for the CrossFit Games.

Based on the Ram 2500 regular cab/longbed platform, a 3-inch lift courtesy of AEV's DualSport SC suspension raises the roll center, allows more wheel travel for the huge 41-inch IROK rubber, and improves handling and stability. Dual ARB air lockers (with onboard air connections) provide additional grab and the gear ratio has been upped to 4.30. When our fearless editor Iain Harrison was out slogging the Prospector XL through the Flagstaff, Arizona, hill country, he confirmed it rode as smooth as a prom queen's thighs.

The lightweight aluminum tray bed not only gives increased storage area for ATVs, a camper, ARB compressor, and larger fuel tank, but fold-down sides allow for ease of loading and unloading. AEV's mounts fasten the bed to the frame and the addition of flares and a steel bumper keep it looking like it was a factory option and not some aftermarket contraption designed to fit any truck on the market.

While you might look at the snorkel and think, "I don't need that," it's there for the obvious purpose of protecting your engine during water crossings as well as keeping the induction high to minimize the amount of dust getting into it. The steel front bumper incorporates plates to protect it from obstacles encountered at steep approach angles and also includes a Warn 16.5ti Winch and 30-inch Vision Xmitter lightbar.

At first blush you might think it couldn't possibly be practical as a grocery getter, but the Prospector XL can serve that purpose whether your groceries are store bought or obtained from hunting waterfowl, feral hogs of the Texas hill country, or mountain-dwelling elk. We liken it to a Swiss Army knife — it's one thing capable of numerous duties. The standard features it offers alone were enough to whet our appetite, but additional touches like a rear vision system, leather package, and differential covers make it a very purpose-driven truck for driving to the office or your favorite honey hole.

With a tray bed, you're not hampered by the usual limitations of a single side that opens and space usually occupied by the wheel humps.

Home on the Ranger

Hellwig's 2019 Ford Ranger Offers Fully Appointed Backcountry Lodging for Overland Adventures

By Patrick McCarthy
Photos courtesy of Hellwig

Anyone who has attempted to plan a family outing knows all too well that the term "camping" can represent a wide range of experiences, depending on who you ask. To some, it means hiking to a remote campsite with nothing but a backpack, and sleeping in a bivvy bag under the stars (or possibly a tarp, if you're feeling fancy). For others, camping signifies a much more comfortable experience in the great outdoors — access to a roomy tent, electricity, full-size stove, and plenty of storage for recreational gear, food, and cold beverages. There will always be purists who decry the latter activity as "glamping," but even if you're a die-hard ultralight backpacker, it's hard to deny the occasional appeal of this form of travel. Plus, it's rather difficult to drag your mountain bikes, kayaks, or hard cases full of guns up a rutted mountain trail on foot. This is where overland truck builds excel.

Hellwig Products has a long history of upgrading trucks. The company was founded in 1946 by Rudy Hellwig, a postwar entrepreneur who noticed a common problem on American highways: vehicles carrying heavy loads often limped along with sagging, bottomed-out suspension. This resulted in a nose-high stance, poor handling, and potentially dangerous instability at speed. At his shop in central California, Rudy produced "Helper Springs" that allowed customers to bolster their vehicles' rear suspension and carry heavy loads more safely. Three generations later, the company is still owned and operated by the Hellwig family and still manufactures its suspension components in the USA.

Above: The Yakima bed rack features attachment points for a shovel, fuel and water cans, and perimeter LED lights, in addition to the Tepui rooftop tent.

Left: Gunmetal gray ICON wheels and Falken Wildpeak A/T3W tires give the truck a trail-ready stance.

TRUCKS • HOME ON THE RANGER | 85

An sPOD Bantam touchscreen interface offers full control of Rigid Industries lights mounted on the bumpers, A-pillars, undercarriage, and bed rack.

When the truck isn't running, this Goal Zero Yeti 1400 provides 1,425Wh of stand-alone electricity. Goal Zero Boulder 100 solar panels can be set out during the day to recharge the unit.

The team at Hellwig recently set out to create an overland-style truck based on the new-body-style Ford Ranger. The build began with a 2019 four-door Super-Crew model with the FX4 off-road package. Its turbo-charged 2.3L motor provides plenty of low-end torque to overcome rough terrain, and the 10-speed automatic transmission makes it equally proficient at long stints on the highway. However, Hellwig had no intention of leaving this truck in stock form.

Unsurprisingly, the first area addressed was the Ranger's suspension. It received a 3.5-inch lift kit from ICON Vehicle Dynamics, as well as Hellwig's own helper springs and rear sway bar — the latter items help the truck comfortably carry all the additional gear we'll discuss below. ICON also provided 17-inch wheels, which were wrapped in 34-inch Falken Wildpeak all-terrain tires. Bushwacker fender flares and Addictive Desert Designs (ADD) Venom R bumpers make room for these larger tires; ADD rock sliders protect the door sills from impacts. Rigid Industries light bars offer clear visibility for dark trails or remote campsites.

The Ranger's exterior received a custom paint job with blue and yellow accents at LGE-CTS Motorsports in California. A T-Rex grille and custom Billet Badges add a little extra visual flair. Inside the cab, the seats and door

2019 FORD RANGER XLT SUPERCREW FX4

ENGINE: 2.3L EcoBoost turbocharged 4-cylinder: 270 hp at 5,500 rpm, 310 lb-ft at 3,000 rpm

TRANSMISSION: 10-speed SelectShift automatic

DRIVELINE: 2WD/4WD with two-speed transfer case

SUSPENSION: ICON Vehicle Dynamics 3.5-inch suspension system, Hellwig adjustable rear sway bar and steel helper springs

WHEELS & TIRES: 17x8.5 ICON Compression wheels, 285/75R17 Falken Wildpeak A/T3W tires

BED RACK & TENT: Yakima Overhaul HD rack with Tepui HyBox rooftop tent and Yakima SlimShady awning

MOBILE KITCHEN: Trail Kitchens bed-mounted kitchen and accessories, BedSlide 1000 Classic, Expedition Essentials ExO Table Lite, ARB Elements freezer/fridge

LIGHTING & ELECTRICAL: Rigid Industries LED lights; Goal Zero Yeti 1400 power station, Boulder 100 solar panels, and Yeti Link car charging kit

MOUNTAIN BIKES: Specialized Levo Turbo bikes on Yakima HoldUp EVO bike rack attached to RIGd UltraSwing hitch carrier

CREATED BY: Hellwig Products
www.hellwigproducts.com

BUILT BY: Old Steel Hotrods and Sickles
Leona Valley, CA

Above: Like an adventurous transformer, this Ranger unfolds to reveal a two-person tent, complete kitchen with stove and freezer/fridge, mobile power station, and four-speaker outdoor sound system.

Below: For additional clearance, load-carrying capacity, and stability, the Ranger was fitted with an ICON lift kit, Hellwig helper springs, and a Hellwig adjustable rear sway bar.

panels were reupholstered with upscale Katzkin leather, and Rockford Fosgate speakers were installed for clearer sound quality.

At this stage, the Hellwig Ranger was substantially improved over its stock form, but it wasn't yet a true adventure rig. For that, attention had to be focused on the bed. A Yakima Overhaul HD bed rack was installed, as well as a Yakima SlimShady roll-up awning and HoldUp EVO bike rack. The latter item is used to carry two matching mountain bikes, namely a pair of Specialized Levo Turbos. The bikes and carrier are attached to a RIGd UltraSwing hitch carrier, which swings conveniently out of the way to allow unrestricted access to the tailgate.

> ### EVEN IF YOU'RE A DIE-HARD ULTRALIGHT BACKPACKER, IT'S HARD TO DENY THE APPEAL OF THIS FORM OF TRAVEL.

A Tepui HyBox rooftop tent was mounted atop the bed rack. Unlatching its hard shell reveals a roomy two-person sleeping area. Beneath it, the sides of the rack were fitted with various accessories — Daystar Cam Cans for fuel and water, a Krazy Beaver shovel, more Rigid Industries LED lights, and a Rockford Fosgate exterior sound system with four speakers and a weatherproof head unit. These electronics are powered by a Goal Zero Yeti 1400 power station, which can be recharged via Goal Zero Boulder 100 solar panels or from the truck's engine using a Yeti Link car charging kit. Additional gear can be stored in the nine Pelican hard cases arranged throughout the bed. An array of single-key BOLT locks were installed to ensure all this expensive equipment doesn't grow legs and disappear.

Lastly, whether it's used for processing game after a hunt or grilling burgers at a tailgate party, a good kitchen setup is a must for any adventure vehicle. Trail Kitchens provided a complete system with flip-down work surfaces, cookware storage compartments, a camp sink, and a Camp Chef two-burner stove. An Expedition Essentials table is mounted on the inside of the UltraSwing carrier for additional prep space. Drinks and perishable items can be stored in the ARB Elements freezer/fridge, which is mounted on a BedSlide platform for easy, slide-out access.

Hellwig's 2019 Ranger serves as an optimal platform for cross-country trips filled with mountain biking, hunting, fishing, and exploring the roads less traveled. Whether your family thinks staying at the Holiday Inn constitutes "roughing it" or they sneer at the idea of using an established campsite, this truck offers a middle ground that everyone can enjoy.

Proof of Concept

The "Ranger Goat" Tacoma Memorializes the Past and Validates the Future of Tactical Application Vehicles

By Patrick McCarthy

Losing a loved one is always traumatic, but it also presents an important turning point. Rather than being overcome by grief, we must find the strength to live on in a way that would make that person proud. Walt Wagner made this difficult choice after his cousin — a former Army Ranger, federal law enforcement officer, and tactical medic — passed away unexpectedly at a young age. The two men had bonded over their love for overland vehicles, and Walt's cousin purchased his 2009 Toyota Tacoma with the intention of turning it into a mutual project. After he passed, Walt inherited the truck and decided to use it to keep that legacy alive.

Walt's cousin had earned the nickname "Ranger Goat" after showing up to his new long-range surveillance detachment with a beard, so the truck was christened with the same name. Walt writes, "His quiet rebelliousness was an inspiration for our build." In addition to its sentimental value, the Tacoma would serve as a proving ground for Walt's new overland vehicle building com-

Two sets of remote-reservoir King shocks are visible between the 37-inch mud tires and bulged fiberglass fenders.

Two-thirds of the rear bench seat were removed and replaced with a Goose Gear storage compartment. Grey Man Tactical seatback panels contain a fire extinguisher, binoculars, and other gear.

TRUCKS • PROOF OF CONCEPT | 89

The Goat's custom long-travel suspension soaks up bumps and makes it easy to maintain high speed over uneven terrain.

Baja Designs LED lights are attached to the bumpers, roof rack, and topper to illuminate dark trails and campsites. Each set of lights can be toggled by an sPOD switch inside the cab.

Opening the bed topper reveals a spare wheel and tire, full-size jack, dual air compressors in an aluminum box, and plenty of room for other equipment.

pany, Tactical Application Vehicles (TAV). "With this truck, we were able to validate everything we want to implement in the expedition vehicles we build for our clients."

The heart of this Tacoma is its long-travel suspension, which was painstakingly tested, modified, and re-tested until it produced the desired results. Rather than settling for off-the-shelf spring and shock combinations, TAV worked with the manufacturers to spec out custom valving and spring rates for a buttery-smooth ride. We're told the company also has plans to set up an in-house shock dyno, something that you typically won't find in the overland vehicle segment — that level of suspension R&D is more common among shops that work on racecars and trophy trucks.

A Total Chaos Fabrication long-travel kit serves as the foundation, with 3.5-inch extended, boxed, and gusseted lower control arms. These were fitted with 2.5-inch King coilovers and secondary King triple-bypass shocks, each with custom TAV-spec valving and adjustment knobs for fine-tuning. In the rear, TAV removed the original axle and replaced it with a much stronger Ford 9-inch unit, complete with a Currie fabricated housing and Nitro Gear billet differential. The axle rides on an Alcan spring pack and King 12-inch-travel remote-reservoir shocks, both customized to TAV's specifications. All four corners were topped off with SOS Performance big brakes, 17-inch Method Race Wheels, and 37-inch Yokohama mud-terrain tires.

This suspension setup allows the Goat to cruise smoothly over whoops and ruts, but the stock 4.0L V-6 seemed lacking in comparison. TAV addressed this by installing a Magnuson supercharger, which added roughly 70 horsepower and an equal amount of torque. Since this would be an expedition vehicle, it would need to

remain reliable on long treks, so a dual-battery system, upgraded alternator, transmission cooler, and high-capacity fuel tank were also added.

TAV reworked the Tacoma's exterior with bulged fenders and bedsides from McNeil Racing, rock sliders, and fabricated bumpers. The front bumper is a one-off custom piece, and houses four Baja Designs LED lights as well as a ComeUp USA winch. A matte gray vinyl wrap gives the body a subdued appearance. Maxtrax recovery devices, a storage case, and area lighting are attached to the Front Runner roof rack.

An AT Overland Equipment Habitat topper provides secure access points on all three sides of the bed, and its roof panel swings open in a 180-degree arc to reveal a spacious Nemo rooftop tent. This setup conveniently doubles as an awning over the tailgate. Extra storage capacity was added by replacing two-thirds of the rear bench seat with a sliding drawer from Goose Gear and attaching Grey Man Tactical organizer panels to the seatbacks. Auxiliary electronics are controlled by an sPOD switch panel attached to the overhead console.

Walt says he uses the Tacoma as a marketing tool for his company at events and trade shows, but it's no squeaky-clean show vehicle. He drives it daily and frequently takes it out on long journeys, including a 1,500-mile, 10-day "Trail of Missions" trip down the Baja Peninsula in Mexico. Over the years, parts have broken, and catastrophic failures have occurred, but these incidents just fueled TAV's improvements to the truck. "The Goat always got us home and is stronger than ever." No matter what happens, it'll be a part of his life and his company forever — "This truck is basically a family member."

One glance at the engine bay tells you this truck isn't a pavement princess. The supercharged V-6 is coated in a healthy layer of dust from the trail.

2009 TOYOTA TACOMA

ENGINE: 4.0L V-6 with Magnuson supercharger and LRA 33-gallon fuel tank

TRANSMISSION: 5-speed automatic with transmission cooler

DRIVELINE: 2WD / 4WD with 2-speed transfer case; TAV-spec rear axle with Nitro Gear billet Ford 9-inch differential and Currie F9 housing

BRAKES: SOS Performance big brake kit

FRONT SUSPENSION: Total Chaos Fabrication 3.5-inch long-travel kit, secondary shock hoops, and cam tab gussets; custom 2.5-inch King coilovers with compression adjuster, and custom triple-bypass shocks with quick-adjust knobs; RCV Performance CV axle shafts

REAR SUSPENSION: Total Chaos Fabrication shock tower; custom King 12-inch travel remote-reservoir shocks and air bump stops; Archive Garage hammer hangers, shackles, and cross-tube; custom Alcan leaf spring pack

WHEELS & TIRES: 17x8.5 Method Race Wheels 704 Trail Series wheels, 37x12.5R17 Yokohama Geolandar M/T G003

BED TOPPER & ROOF RACK: AT Overland Equipment Habitat topper/tent with Revive Wraps MultiCam Black vinyl wrap, Front Runner roof rack

BODY MODIFICATIONS: McNeil Racing fenders and bedsides, TAV custom front bumper, CBI Offroad custom rear bumper, Revive Wraps matte gunmetal gray vinyl wrap

LIGHTING & ELECTRICAL: Baja Designs LED lights; Spyder Auto headlights; ComeUp USA Seal Gen2 wireless winch; Garmin Overlander navigation; sPOD 4x4 switch panel; TAV custom dual battery system; DC Power alternator; dual air compressors

BUILT BY: Tactical Application Vehicles, LLC Albuquerque NM
www.tavllc.com

It only takes a few seconds to deploy the pop-up roof and set up camp. The truck also includes a deployable awning and shower enclosure with hot and cold running water.

As Americans, we take great pride in our unique national treasures. The Bill of Rights, National Parks, baseball, barbecue, rock and roll — the list goes on. In addition, our cultural melting pot has given us access to a huge variety of iconic creations from foreign shores; we didn't invent pizza or tacos, but we've certainly embraced them. So, it's always surprising to come across an item that's essentially unobtainable in America. Such has been the case for the 70-Series Toyota Land Cruiser.

Produced from 1984 through the present (yes, it's still in production), the 70-Series is an immensely popular vehicle for militaries, government organizations, and off-road adventurers around the world. However, it was never sold in the United States — we got the rounder and more luxurious 80-Series, sold here from 1990 to 1997. Although it's possible to bring over some foreign-market 70-Series Land Cruisers under the 25-year-old vehicle import law, making one street-legal comes with a long list of additional headaches and costs, especially if you live in a state with strict emissions regulations.

Forbidden Fruit

Tim McGrath's Heavily Modified Maltec Land Cruiser is the 79-Series Truck America Never Got

By Patrick McCarthy
Photos by Tim McGrath

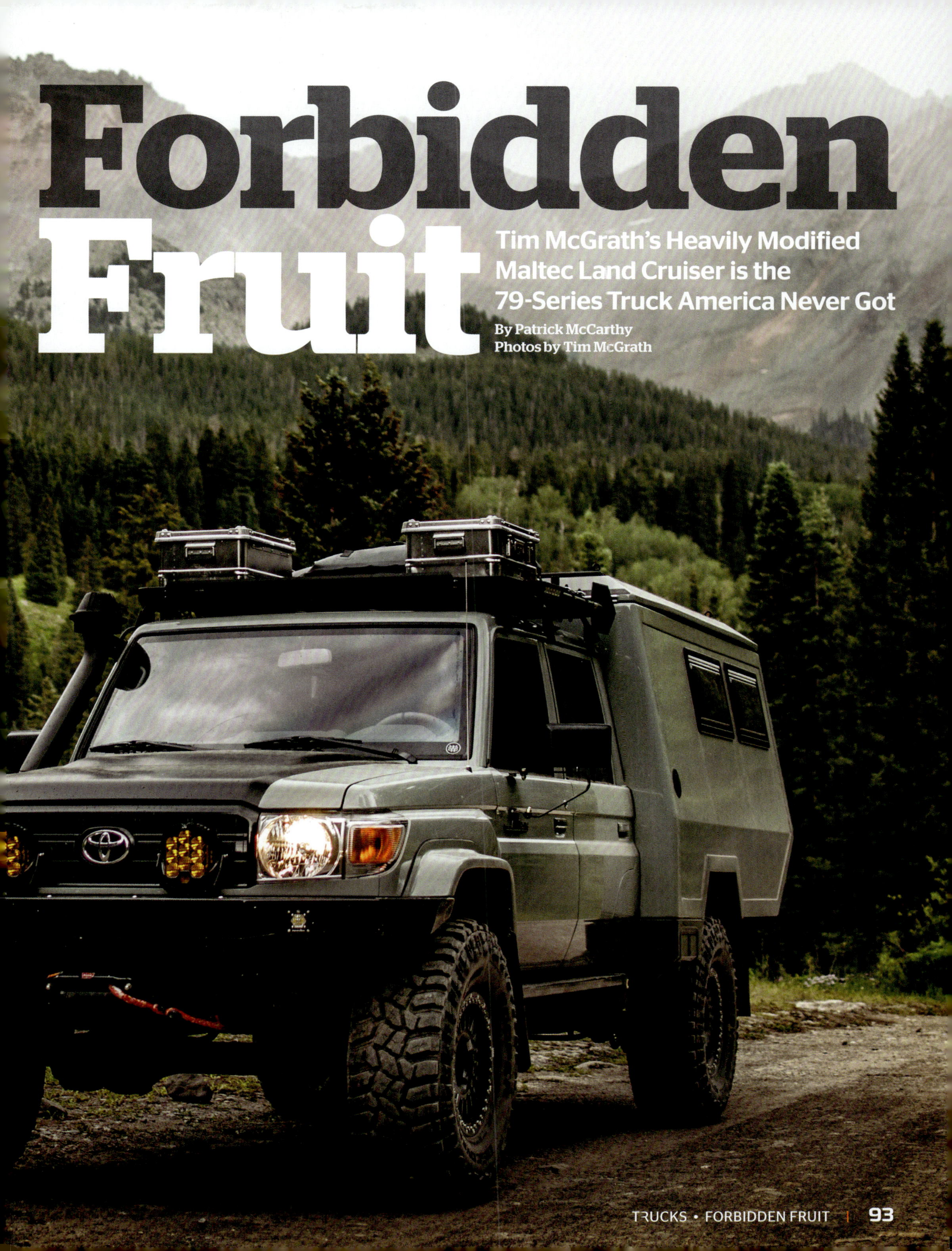

TRUCKS • FORBIDDEN FRUIT | 93

The Front Runner roof rack holds two Alu-Boxes and a large dry bag for gear storage. Additional rails atop the camper can be used to retain a kayak or paddleboards.

Despite its many creature comforts, this Land Cruiser is no pavement princess. It can still go just about anywhere and take Tim's whole family with it.

Tim McGrath, founder and lead designer for overland apparel company Sackwear, fell in love with the 70-Series Land Cruiser, especially its 79-Series pickup truck sub-model. "The people that know about the 79 wish they sold them here in the States," he says. Knowing the difficulties of legalizing an imported 79-Series, he began looking for alternative ways to achieve the appearance and rugged functionality of one of these trucks. This led him to Maltec, a company in Germany that builds custom Land Cruisers that — despite their appearance — are actually based on the easily importable 80-Series chassis. They agreed to build him a North American-spec truck that features a modified 70-Series cab and carbon-fiber camper on top of an 80-Series frame.

The build began with a 1993 80-Series Land Cruiser. After removing the original body, its frame was stretched to match the desired wheelbase for the camper conversion. A four-door cab from a 79-Series donor vehicle was mounted onto the 80-Series frame, and the back of that cab was cut out to create a pass-through into the carbon-fiber camper shell that was added next. Normally, having a custom vehicle built halfway across the globe would be rather nerve-wracking, but Tim says the builders listened to his needs and were extremely communicative. "Maltec did a great job keeping me connected with the progress, and sent me lots of emails with photos. I trusted their expertise and craftsmanship since they build really awesome rigs."

1993 TOYOTA LAND CRUISER

DRIVETRAIN: 4.2L 1HD-T turbo-diesel inline-6, 5-speed manual transmission, 4x4 with 2-speed transfer case

SUSPENSION: Old Man Emu springs and shocks

WHEELS & TIRES: 17-inch Braid Dakar Beadlock A wheels, 37x12.5R17 Cooper Discoverer STT Pro tires

BODY MODIFICATIONS: 79-Series Land Cruiser cab with rear cutout; Maltec aluminum front bumper, skid plates, fender flares, and carbon-fiber camper; Front Runner roof rack, awning, and camper roof rails; Alu-Cab exterior hot/cold shower, two 42L Alu-Boxes and Halite dry bags for storage

INTERIOR MODIFICATIONS: Maltec cabinets, gray and black leather door panels, suede headliner, and teak wood camper flooring; four Recaro Sportster CS leather seats, Webasto heater, 15-gallon fresh filtered water tank, water boiler, hot/cold sink, three-burner stove, espresso machine, upper and lower beds (sleeps four)

LIGHTING & ELECTRONICS: Dual AGM house batteries, two 100W SunWare solar panels, Victron Energy 2,000W power inverter, Alpine Halo 11-inch head unit/navigation, Simarine PICO touchscreen information panel, two Dometic refrigerators, LED camper lighting with charge ports, Warn Zeon 10-S Platinum winch with Factor 55 fairlead and FlatLink E, Baja Designs S1 bumper lights and LP9 Pro driving lights, KC Hilites Cyclone rock lights

BUILT BY: Maltec, Menden, Germany, www.maltec.org

In addition to the body modifications, Maltec installed a 4.2-liter 1HD-T turbo-diesel engine and five-speed manual transmission, a configuration that was also unavailable in U.S.-spec Land Cruisers. The truck's underbody is armored with a variety of Maltec skid plates to fend off rocks on the trail; it rides on OME 3-inch-lift springs and OME shocks, 17-inch Braid beadlock wheels, and 37-inch Cooper tires.

Tim says this combination balances a spacious interior and compact exterior, with "enough room to travel and sleep four while still remaining small and capable." He explains, "There's not a lot of room, but it's doable — I guess that's the trade-off. I can wheel this thing to places where most campers can't go. I love that we can set up someplace crazy and stay comfortable, warm, and dry at night. We can even cook inside and watch a movie." It wasn't an easy or inexpensive process, taking a year to complete and costing north of $200,000, but he doesn't regret it for a second.

Over the course of the last year, Tim has taken his Land Cruiser out on family expeditions at least once a month. In one of his most memorable experiences, he and his daughter drove to Colorado, arriving late in the evening to a dark and narrow trailhead. They continued onward, winding up a steep mountain road to a lake just above the tree line at 12,000 feet. He recalls, "The truck tackled the obstacles without any issues and delivered us safely. We were the only ones there under a star-filled sky, and had paddle boards to keep us entertained the next day."

Maltec built the camper with luxurious teak flooring, custom cabinets, Dometic windows, and a fully enclosed pass-through into the cab.

A triple-burner stove and espresso machine allow Tim and his family to enjoy a hot breakfast without leaving the comfort of the camper.

Decked Out for Bug Out

This Toyota Tacoma Is a Daily Driver, Weekend Warrior, and an Escape Plan, All Rolled Into One

By Martin Anders
Photography by Mike Shin

If the city comes crumbling down around you and you have no choice but to bug out, what kind of vehicle would you choose to get out of town in? It sounds like a simple question, but reality makes it a lot tougher to answer than we'd like it to be.

Ask 10 people this question, and you're bound to get at least 10 different answers. Some might say an old carbureted truck, others swear by diesel power, yet others still would ride off on a motorcycle. Then there are those who would reach for their paddles instead (see "Bug-Out 'Yak" on page 88). Because everyone's situation and needs are different, there's no one-size-fits-all answer. What type of area you live in and the number of people in your household are just two in a long list of variables that determine what type of transportation you end up selecting.

For Mike Shin, choosing his daily driver (and just-in-case bug-out truck) was dictated by several factors. After a couple of outings over a few dirt trails in his previous ride, a two-wheel drive Nissan Xterra, Shin quickly realized that he needed a ride swap if he were to drive more aggressive routes. While the Xterra was great to run errands around town, it was not suited for the unpaved regions of the mountains and deserts of Southern California — the very areas he might need to bug out to one day.

Make and Model

Shin drew inspiration from go-anywhere Australian Outback-style 4x4s. One of his dream trucks was the venerable Toyota Land Cruiser Hardtop 150. He considered traveling to his wife's home country of Guatemala to drive one back, but soon realized that the logistics and legalities of owning such a vehicle in the United States was more work than he was willing to take on. Instead, he looked at more readily available stateside options. Shin quickly discovered the 2013 Toyota Tacoma Double Cab 4x4 TRD Sport Package and figured it would more than meet his requirements.

From Show to Go

The ball really got moving when Shin, a former employee at Toyo Tires, got the call to display his truck at the Toyo Tires booth at the 2013 Specialty Equipment Market Association (SEMA) Show being held in Las Vegas, Nevada, with the caveat that he build a show- and off-road-worthy truck out of his Tacoma in less than three months' time — and on his own dime. Considering the time and budget concerns, it was far from certain that he would be able to pull this endeavor off. Even so, he was up to the challenge.

An ARB Deluxe Bull Bar replaces the factory front bumper. The All Pro Off-Road Front IFS Skid Plate was added to armor up the vulnerable IFS third member and steering components. A weather-sealed Superwinch Tiger Shark 11500 Winch in the front bumper can pull up to 11,500 pounds of trouble with its 6hp motor.

The high positioning of the ACAIS snorkel air inlet allows for cleaner, colder air to be driven into the engine's induction system, helping to improve fuel efficiency and power.

ReadyLIFT's Off-Road Heavy Duty Steering Kit consists of heavy-duty aftermarket tie-rod assemblies that are suited for lifted trucks running larger tires.

Suspension

The Tacoma was lifted 2 inches for additional ground clearance to get over natural and manmade obstructions. Shin opted for an Old Man Emu Lift Kit for the front that consisted of sets of Nitrocharger shock absorbers and coil springs. He matched the rearend with Old Man Emu Dakar Leaf Springs and shocks, as well. These suspension upgrades not only improve the ride, handling, and load-carrying capability of a heavily laden truck, but also decreases the chance of suspension-component failure. Because of the 2-inch height increase, an Old Man Emu Driveshaft Spacer kit was installed to reduce driveline vibration common to lifts on Tacomas of this type.

Shin further beefed up the frontend by installing a set of ReadyLIFT Off-Road Upper Control Arms. These arms are stronger than stock and feature zerk fittings that make re-greasing its urethane bushings a breeze. Because the wheel and tire combination he's running is heavier than stock, he went with ReadyLIFT's Off-Road

Rays Gram Lights 57JX6 rims in 18x8-inch sizing are mounted with Toyo Tires' all-new Open Country R/Ts.

Engine

Its 1GR-FE model V-6 engine displaces 4 liters and runs on regular-grade fuel. That's good enough to churn out a factory-rated 236 horsepower and 266 lb-ft of torque. To help it breathe easier, an Australian-made Airflow Cold Air Induction System (ACAIS) snorkel was installed to force in air that is free of water and other contaminants. According to Airflow, the high positioning of the ACAIS' snorkel air inlet also allows for cleaner, colder air to be driven into the engine's induction system. Colder air contains more oxygen, helping to improve fuel efficiency and power.

To keep the entire system free flowing, Shin coupled the ACAIS with a custom-fitted MagnaFlow Race Series exhaust system. The fully stainless-steel cat-back exhaust system optimizes exhaust flow and is mounted just behind the factory catalytic converter. We noticed that it also gives the truck a refined yet throaty sound.

CBI Off-Road Rock Sliders help protect the doors and doorsills from impact with obstacles.

Heavy Duty Steering Kit to avoid possible parts breakage down the road. The kit consists of heavy-duty aftermarket tie-rod assemblies that are suited for lifted trucks running larger tires.

Differentials

This Toyota drives power to all four wheels with aftermarket ratio ring-and-pinion gears made by Nitro Gear and Axle, that are encased in the factory 8-inch front and 8.4-inch rear clamshell IFS differential housings. The stock 3.72 gear ratio is better suited for economy and the truck's standard 30-inch tires, but it doesn't cut it with the larger wheels and tires that Shin went with. Due to the increase in rolling mass of larger 33-inch tires, both power and fuel economy are lost with the factory setup. The new ring and pinion by Nitro Gear and Axle "lower" the ratio to 4.56, which better compensates for the larger tires.

Body Armor

To protect the truck's body and better increase approach and departure angles, Shin added some heavy-duty truck armor. Up front an ARB Deluxe Bull Bar replaces the factory front bumper. Stronger and capable of mounting a winch and several lights, the ARB bumper has become ubiquitous in the off-road world and is available for many makes and models of trucks.

Underneath, a laser-cut 3/16-inch steel All Pro Off-Road Front IFS Skidplate was added to armor up the vulnerable IFS third member and steering components. Running along the bottom of the truck body between the front and rear wheels are CBI Off-Road Rock Sliders. These rock sliders help protect the doors and doorsills from impact with obstacles (fallen tree branches, boulders, etc.) and keep the body in pristine shape even if the sliders themselves are bumped.

A CBI Off-Road Trail Rider 2.0 bumper with swing-away tire carrier protects the rear end. Tucked below the spare tire in the rear is a Hi-Lift X-TREME Jack which can be used not only for jacking the truck up to swap out a flat tire, but also for manual winching and clamping.

A CBI Off-Road Trail Rider 2.0 bumper protects the rear. Because having extra fuel on hand is a bug-out essential, it's fitted with two 5-gallon Jerry Can fuel carriers and a spare wheel and tire. The tire carrier swings away, allowing for easy access to the tailgate and bed. It even conceals a fold-down camp table further increasing its usability. The bumper's higher undercut allows for the truck to clear steeper departure angles that the stock bumper can't.

Storage and Gear

Storage is always at a premium whether you're packing for a camping trip or trying to haul you, your loved ones, and your gear out of a bad situation. Shin wanted to maximize the organizational space of his truck bed with the use of a bed rack.

The All Pro-Off Road Expedition Series Pack Rack helped him do just that all without compromising the hauling capacity of the truck's bed. The Rack Pack allows him to carry an ARB Series III Simpson Roof Top Tent up top that comfortably sleeps two adults and an ARB Awning 2000 that deploys to the side, providing about 53 square feet of overhead coverage from the elements.

Keeping clean is a real morale booster — imagine being able to take a warm shower when bugging out. A Road Shower sits on the side of the rack and holds 5 gallons of water, heats up in the sun, and works by either having gravity push water out of its 55-inch length hose or alternatively, the tank can be pressurized with an air compressor or bike tire pump to provide a more powerful jet of water.

On the opposite side of the Pack Rack sits a Rotopax 2-gallon water container and a Rotopax First Aid+Preparedness Kit. The efficient kit contains everything from medical supplies and a shovel to toilet paper and zip ties.

To add even more storage area, Shin custom-mounted an ARB 52x44-inch Steel Roof Rack Basket above the truck's cab using a fitment kit made for a Toyota Hilux. The roof rack basket allows for gear and other supplies to be stored as well as a high position for roof rack lights to be mounted.

Lighting

For better forward view in low light and blacked-out moonless nights, Shin decked his truck out with a wide range of lighting options. He went to The Retrofit Source (TRS) for a set of OEM-quality Morimoto FX-R Bi-Xenon HID projectors to retrofit his stock halogen lights. The reason for going with an HID retrofit is to improve light quality, as the factory halogens are generally pretty dim, especially when in off-road environments. The problem with sticking any cheap aftermarket HIDs in existing halogen housings is that they typically cast an uncontrolled beam pattern due to higher light output. This ends up blinding other drivers while giving the user only mediocre visibility.

Opting for OEM-quality HIDs results in a piercing beam that is controlled and distributed with a crisp and focused cut-off beam pattern, delivering maximum visibility to the driver with higher light output that doesn't also blind oncoming drivers. To install the TRS-sourced HID projectors, Shin relied on a company called Essential Lites to do the painstaking work of retrofitting them into his factory headlights.

He continued by adding dual rows of high-mounted lights to the roof rack. Sitting on the top row is a Rigid

The All Pro-Off Road Expedition Series Pack Rack bed rack helps create organized storage space over the truck bed without compromising hauling capacity. A bevy of gear is attached to it, including an ARB Series III Simpson Roof Top Tent, ARB Awning 2000, and a Road Shower.

Top left: These Rigid Industries 38- and 40-inch E-Series LED light bars are configured in a spot-and-flood-light combination.

Left: Each of the 9-inch ARB Intensity LED Driving Lights that are mounted to the front bumper contain 32 LEDs, producing 8,200 raw lumens.

Above: Ram Mount's versatile No Drill Laptop Mount can be configured to use with a tablet.

Top right: A Scan Gauge II monitors the vehicle's performance and is programmable to display information, such as trip data, transmission temperature, fuel economy, engine speed, among other statistics.

Industries 38-inch E-Series LED Light Bar, which is configured in a spot and flood light combination. This combination is rated at 17,480 raw lumens and allows him to see a wide swath immediately forward as well as out to more than 1,300 meters ahead of the vehicle. If that isn't enough, a second 40-inch E-Series LED Light Bar sits just under the 38-incher. Also in spot-and-flood-combination configuration, this bar spits out 18,400 raw lumens of light up to a distance of 1,400 meters. For those keeping count, that's a range of almost 13 football fields.

As if he plans on exploring the eternal darkness of a black hole, Shin found a need to further mount a pair of 9-inch ARB Intensity LED Driving Lights to the front bumper. The flood and spot combination lights each contain 32 LEDs that produce 8,200 raw lumens and a spot reach of almost 1,000 meters.

Not to be outdone, the rear end was treated to a bank of LED lights as well. Rigid SR-M Back-Up lights, a Rigid SR-M Bed Light, and a Rigid Q-Series Camp Light mounted on the tire carrier round out the rear facing light fixtures.

Electronics

A Scan Gauge II monitors the vehicle's performance and is programmable to display information such as trip data, transmission temperature, fuel economy, engine speed, and vehicle speed, among other statistics. What's really useful too is that it is capable of displaying trouble codes, so you can troubleshoot problems.

Ram Mount Phone and No Drill Laptop Mounts help keep what otherwise would be loose electronics in place, even over the roughest of turf. The versatile No Drill Laptop Mount, as its name implies, requires no drilling for installation into your vehicle and, as seen here, can be configured to use with a tablet. Other than accessing electronic maps over his phone or tablet, Shin also carries an old-fashioned Thomas Guide (remember those?) and a compass for backup land navigation.

Never Done

Shin's Tacoma fits each of the roles he initially outlined quite nicely. It's a reliable daily driver that's a blast to take out for the occasional trail run. If push ever comes to shove, it looks as if this pickup will be a capable rolling urban escape plan as well. But automotive enthusiasts know that a project is rarely ever complete. When asked what the next step for his truck was, Shin mischievously smiled and said that he was done with it…somehow we're not so convinced.

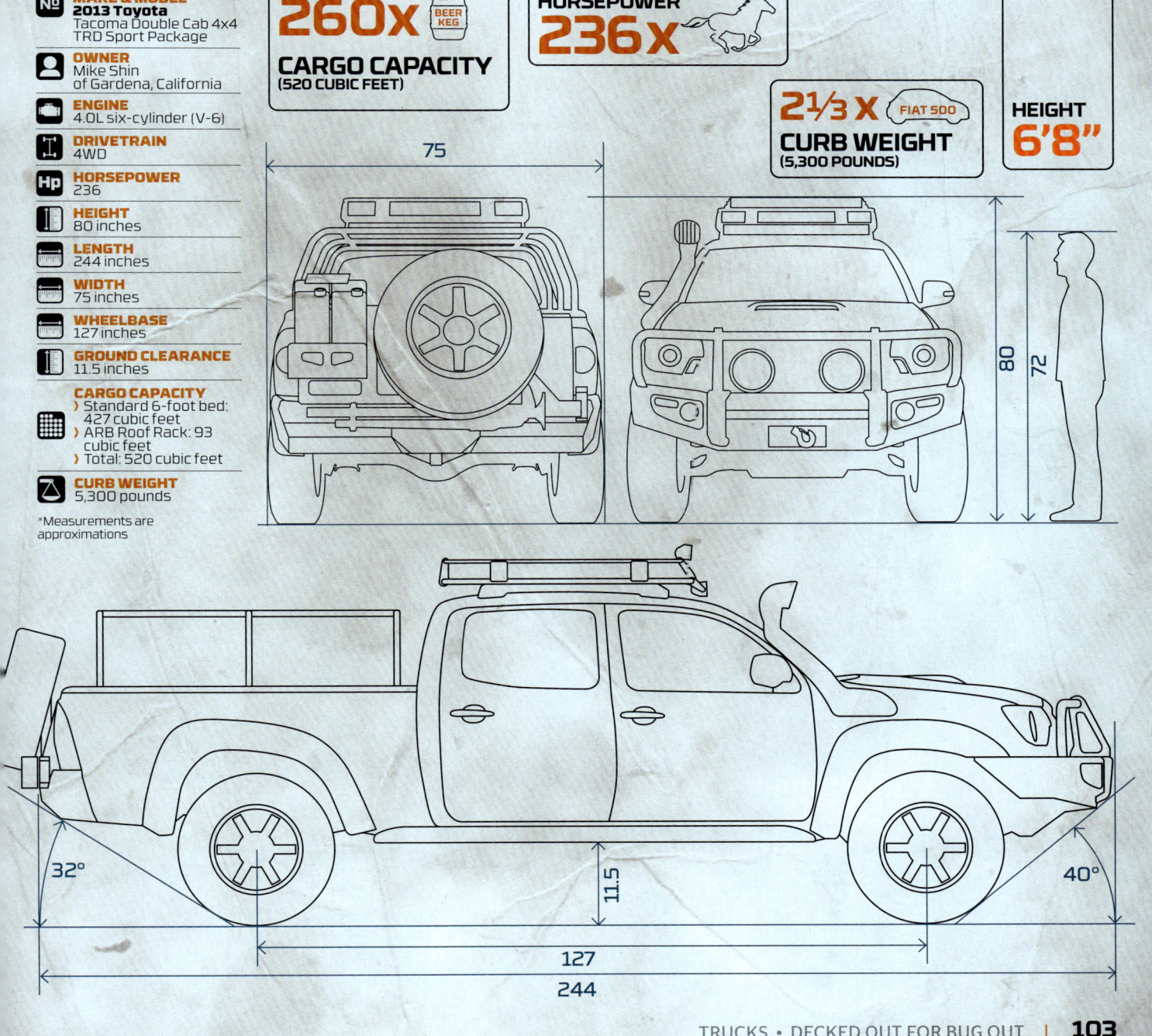

MAKE & MODEL
2013 Toyota Tacoma Double Cab 4x4 TRD Sport Package

OWNER
Mike Shin of Gardena, California

ENGINE
4.0L six-cylinder (V-6)

DRIVETRAIN
4WD

HORSEPOWER
236

HEIGHT
80 inches

LENGTH
244 inches

WIDTH
75 inches

WHEELBASE
127 inches

GROUND CLEARANCE
11.5 inches

CARGO CAPACITY
› Standard 6-foot bed: 427 cubic feet
› ARB Roof Rack: 93 cubic feet
› Total: 520 cubic feet

CURB WEIGHT
5,300 pounds

*Measurements are approximations

260x CARGO CAPACITY (520 CUBIC FEET)

HORSEPOWER 236x

2 1/3 x CURB WEIGHT (5,300 POUNDS) FIAT 500

HEIGHT 6'8"

TRUCKS • DECKED OUT FOR BUG OUT | 103

Armored Taco

A Bug-Out Toyota Tacoma Fit for a U.S. Marine

By Mike Shin

icture this. You're in one of America's beautiful national parks with your family for the weekend. With the family hauler packed and the sun beginning to set behind the mountains, you begin piloting the winding roads back to civilization.

The radio suddenly gives off an intrusive shrill. Your gaze goes back to the road while in the background you faintly hear that calm voice reciting a message from the Emergency Alert System, only this time, it doesn't say, "This is only a test."

Highways are at a complete stop. All lanes in both directions jammed with cars going nowhere fast and with no end in sight. After an hour and a half with no information coming over the radio, people begin abandoning their cars to go on foot, carrying with them what they can. There are chirps and flashes of lights as car alarms are armed. Worried owners perform quick walks around their vehicles, making sure everything is secure. As they walk away, some look back warily at their parked cars as if to say: "Don't worry. I'll be back to get you when whatever this is all blows over."

The Pelfreybilt Offroad lightweight aluminum bumper and the IFS aluminum skidplate also by Pelfreybilt provide protection from hazards. The bumper also hides a Warn Zeon 10-S Winch capable of pulling 10,000 pounds.

Rather than get stuck in the impromptu parking lot, you find a part of the shoulder that leads to an elevated parallel dirt road and pull off to collect your thoughts. The phone network is down, judging by the telltale busy signal, as well as the data connection, and the browser won't refresh. As you look off miles and miles away in the horizon toward the city, where home is, you see the unmistakable orange glow of fire, and it can't be anything good. The pulsating glow and clouds of smoke is much too large to be localized.

This is widespread, you think to yourself. As you contemplate what to do next, a thick dark haze begins to form over the highway almost like fog. You squint to get a better look through the dying light and see several figures running toward your direction on the highway below. Seconds later a swarm of terrified people emerge from the haze darting in between the parked cars. Running for their lives. They are the ones who had abandoned their cars earlier.

Although the aforementioned scenario is fictional, almost reminiscent of a current popular cable television show, some can't help but wonder, "What if?" For Sean Jennings, as unlikely as the scenario sounds, he's not one to take chances.

An adventurer at heart, Jennings drew upon his experience in the U.S. Marine Corps and his two tours in Iraq, which put him in a mindset that being prepared isn't a suggestion, it's a way of life.

The Modifications

While this 2013 Toyota Tacoma was built for recreation, Jennings added that he chose the Tacoma's midsize truck platform for Toyota's unsurpassed reliability and felt that it would be a more than adequate bug-out vehicle if the need ever arises. Considering the modifications done to this Tacoma, we're in agreement.

Since "Go anywhere" can literally mean just that, the Tacoma's independent front suspension was outfitted and modified for long travel. Both factory upper and lower arms were swapped for the Total Chaos +2 Long Travel Race Series Kit complemented by Fox 2.5DSC coilovers. A Total Chaos secondary shock hoop was added to properly install the Fox Triple Bypass system. With the front suspension sorted out, suspension travel was no longer much of an issue. The rear suspension was upgraded with Fox 2.0 DSC extended travel shocks and bumpstops with Pelfreybilt shock relocation hoops welded onto the frame. The factory leaf packs were swapped for All-Pro Expedition units to withstand heavier loads.

Crucial to any overland build are tires. Having the right size tire — as well as the right kind — is important when

Fox Triple Bypass shocks offer compression and rebound adjustments to further refine the ride.

you've got to run for the hills or if you're just going on an off-road excursion with friends. Meaty sidewalls and the right track were important to Jennings, who opted for 35x12.50x17 Toyo Open Country R/T tires mounted onto Method Race Wheels' 105 beadlock model. Although 35-inch tires are a great size for any overland rig, getting them to fit properly on the Tacoma is a slight challenge.

To achieve the proper clearance, a cab-mount chop was required. What this modification consists of is cutting a portion of the frame located on the backside of the inner fenderwell, allowing the tires to turn lock to lock without rubbing against the body and potentially causing damage to the tires and the truck itself. Further trimming and massaging of the front fenders, including the Bushwacker over-fenders, were required to ensure that the tires would clear under full suspension travel.

Four-wheel-drive enthusiasts have always relied on their rig's drivetrains and their driving skills to get through any tough situation the trail throws their way. Jennings, having traveled with his Tacoma through many a trail, wanted to ensure the chips were stacked in his favor when out in the rough. Installed on both axles are ARB Air Lockers activated by an onboard ARB Twin Air compressor. When activated, the Lockers will lock both axles 100 percent, achieving even greater traction when the factory 4-Lo setting won't do.

Jennings knows keeping the shiny side up on his rig is always ideal, but he also knows having body armor for the Tacoma was necessary for his build. Pelfreybilt Offroad was called on to outfit the truck with their line of products consisting of their aluminum front bumper and Hi-Clearance rear bumper. These components drastically improve the vehicle's approach and departure angles while providing ample protection from the terrain and road hazards. The Tacoma's undercarriage also received protection with an aluminum front IFS and transmission skidplate and Pelfreybilt's rock sliders round out the Tacoma's road armor.

The Interior

Inside, the Tacoma is decked out for long trips. The factory seats were redone with comfort in mind. Up front

Total Chaos Upper and Lower arms are part of their +2 Race Series Long Travel kit, increasing the track, suspension travel, and height. The Fox 2.5 DSC Coilovers with remote reservoir ensures no terrain is impassible.

Katzkin custom embroidered Jennings' online handle, "Defconbrix," into the heated and cooled seats for a personal touch.

are heated and cooled leather seats with suede inserts by Katzkin. The rear bench also received the same leather and suede treatment.

Since a road trip wouldn't be a road trip without music, a trick custom fiberglass enclosure was built for the audio system, consisting of amplifiers and a slim subwoofer, all tucked away neatly behind the rear seats. A trio of switches control different functions on the truck such as the onboard ARB Twin Air Compressor to actuate the front and rear ARB Air Lockers. What really caught our eye inside this adventure rig was the sPOD SE Touch Screen controller. This unit can act as switches for eight different auxiliary lighting systems; this one was wired up to the bevy of Rigid Industries LED lights outfitted on the truck. From the rock lights to the lightbars, they're all controlled through the customizable touch screen.

Storage was addressed with Truck Vault's All Weather series two-drawer locking cargo system installed in the bed, in addition to a Line-X coated Cargo Glide 600XL shelf. The Truck Vault was essential for Jennings' storage needs, as it would carry everything from his rifles to his recovery gear. The addition of an A.R.E. Z-Series truck cap keeps everything under lock and key.

The Shelter

True to the overland theme, Jennings then added an XVenture XV-2 Off-Road Trailer complete with an 89x18-inch folding Galley table, which includes a three-burner range stove and sink. He then took it a step further and outfitted the trailer to be a sustainable shelter with a CVT Mt. McKinley Roof Top Tent. Capable of fitting four people, this tent ensures his family will stay out of the elements. A CVT 55-inch awning provides shade and the XV-2 is also outfitted with a 20L water tank with an electric pump and a propane water heater allowing the luxury of a hot shower.

The trailer also sustains it's own power via a deep cycle battery and an onboard power distribution center, easily allowing Jennings to hook up additional lights or appliances such as the ARB 63-quart fridge/freezer tucked in the XV-2's storage compartment.

MAKE & MODEL	2013 Toyota Tacoma Double Cab 4x4 Double Cab Shortbed
ENGINE	4.0L Six-Cylinder (V-6)
DRIVETRAIN	4WD
HORSEPOWER	236
HEIGHT	80 Inches
LENGTH	209 Inches
WIDTH	77 Inches
WHEELBASE	127 Inches
GROUND CLEARANCE	11.5 Inches
CURB WEIGHT	5,500 Pounds
APPROACH ANGLE	54 Degrees
DEPARTURE ANGLE	36 Degrees

Anyone who has fished likely knows that going out into a body of water allows you access to a variety of fish and fishing grounds versus being on the shoreline. Luckily for Jennings, he's got that covered with his Flycraft inflatable fishing craft. The two-man vessel can also easily be an escape vehicle on water should options on land run out.

But say options on land call for two wheels instead of four or on foot, this Marine has one more trick up his sleeve. Jennings took a 125cc Honda Grom and outfitted it with knobby Maxxis Moto-Off Road Tires, giving the mini street bike a whole new level of capability. However, Jennings wasn't finished there. From his experience being out in the woods, he knows it gets dark, real dark. With this the halogen headlight on the Grom was dropped in favor of a single custom-mounted ARB Intensity LED Spot light. This single light is capable of producing over 8,000 lumens and throwing light over 900 meters giving this Honda Grom enough light to ride confidently during the darkest of nights.

Now, it's obvious this Tacoma didn't get to this level of preparation overnight. There have been several iterations of this build before it got to where it is today. Many different parts were installed and removed in a game of trial and error. But in the end, Jennings found that this current setup was the right balance of what would encompass his needs for recreation and survival. While we've seen an overland rig or two in our time, Sean Jennings' Tacoma definitely reinforces the saying, "It's better to have it and not need it, than to need it and not have it."

But don't count on Jennings being done just yet. He still has plans for more upgrades to his ultimate survivalist rig.

The XVenture XV-2 Off-Road Trailer is a fully capable trailer especially the way Jennings has outfitted his. Equipped with the same Method 105 Series Beadlock wheels and 35-inch Toyo Open Country R/T Tires as the Tacoma, the XV-2's overland capabilities are further enhanced.

TRAILER	Schutt Industries XVenture XV-2 Off-Road Trailer
LENGTH	151.1 Inches
WIDTHS	75 In. (52 In. W/Tires)
CURB WEIGHT	1,190 Pounds
WATER HEATER	Camp Chef Triton 5L
BATTERY	Deep Cycle
WATER TANK	20-Liter
PROPANE TANK	20 Pounds

Never leave home without it. Jennings' Truck Vault drawers are filled with the essentials, from firearms to his Victor Axe and Hatchet to his ARB recovery gear.

TRUCKS • ARMORED TACO | **109**

Jeeps

RUBIGONE

A Dream Wrangler That is Ready for Play or Survival

By Sean P. Holman
Photos By Jorge Nuñez

You don't have to wait for the end of the world or roving groups of undead to feel the need to bug out for a bit. Long days strapped into an office chair next to a cubicle mate who wants to tell you all about her 15 cats, sitting for hours in a freeway parking lot without an ETA home, or living next door to a wingnut neighbor who always seems to place those "Hope" and "Change" signs on your side of the property line are all acceptable reasons for needing some time away.

Recreation is life's best medicine and leaving civilization with a few of your favorite firearms and enough gear to be self-sufficient for a couple days is an age-old tradition guaranteed to give you the recharge you've

ARMORED FENDERS

These Crusher Flares by Poison Spyder laugh off rock hits like a .50 cal pokes holes through watermelons. Featuring all-steel construction, Crusher Flares replace the vulnerable plastic stock fenders, while giving the Jeep enhanced aesthetics and improved clearance for the trail.

BRAND: Poison Spyder Customs
MODEL: JK Front Crusher Flares
MSRP: $495 (pair)
URL: www.poisonspyder.com

GRAB HANDLES

MasterCraft Safety makes climbing aboard lifted Wranglers quick and easy with its high-quality 4-piece grab handle kit. The front handles wrap around the roll bar with three mounting straps, ensuring they won't move around on you, and the rear straps bolt-in using existing hardware on the Sound Bar.

BRAND: MasterCraft Safety
MODEL: 4-piece JK Grab Handle Kit
MSRP: $67
URL: mastercraftsafety.com

COMMUNICATION

Sometimes you need to break cover and communicate with the outside world. For those instances, communication duties are handled by an ICOM two-way radio, which has been modified to reach all frequencies.

BRAND: ICOM
MODEL: IC-706MKIIG
MSRP: $1,069
URL: www.icomamerica.com

WHEELS

Finding yourself in intense situations calls for a wheel that is up to the mission at hand. These 17x8.5-inch Walker Evans aluminum wheels feature high-pressure cast construction for strength and full-face beadlock rings, which protect the wheel face and valve stem while keeping the tire on the wheel, even if you roll over a spike strip.

BRAND: Walker Evans
MODEL: 17-inch Beadlock Racing Wheel
MSRP: $395
URL: walkerevansracing.com

TIRES

Crawling over anything takes a big tire, and the large-lugged Goodyear Wrangler MT/R* tires are huge. At 40-inches tall, there isn't much that can stop the forward progress of these big meats. Each tire is rated at 3,195-pounds of carrying capacity, so tires will be least of your worries when you load up for your adventure away. Goodyear developed the MT/R with excellent highway manners, but that doesn't mean they won't hold their own in the slop. (* Spare tire is a Toyo Open Country M/T)

BRAND: Goodyear
MODEL: Wrangler MT/R
MSRP: $605
URL: www.goodyear.com

ROCK SLIDERS

Running a long wheel-base rig in tight places sometimes requires pivoting and sliding. Red Rock Fab sliders keep rocks out of the doors, the sheetmetal unscathed, and allow the big Jeep to slither over obstacles without getting hung up.

BRAND: Red Rock Fab
MODEL: Rock Slider
MSRP: Discontinued
URL: www.redrockfab.com

BODY ARMOR

Working together with the rock sliders, the 3/16th-inch-thick JK Body Armor panels are precision fit to the Wrangler JK's subtle body shape and add reinforcement to an area of the Wrangler that could dent at the slightest contact with anything harder than dry brush.

BRAND: Poison Spyder Customs
MODEL: JK 4-door Body Armor
MSRP: $229
URL: www.poisonspyder.com

earned. Doing it in a vehicle that gets you further away will almost certainly ensure your peace and isolation. In the spirit of bugging out of everyday life, Bob Tulley of Corona, California's Wrangler fits the bill.

Starting life as an '08 Jeep Wrangler Rubicon and fully upgraded by Off Road Evolution in Fullerton, California, this rig is overbuilt by most standards, yet remains civil enough to be a daily driver. Based on the long-wheelbase, 4-door Wrangler JK Unlimited, it's big

1 LED LIGHT BAR
Traveling on a moonless night is not a problem with Rigid Industries' 50-inch SR-Series Hybrid LED light bar. With an output of more than 16,000 lumens and a draw of just 173 watts, the SR is as bright as it is efficient and easily cuts through the darkest nights.

BRAND: Rigid Industries
MODEL: 50-inch SR-Series
MSRP: $1,200
URL: www.rigidindustries.com

2 FRONT BUMPER
Stock Wrangler bumpers are no match for rocks and locked gates, but this beefy replacement from Red Rock Fab with its reinforced stinger, provisions for the factory foglights, and heavy-duty shackle mounts will stand up to any obstacle.

BRAND: Red Rock Fab
MODEL: Front Bumper
MSRP: Discontinued
URL: www.redrockfab.com

3 WINCH
Going alone? Then it's wise to have a self-recovery winch at the ready. Not only will it allow you to extract yourself from a sticky situation, but it's also useful for moving debris out of your path. The Warn 9.5ti is one of the best available in this class of winch, and with a 9,500-pound rating, pulling stuck vehicles out is no problem.

BRAND: Warn
MODEL: 9.5ti
MSRP: $1,521
URL: www.warn.com

4 STEERING
Stock steering systems aren't designed for the loads created by giant tires, so a hydraulic steering assist system, like the PSC Motorsports one used here, is a mandatory upgrade. The PSC system uses a hydraulic ram to aid the steering system and makes piloting the Jeep through a sea of obstructions a breeze.

BRAND: PSC Motorsports
MODEL: Jeep JK Trail & Street Cylinder Assist Kit
MSRP: $1,323
URL: pscmotorsports.com

5 FRONT AXLE
When you need an axle upgrade that can take a .357 round better than a sandbag and manage huge tires, Dynatrac is where you go. The front ProRock 60 has more ground clearance than the stock Dana 44 axle and comes with bigger brakes for shedding speed in a hurry. The Jeep will likely fall apart before these cast-iron-and-steel monsters fail in the field.

BRAND: Dynatrac
MODEL: ProRock60 Front
MSRP: $7,338
URL: www.dynatrac.com

enough to take you and a buddy away for the weekend (or the family away from Armageddon), but still compact enough to fit on most trails. The race-inspired suspension, beefy underpinnings, and massive rolling stock add to the "just-in-case" factor and allows the Jeep to climb over boulders to get you to the high point, or over the top of the boss's Prius; you'll know if you ever find it blocking the parking lot exit.

The stock 3.8L V-6 doesn't make big power so it relies on proper gear-

REAR BUMPER

Carrying a couple hundred pounds of wheel and tire is not easy on a vehicle, so a Red Rock Fab rear bumper and tire carrier was chosen to support the spare. It is also a good place to mount communications antennas, auxiliary lighting, and recovery shackles.

BRAND: Red Rock Fab
MODEL: Rear Bumper and Tire Carrier
MSRP: Discontinued
URL: www.redrockfab.com

REAR AXLE

Like the front axle, the rear of this Jeep employs a Dynatrac ProRock60, which has more ground clearance than the stock Dana 44. Also like the front, it's stuffed with upgraded axleshafts, an ARB-selectable Air Locker, and 5.38 gears for big gains in strength and capability over the stock axles.

BRAND: Dynatrac
MODEL: ProRock 60 Rear
MSRP: $4,349
URL: www.dynatrac.com

CORNER ARMOR

When traversing extreme terrain, rear vehicle corners and taillights are especially susceptible to being reshaped by the topography. To keep the body square, a set of Poison Spyder Customs 1/8th-inch-thick steel Crusher Corners are bolted in place and work in conjunction with the rear Crusher Flares, even including provisions for superbright flush-mounted LED lights.

BRAND: Poison Spyder Customs
MODEL: JK Rear Crusher Corners
MSRP: $666
URL: poisonspyder.com

LED LIGHTING

Flush-mounted LED lights are not going to get knocked off on the trail like the protruding factory lights will. LEDs are incredibly bright and draw little power, plus there is no filament to get damaged from bouncing around off-road. Extremely durable and vibration-resistant, there is no bulb to replace.

BRAND: Poison Spyder Customs
MODEL: 24-LED Taillight
MSRP: $33
URL: poisonspyder.com

REAR SUSPENSION

Notice the rear suspension? No? Well that's the point. EVO MFG's Double ThrowDown rear-suspension system mounts everything above the rear axle, so nothing is hanging down to hang you up. The cantilever suspension uses any existing long-arm suspension kit and adds four horizontally mounted King shocks (two bypass and two reservoir) to get 14 inches of real-wheel travel without having to cut into the body. Also available are King Rock Stop hydraulic bumpstops.

BRAND: EVO MFG
MODEL: Double ThrowDown System
MSRP: $4,928
URL: www.evomfg.com

JEEPS • RUBIGONE

1. AUXILIARY LIGHTING
There is no such thing as too much lighting, and Baja Designs' SolTek LED lights are performers. With an output of 2,880 lumens, the SolTek LEDs pack a punch for their size and are designed to be nearly unbreakable, making these lights a perfect choice for front-bumper applications.

BRAND: Baja Designs
MODEL: SolTek LED
MSRP: $450
URL: www.bajadesigns.com

2. FRONT SUSPENSION
Regardless of what long-arm kit you start with, you can easily add coilovers with EVO MFG's front coilover system. When paired with EVO-spec 14-inch King reservoir shocks, this coilover system will match the rear suspension's 14 inches of travel for a very balanced suspension system. Whether you require slow control in a technical section of trail or need to make a fast getaway, the EVO MFG suspension upgrades are up to the challenge.

BRAND: EVO MFG
MODEL: Front Coilover System
MSRP: $2,370
URL: www.evomfg.com

3. LIGHT BAR MOUNT
Poison Spyder Customs' JK light bar mount is a solid place to mount your full-width LED light bar. Putting the light source high above the hood allows the light to penetrate deeper into the darkness, giving you the ability to see any lurking dangers that much quicker.

BRAND: Poison Spyder Customs
MODEL: JK Light Bar Mount
MSRP: $274
URL: www.poisonspyder.com

4. TRAIL FRIDGE
Ice for perishables is hard to come by in the backcountry, and when it melts it usually makes the sandwich bread soggy. Instead of using an ice chest, ARB's exceptional fridge freezer runs off of your 12-volt electrical system and will keep its contents at a user-selected temperature as long as you have battery power. Once down to the specified temp, a low power draw means you'll still be able to start your rig in the morning.

BRAND: ARB
MODEL: 50-Quart Fridge Freezer
MSRP: $880
URL: www.arbusa.com

5. FIRE EXTINGUISHER MOUNTS
Dual 5-pound fire extinguishers are mounted on the rollbar's rear downtube with a set of Kartek heavy-duty quick-release fire extinguisher mounts. These mounts are TIG welded and feature a sturdy quick-release design. They're good for when you find yourself rubber-side up and on fire.

BRAND: Kartek
MODEL: Heavy-Duty Quick-Release Fire Extinguisher Mount
MSRP: $51
URL: www.kartek.com

6. SEATS
Regardless of how capable the vehicle is, you won't be covering much ground if the occupants aren't comfortable. MasterCraft Safety's Baja RS suspension seats blend the proven safety and performance of its race seat in a chair that reclines, enhancing functionality in any vehicle that sees everyday use. Optional seat heaters and a palette of color choices mean they'll match any interior.

BRAND: MasterCraft Safety
MODEL: Baja RS
MSRP: $576
URL: www.mastercraftsafety.com

7. SPORTS CAGE
While the Wrangler does come from the factory with a minimal cage, it leaves the front passengers without full protection and won't be enough if you are at some point likely to take a tumble. To reinforce the stock structure, Rock Hard 4x4 offers this completely bolt-in sports cage that extends the factory protection all the way to the A-pillar.

BRAND: Rock Hard 4x4
MODEL: Ultimate Sports Cage
MSRP: $650
URL: www.rockhard4x4.com

8. NAVIGATION
When escaping from something or to something, it's good to know where you're going. The Lowrance family of GPS units is a great choice to keep tabs on where you are and where you'll end up.

BRAND: Lowrance
MODEL: GlobalMap 540C
MSRP: $800
URL: www.lowrance.com

9. ON-BOARD AIR
Being able to make your own compressed air is helpful for more than just airing up tires. With a powerful on-board air system, you can run pneumatic tools, making your rig a mobile workshop. Using a York compressor, the Kilby Air Boss system uses engine power to compress air and hold it in a 2.5-gallon storage tank, ensuring it's ready when you need it.

BRAND: Kilby Enterprises
MODEL: Air Boss
MSRP: $1,450
URL: www.kilbyenterprises.com

10. AUXILIARY POWER
Running lights, lockers, and the myriad of other accessories that are installed to a vehicle can tax the factory wiring, so Precision Designs has developed a system to power any accessory separate from the factory wiring. The sPod system makes it easy for Jeep owners to add accessories without damaging the power system or cutting into any factory-installed wiring.

BRAND: Precision Designs
MODEL: sPod
MSRP: $435
URL: www.4x4spod.com

11. DUAL BATTERIES
When you are loaded down with electrical accessories, you better be able to back them up with dual batteries. A dual battery setup will allow the use of accessories off of one battery, while preserving the other for starting the vehicle. Once running, the vehicle's electrical system charges both batteries.

BRAND: Optima
MODEL: BlueTop Group 34/72
MSRP: $250
URL: www.optimabatteries.com

ing. The factory 4.10 gearing has been replaced with 5.38s that are able to turn the 40-inch Goodyear Wrangler MT/R tires at highway speeds. Paired with the Rubicon's low 4:1 transfer case and EVO MFG suspension, this Wrangler can creep or blast over just about any terrain. Proven on trails such as Dusy-Ershim and the Rubicon, Tully's Jeep is also used by his company to service and maintain rural telecommunication towers that can only be accessed by rough and desolate dirt roads, so its dependability in backcountry has been validated. We should all be so lucky to have a work truck like this one.

Whether you enjoy trail riding and discovering new places filled with old history or are doing some recon for your escape route, this Wrangler is built to bug out on demand. In the meantime, it provides all sorts of fun and relaxation, and a much-needed respite from everyday life's frustrations. Now we just need to win the lottery to afford one.

Military Buildup
Taking Brinkmanship to the Limit
By Sean P. Holman, Photos By Henry Z. De Kuyper

e Prepared" is the enduring motto of the Boy Scouts, and worthwhile mantra for life, but there are those out there who tend to be a little more prepared than others. For example, some of us might have few gallons of water in the garage and a favorite backcountry camping spot we'll head to if things go bad, while others have a decommissioned missile silo they've renovated as a Doomsday safe house. If you fall in the latter group, then we have just the rig you've been looking for.

Designed and built by VWERKS as a buzz model to showcase their military and civilian accessory and vehicle programs, the Recon started life as an '11 Jeep Wrangler

BODY MODIFICATION

The Recon features a JK-8 pickup conversion kit that has been stretched a full 10 inches behind the rear axle to increase cargo room. For those Wrangler Unlimited owners who rather have room for payload than rear doors and a rear seat, this conversion is a worthwhile upgrade.

MAKE: VWERKS
MODEL: JK-8 Conversion and Stretch
MSRP: $12,888
URL: www.vvwerks.com

SUSPENSION

The VWERKS 4-inch heavy-duty suspension includes remote-reservoir Fox shocks, taller Super HD coil springs, and ups the payload capacity to 2,500 pounds. This puts the Recon on par with some 1-ton trucks, while maintaining the footprint of a midsize and the coil-sprung ride quality of a Jeep.

MAKE: VWERKS
MODEL: 4-inch Heavy-Duty Suspension
MSRP: $8,971
URL: www.vvwerks.com

WHEELS AND TIRES

Bad roads require specialized equipment, such as a wheel and tire package designed for unforgiving environments, and the pairing on the Recon is exceptional. Hutchinson Rock Monster wheels are street legal and DOT-compliant beadlocks that will allow the tires to be run at low pressures without coming off the wheel and 39-inch BFG Krawler tires deliver maximum off-road traction and huge ground clearance for running over K-Rails and trails, alike.

MAKE: Hutchinson/BFGoodrich Tires
MODEL: Rock Monster/Krawler T/A KX
MSRP: $8,352
URL: www.vvwerks.com

PROTECTION

Featuring VWERKS Premium Rock Rails, which keep the body of the Jeep off of obstacles, the Recon's body sides are well protected on or off the trail. These rock sliders are also useful for pivoting in tight quarters or as a step for easier ingress and egress for your crew.

MAKE: VWERKS
MODEL: Premium Rock Rails
MSRP: $1,125
URL: www.vvwerks.com

ARMORED FENDERS

The Wrangler's stock plastic "fenders" have been replaced by front and rear GenRight Tube Flares. These tube fenders work in conjunction with the rock rails to help protect the body and provide increased clearance for taller tires. Available in steel or lightweight aluminum, the flares are perfect for taking glancing blows from trees or bodies.

MAKE: GenRight Off Road
MODEL: JK Tube Flare
MSRP: $1,000
URL: www.genright.com

DRIVETRAIN

After undergoing extreme modifications, more often than not the stock drivetrain is no longer up to the task of its new mission. In the case of the Recon, which needs power to get out of questionable situations as well as to haul around additional cargo and weapons systems, a 5.7L Hemi V-8 was added. The 390hp Hemi is a major upgrade from the anemic 202hp 3.8L V-6 that formerly resided in the engine compartment. Additionally, the conversion adds a five-speed 5-45RFE automatic transmission and a stout Advance Adapters Atlas II transfer case with a 4.3:1 low range.

MAKE: VWERKES
MODEL: Hemi Conversion w/ Atlas II
MSRP: $34,024
URL: www.vvwerks.com

FRONT BUMPER

The VWERKS front Premium Bumper offers protection for the grille and mounting points for a winch and auxiliary lighting. There are also sturdy attachment points for recovery shackles.

MAKE: VWERKS
MODEL: Front Premium Bumper
MSRP: $1,716
URL: www.vvwerks.com

HEAT EXTRACTION HOOD

The VWERKS JK Premium Hood is made from lightweight ABS plastic and incorporates functional heat extractor vents to help shed heat from the big Hemi V-8. Like the rest of the Recon, the hood has been painted Military Flat Green.

MAKE: VWERKS
MODEL: JK Premium Hood
MSRP: $2,446 (painted)
URL: www.vvwerks.com

CANVAS SOFT TOP

Covering the Recon is a custom soft top made from durable canvas, which protects the passengers from the elements, as well as conceals the contents of the Recon from prying eyes.

MAKE: VWERKS
MODEL: Removable Canvas Top
MSRP: $5,990
URL: www.vvwerks.com

HALF DOORS

Half doors give the driver increased visibility in places where technical driving is critical, while still protecting and restraining occupants. Half doors also weigh less than the full steel doors, helping to offset some of the weight gain added in other areas.

MAKE: Mopar
MODEL: Front Half Door Kit
MSRP: $1,300 (unpainted)
URL: www.mopar.com

STEERING

Attempting to turn 39-inch tires with the stock steering system would cause havoc on the steering system and lead to imminent failure. To help the stock steering box and pump out, VWERKS added a hydraulic assist system from PSC. The PSC system uses a hydraulic ram to assist the stock steering system by taking up most of the increased load.

MAKE: PSC Motorsports
MODEL: Jeep JK Trail & Street Cylinder Assist Kit
MSRP: $1,323
URL: www.pscmotorsports.com

WINCH

The whole point of having a capable escape vehicle is moot if you can't self-recover from getting stuck. To keep your contingency plan in effect, a 9,500-pound-rated Warn thermometric winch has been mounted to the front bumper as added assurance that you'll reach your destination.

MAKE: Warn
MODEL: 9.5ti
MSRP: $1,521
URL: www.warn.com

LIGHTING

Away from the soft glow of urban light pollution, the backcountry can suddenly become a very dark place. VWERKS chose PIAA's 520 ATP (All Terrain Pattern) lights to cut through the night. These lights use PIAA proprietary ATP technology, which cast a beam that is optimized for height, width, and distance and should easily light up the eyes of any looming zombies.

MAKE: PIAA
MODEL: 520 ATP
MSRP: $287
URL: www.piaa.com

TOOLS

Mounted to the front bumper and within easy reach is a deluxe tri-fold shovel and military pick axe. These tools have multiple uses and could come in handy in a variety of situations.

MAKE: VWERKS
MODEL: Tri-fold shovel/military pick axe
MSRP: $40/$16
URL: www.vvwerks.com

Unlimited and ended up as a 1-ton, all-terrain, armored pickup.

The puny, stock 3.8L V-6 was ditched for a hairy-chested 390hp 5.7L Hemi V-8, and a JK-8 pickup conversion kit was then used to turn everything behind the B-pillar into a cargo box. The frame was reinforced and upgraded to 1-ton capacity and stretched 10 inches behind the rear axle, giving the Recon more cargo space, while keeping the stock 116-inch wheelbase intact to ensure maneuverability. Lining the bed is 7/16-inch steel plate, which both protects the rear gunner and provides a solid platform to stand on.

Other areas of the chassis that were upgraded include a Dynatrac ProRock 60 front axle with an ARB Air Locker and a massive Dynatrac ProRock 80 rear axle with a Detroit Locker. Both axles run 5.38 gearing and upgraded axleshafts, bringing the vehicle's undercarriage as close to mechanically bulletproof as possible.

1 TIRE CARRIER

The stock tire carrier is not designed for the weight of 39-inch tires, so it was replaced with a GenRight JK Steel Rear Tire Carrier. Also available in a lightweight aluminum model, the GenRight carrier mounts to the factory tailgate hinges and is designed to work independent of the bumper. The huge 1.75-inch tubing is strong enough for tires as large as 42 inches and the four-point mounting method is rattle-free.

MAKE: GenRight Off Road
MODEL: JK Steel Rear Tire Carrier
MSRP: $800 (unpainted)
URL: www.genright.com

2 REAR BUMPER

The VWERKS Premium Rear bumper has the functional aesthetic of something that came straight from the surplus yard. This simple bumper is made strong and has clevis mounts for recovery, as well as a military pintle hook.

MAKE: VWERKS
MODEL: Premium Rear Bumper
MSRP: $2,734
URL: www.vvwerks.com

3 AXLES

Underpinning the Recon are a pair of the best axles you can buy. The front Dynatrac ProRock 60 and rear Dynatrac ProRock 80 are stuffed with 5.38 gears, upgraded axleshafts, and lockers. Both axles feature brakes from a 1-ton Ford truck and can easily handle the bigger tires and added weight of the Recon.

MAKE: Dynatrac
MODEL: ProRock 60/ProRock 80
MSRP: $28,917
URL: www.dynatrac.com

4 ARMOR

Lining the bed is a 7/16-inch steel plate, which is strong enough to deflect the energy coming from an IED. It also reinforces the cargo area floor and acts as a platform for the rear gunner.

MAKE: VWERKS
MODEL: Armor Package
MSRP: N/A
URL: www.vvwerks.com

5 ON-BOARD AIR

On-board air is for more than just activating lockers. Having your own source of air means having the ability to optimize tire pressures for the terrain your are traversing. An on-board compressor, when used in conjunction with a high-volume air tank, also gives you the ability to run pneumatic tools for making repairs in the field. The Recon pairs a high-output ARB twin on-board compressor with a Viair 2.5-gallon tank for maximum flexibility.

MAKE: ARB/Viair
MODEL: 12V Twin On-Board Compressor/2.5 Gallon Air Tank
MSRP: $545/$98
URL: www.arbusa.com/ www.viaircorp.com

Weapons of the VWERKS Recon

1. MA DEUCE
If you ever find yourself in a situation where you need to shoot your way out, there isn't a better friend than a belt-fed, fully automatic .50 caliber machine gun. Even if you don't pull the trigger, the menacing look of this beast will be enough to keep any miscreants at a safe distance. Mounted on a 360-degree swivel, it is a setup that would make international warlords jealous.

MAKE: Kelsey Hayes Wheel Company
MODEL: M2HB Browning Machine Gun
CALIBER: .50 BMG

2. M2HB MOUNT
The "Fifty" is mounted on a Crane Technologies MK93 Gun Mount with a 100-round ammunition can holder. It sits on a full 360-degree rotary mount, also made by Crane Technologies, that allows the gunner an unobstructed view around the entire vehicle.

MAKE: Crane Technologies
MODEL: MK93 Gun Mount
MAKE: Crane Technologies
MODEL: Rotary Mount

3. M240 BRAVO
As long as you are helping others get to safety, you might as well put them to work. The passenger-side mounted, .308-chambered, M240 "Bravo" is easily fired from the passenger seat. With 180-degrees of swivel, full-automatic shooting, and a Trijicon TA 648 ACOG (6x48) optic, you won't have to worry about any threats flanking your starboard side.

MAKE: FN Herstal
MODEL: M240B
CALIBER: 7.62x51mm NATO

4. SWING ARM
From the passenger side, a swing arm mechanism is augmented with a Crane Technologies M240 adaptor to give the side gunner the capability to cover the entire right side of the vehicle in a 180-degree arc of fire. With the "240" being fed by its mounted 600-round ammunition can it will easily get the VWERKS Recon out of harms way.

MAKE: Crane Technologies
MODEL: M240 Adaptor

A VWERKS 4-inch suspension system with heavy-duty coil springs increases payload capacity to 2,500 pounds and adds enough room for a set of 39-inch BFGoodrich Krawler T/A KX tires mounted on 17-inch Hutchinson beadlocked wheels. Keeping everything under control are a set of adjustable Fox Racing reservoir shocks and the entire suspension package guarantees that the Recon can take on any obstacle, from a burned-out car blocking the road to a boulder-strewn field far away from civilization.

At the heart of the VWERKS Recon is a bed-mounted, belt-fed M2HB .50 caliber full-automatic machine gun. Using a Crane Technologies 360-degree rotary-mount and 100-round ammo can, the M2HB can engage soft or hard targets, such as vehilces, from any direction. On the passenger side and mounted to a full swing arm setup that is capable of covering 180-degrees, is a fully automatic .308 Winchester-chambered FN Herstal M240B, making the Recon as formidable as it is impressive. With that kind firepower, you can probably stick your wife or kid behind either of the triggers and just drive behind the wall of lead the Recon can put out. Think of it as a Jeep-mounted Phalanx CIWS and you'll get the idea.

While the game of brinkmanship is all about out-escalating your opponent, the tools on the Recon will ensure no one ever calls your bluff. Whether you are escaping through a war-torn neighborhood, a rowdy crowd of riotous thugs, or disaster-scared cityscape, you can rely on the Recon to get you and your family safely to your emergency shelter, and, if need be, you will be more than capable of holding your ground. Knowing that you have that kind of insurance policy for safety is priceless.

JEEPS • MILITARY BUILDUP | **121**

Extreme Rock Crawler

Falken Designed WildPeak Tires to Conquer Any Terrain If SHTF, and Built a Jeep to Prove It

By Patrick Vuong
Photography By Jorge Nuñez

No warrior likes the idea of retreating, but let's be real for a second. If there's a potential nuclear meltdown as in Fukushima, mass looting and lawlessness like after Hurricane Katrina, or an inbound natural disaster similar to Superstorm Sandy, it's clear that GTFO is often a good option. And for some, the only option. But how do you bug out when the airport's shuttered, the freeways are clogged, or the streets are littered with downed power lines?

You'll need a nimble yet powerful vehicle to get you out of an urban jungle quickly if a FUBAR situation arises. But don't expect your truck with a measly 3-inch lift kit and stock axles — let alone your Toyota Prius — to do the same job. It takes serious engineering, sizeable resources, and the right platform on which to build a reliable bug-out vehicle that runs on four tires.

Enter the JK Recon. This one-of-a-kind Jeep was built by Falken Tire Corporation to be an extreme rock crawler and, more importantly for our purposes, serve as a survival vehicle when SHTF.

The JK Recon can easily pound dirt or pavement, roll over rubble, scramble over fallen trees, cut through shallow streams, or crawl up the steepest rock faces. It can do so thanks to an arsenal of heavy-duty parts and a set of WildPeak A/T Tires (naturally) wrapped around 18x9.5-inch Raceline RT Monster wheels. This Wrangler can steer clear of and climb over almost any hurdle it might encounter.

Off-Road Origins

The JK Recon was birthed when Falken decided to put its money where its mouth was. The tire manufacturer didn't want to just claim its WildPeak all-terrains provided an unusually smooth and quiet ride on asphalt while offering tremendous traction in mud, rock, or dirt — Falken wanted to prove it. The best way to do that was to build something with a purpose.

About four years ago, the Falken Off-Road Team decided to enter the King of the Hammers, an annual race held in Johnson Valley, California, that combines desert racing with rock crawling. The team needed a pre-runner that could serve as both a chase vehicle and a service truck to support the racers. And Falken needed a platform to prove WildPeak's worthiness. So, bam, the JK Recon was conceived.

Falken chose to start its project with an already capable four-wheeler — a new Wrangler Unlimited Rubicon. But the company wanted to give the four-door Jeep an extreme makeover to match its future extreme capabilities.

"The most challenging part of the build was making the vehicle different from any other JK on the trail," says Nestor Cabrera, Falken's off-road supervisor. "We wanted people to be able to tell this Jeep apart from all the other cookie-cutter Jeeps on the road."

The custom military desert-tan paintjob definitely helped in that regard, but the changes had to be more than skin deep. So, Falken tasked David Chappelle of Chappelle's Exhaust and Kustom Shop with turning the Jeep into a hardcore yet versatile pre-runner truck. The El Cajon, California-based fabricator started the transformation by gutting the rear passenger area and installing a custom truck bed. The bed is large enough for a spare tire and two storage compartments that house jacks, tools, supplies, and emergency straps. (The storage area could also be used to secure long-guns and ammo — hey, just saying…)

Kit Up

To get the Falken support team where it needs to be in the desert (chasing race rigs that fly at 100 mph) or on the rocks (winching out trucks stuck on gnarly boulders), the JK Recon's handling had to be top notch. So, Chappelle installed a PSC Motorsport hydraulic-assist steering kit and a Dana 60 high-steer kit, which consist of a skid plate, custom tie rod, and custom drag link.

Underneath an AEV Heat Reduction Hood, the JK is powered by the stock 3.8L V-6 engine and given a mild boost with the additions of a K&N cold-air intake, a Dynomax exhaust, and a Griffin radiator. Falken's rig can climb over almost any terrain, in

FALKEN JK RECON

MAKE: Jeep
MODEL: Wrangler Unlimited Rubicon
YEAR: 2009
ENGINE: 3.8L V-6
DRIVETRAIN: 4WD

large part because of its Rubicon 4:1 transfer case, ARB Air Lockers, and Dynatrac ProRock 60 High-Pinion axles (both with a 5.38 gear ratio). These heavy-duty components ensure the Jeep maintains aggressive traction in slick, slanted, or tenuous conditions.

But what about on the way down? Without a rugged suspension system, a bug-out vehicle could suffer serious damage to its body and undercarriage, perhaps even becoming inoperable.

Fortunately, the JK Recon sports long-travel coilovers (double bypass) from King Off-Road Racing Shocks in the front and King's cantilever long-travel coilovers (also double bypass) in the rear. Billet long-arms complete

1 TIRES
This tire is the *raison d'être* of the JK Recon. Falken built this Jeep pre-runner to prove that these meats could thrive on any terrain you could drive to.
MAKE: Falken Tire
MODEL: WildPeak A/T
SIZE: 37x13.50R18
MSRP: $1,800
URL: www.falkentire.com

2 WHEELS
These forged aluminum beadlocks are meant for hardcore competition, so they're more than capable for bugging out.
MAKE: Raceline Wheels
MODEL: 18x9.5 RT-235 Monster Forged
MSRP: $1,500
URL: www.racelinewheels.com

3 SUSPENSION: FRONT
The long-travel kit with King coilovers (double bypass) soaks up the abuse of hard landings.
MAKE: King Off-Road Racing Shocks
MODEL: Long-travel kit
MSRP: $1,500
URL: www.kingshocks.com

4 SUSPENSION: REAR
The rear suspension features a cantilever long-travel kit with King coilovers (double bypass).
MAKE: King Off-Road Racing Shocks
MODEL: Cantilever long-travel kit
MSRP: $1,500
URL: www.kingshocks.com

5 DOORSILL GUARD
These custom-built sliders keep the doorsill from eating rock damage, which could prevent the door from opening or cause body damage during a treacherous climb.
MAKE: Chappelle's Exhaust and Kustom Shop
MODEL: Customer sliders
MSRP: $1,500
URL: www.chappelleskustoms.com

6 ROLLCAGE
This custom-built 'cage ensures that the entire rig doesn't collapse on the driver and passenger in the case of a nasty spill or roll.
MAKE: Chappelle's Exhaust and Kustom Shop
MODEL: Custom rollcage
MSRP: $2,500
URL: www.chappelleskustoms.com

SKIDPLATES
(NOT SHOWN)
Like ceramic plates, skidplates keep the guts of the rig from suffering.
MAKE: ASFIR
MODEL: Full JK package
MSRP: $1,000
URL: asfir4x4.com

the suspension system. This combo ensures that the Wrangler can absorb harsh landings whether due to massive whoops in the sand or drop-offs from high boulders. The shocks also help to keep the driver from jostling too much in his Master-Craft Baja RS Seat or unleashing his breakfast all over the dashboard.

Like a plate added to a chest

1 REAR BUMPER

This custom one-off is based on an older version of the JK Rock-Brawler from Poison Spider and provides sturdy structural armor.

MAKE: Poison Spider Customs
MODEL: JK RockBrawler Rear Bumper
MSRP: N/A
URL: shop.poisonspyder.com

2 FRONT BUMPER

The 1/4 Pounder Front JK Bumper from Off Road Evolution provides strength and high clearance, thanks to heavy-duty ¼-inch-thick ASTM A36 steel construction. This version comes with a stinger, which has a few purposes other than looking like a boner bar: grille guard, tow spot, and rollover prevention, among others.

MAKE: Off Road Evolution
MODEL: 1/4 Pounder Front JK Bumper
MSRP: $650
URL: www.offroadevolution.com

3 AXLES

The ProRock 60 is practically bulletproof, has no problem managing large tires, and provides more ground clearance than a stock Dana 44.

MAKE: Dynatrac
MODEL: JK ProRock 60
MSRP: $15,000
URL: www.dynatrac.com

4 HOOD

This all-steel hood sucks in fresh air to keep everything underneath from overheating.

MAKE: American Expedition Vehicle
MODEL: JK Heat Reduction Hood
MSRP: $950
URL: www.aev-conversions.com

5 WINCH

A quick recovery is key whether you're in competition or survival mode. This workhorse ensures the JK Recon never gets stuck for very long.

MAKE: Warn Industries, Inc.
MODEL: 9.5xp air station
MSRP: $1,500
URL: www.warn.com

6 HEADLIGHTS

These LED headlights give you a clear line of sight in times of poor visibility.

MAKE: Truck-Lite
MODEL: 7-inch Round LED Headlamp
MSRP: $500
URL: www.truck-lite.com

rig, Chappelle outfitted the Jeep with assorted armor: a custom rollcage, custom sliders, a skidplate from ASFIR 4x4, and a 1/4 Pounder Bumper with a stinger from Off Road Evolution. And no chase team would be complete without the right tools to recover its race truck, so he installed the always-reliable Warn 9.5xp winch.

Based on a unique yet strong chassis, powered by a bevy of heavy-duty parts, and rolling on rugged all-terrain meats, the JK Recon is a unique pre-runner that doesn't just look like a survival vehicle, it rides like one, too. It's thrived in some of the most brutal terrain in North America, from the Blue Ridge Mountains of Tennessee to the red rock of Moab, Utah. "This vehicle has conquered every trail that has been placed in its path," Cabrera says. "It has been the perfect test bed for the WildPeak all-terrain tires."

It is a formidable mechanized steed — for the streets, on the trails, or in the backcountry — and that makes it the ideal bug-out rig for when shit truly does hit the fan.

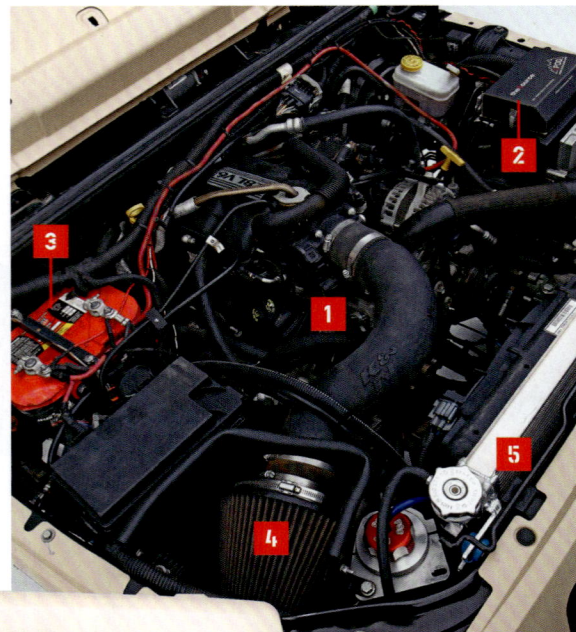

1 ENGINE

Having been a proven winner off-road, the stock engine was capable enough as is. Falken didn't see the need to swap it out or tinker with it.

MAKE: Jeep
MODEL: 3.8L V-6
MSRP: N/A
URL: www.jeep.com

2 AUXILIARY POWER

The sPOD Source allows the accessories to be powered separately from the factory wiring.

MAKE: Precision Designs
MODEL: sPOD Source
MSRP: $420
URL: www.4x4spod.com

3 BATTERY

Optima has earned a reputation for long-lasting, reliable batteries that are vibration resistant, spill-proof, and mountable in almost any position.

MAKE: Optima Batteries
MODEL: Redtop
MSRP: $200
URL: www.optimabatteries.com

4 AIR INTAKE

For an engine to work to its maximum potential, it needs clean, dry air — a lot of it. K&N delivers.

MAKE: K&N Engineering
MODEL: Performance Intake Kit
MSRP: $288
URL: www.knfilters.com

5 RADIATOR

The Griffin radiator is made of strong yet lightweight aluminum, helping to keep the weight down while cooling the engine.

MAKE: Griffin Thermal Products
MODEL: Radiator
MSRP: $595
URL: www.griffinrad.com

STEERING
(NOT SHOWN)

Stock steering systems and beefy tires don't mix, so this hydraulic steering assist kit was installed to make piloting the JK Recon much easier.

MAKE: PSC Motorsports
MODEL: Hydraulic steering-assist kit
MSRP: $1,500
URL: www.pscmotorsports.com

EXHAUST
(NOT SHOWN)

This exhaust lets the JK Recon breathe more efficiently while giving it a gnarly growl.

MAKE: Dynomax Performance Exhaust
MODEL: Custom
MSRP: $350
URL: www.dynomax.com

6 SEATS

This race-style seat keeps the driver from bouncing around and comfy for the long haul.

MAKE: MasterCraft Safety
MODEL: Baja RS
MSRP: $800
URL: www.mastercraftsafety.com

7 GLOVEBOX

This secured lockbox could house valuables or a pistol.

MAKE: Tuffy Security Products
MODEL: JK Security Glove Box
MSRP: $158
URL: www.tuffyproducts.com

8 STEREO COVER

This ingenious security cover (not shown) hides the stereo or GPS unit when locked in place to prevent thieves from spotting the equipment in the first place. Unlocked, it slides up and away. The top can be used as a tray for maps or sunglasses.

MAKE: Tuffy Security Products
MODEL: JK Flip-N-Lock Stereo Cover & Tray
MSRP: $149
URL: www.tuffyproducts.com

9 ON-BOARD AIR

Having your own compressed air means you can deflate your tires to the right psi, depending on the terrain, then air up once you're back on pavement. The Power Tank can also be used for pneumatic tools.

MAKE: Power Tank
MODEL: 20-pound tank
MSRP: $550
URL: www.powertank.com

Texas Instruments

Starwood Motors Shows Off the Black Jeep of the Family

By John Schwartze
Photos by Tristan Buster

It's been said that everything's bigger in Texas. Sometimes the Lone Star State seems like the last refuge for true freedom. You won't find the tyrannical firearms regulations there like the ones many of us face elsewhere in the country. Its residents are blissfully beyond the reach of rules that blame misspelled words on one's pencil. Do you car buffs also get emails from SEMA tipping you off to proposed legislation under the pretense of safety and environmental protection that limits the modifications you'll be able to make to your vehicles? Try making those same ideas fly in Texas. You'll quickly be told not to let the door hit you where the good lord split you.

So aside from my diatribe that retirement or permanent relocation to Texas may be in my future, we at RECOIL do so enjoy seeing the vehicle builds that come out of that state. The name Starwood Motors has graced these pages before, as they've had a hand in other builds such as John Wayne Walding's F-250. We caught a glimpse of this 2014 Wrangler they built and knew that our readers would also be interested in a 4x4 outfitted with necessities like a .50-caliber machinegun and a Browning 1919. So let's check out another creation that represents the 28th state in fine form.

Owner Chris Thompson had been pining over Jeeps since his high school days because his friends all had Wranglers. After spending several years in the Marines riding around in Humvees, his urge to eventually own a Jeep was punctuated by the desire to add a machinegun to it. After seeing an ad for Starwood Motors' "Full Metal Jacket" Wrangler package in an issue of *duPont REGISTRY*, the die was cast for Chris to pick up the phone and start the collaboration.

The Wrangler Full Metal Jacket option offered by Starwood comes with enough options to make your head spin. Chris decided to take it a step further by adding a Magnuson supercharger, K&N filter, and DiabloSport tuning software to the motor. ARB front and rear air lockers and air compressor, along with Rubicon Express driveshafts, a Fox ATS steer-

1 MACHINEGUN
MAKE: Surplus
MODEL: M2 .50 Caliber
URL: www.scalpelarms.com
www.jbiarmory.com

2 DOOR GUN
MAKE: Surplus
MODEL: 1919 converted to .308
URL: www.scalpelarms.com
www.jbiarmory.com

3 MACHINEGUN LIGHT
MAKE: SureFire
COLOR: Hellfighter 4
URL: www.surefire.com

4 TURRET
MAKE: H&H Tool Shop
MODEL: Custom
URL: www.hhtoolshop.com

5 LIGHTBAR
MAKE: Rigid Industries
MODEL: 50-inch
URL: www.rigidindustries.com

6 LIGHTS
MAKE: Rigid Industries
MODEL: Dually
URL: www.rigidindustries.com

7 BUMPERS
MAKE: Smittybilt
MODEL: Stinger JK
URL: www.smittybilt.com

8 WINCH
MAKE: Warn
MODEL: Zeon 10s
URL: www.warn.com

9 SIDE STEPS
MAKE: AMP Research
MODEL: Powerstep
URL: www.amp-research.com

10 PISTOL MOUNT
MAKE: Gunner Fab
MODEL: Pistol Mount, 4-Door JK
URL: www.conditionzeromounts.com

ing stabilizer, Curry Rock Jocks axles, King coilovers, and a Rubicon long-arm system make this thing look like a real-life version of those Stompers that children of the '80s remember playing with.

Smittybilt body armor and bumpers with Starwood's Kevlar finish help protect the exterior from the elements. Rigid Industries lights keep the path illuminated, while PROCAR seats, Gunner Fab rifle and pistol mounts, Tuffy lock boxes, an Alpine stereo and backup camera system, and a Poison Spyder cage keep all the occupants safe and privy to their surroundings.

And who can forget the fun stuff? The turret was built and designed by H&H Tool Shop and sent to Starwood to install. It was fitted with an M2 .50-caliber machinegun that was essentially a brand-new Korean War gun. The door gun is a

1 WHEELS
MAKE:
KMC Wheels
MODEL:
22-inch XD Bombs
URL:
www.kmcwheels.com

2 TIRES
MAKE:
Nitto
MODEL:
40x15.5x22 Mud Grappler
URL:
www.nittotire.com

3 CARGO NET
MAKE:
Safari Straps
MODEL:
Jeep JK 4DR
URL:
www.safaristraps.com

4 ROLLCAGE
MAKE:
Poison Spyder
MODEL:
Trail Cage
URL:
shop.poisonspyder.com

1919 chambered in .308 with a pistol grip converted to a spade grip. Both guns came from Scalpel Arms and had never been fired. Gotta love that military surplus.

Although Chris has sold the Jeep, here's a lesson in freedom at its finest. Ninety percent of the time Chris drove the Jeep around, it was with the guns mounted and the police just stopped him to take pictures and ask questions. God bless the USA; let's try and keep Chris' case study in judicial respect for law-abiding citizens going for the rest of us. It's an election year, and we need it more than ever.

Going Commando

Roamr's V8-Powered 1973 Jeep Commando is Ready for the Roads Less Traveled

By Patrick McCarthy
Photos by John Schwartze

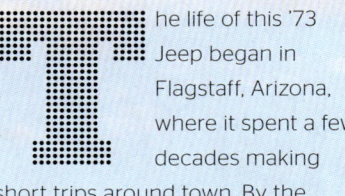

The life of this '73 Jeep began in Flagstaff, Arizona, where it spent a few decades making short trips around town. By the looks of its frame and undercarriage, it didn't see any off-road use back then, and certainly didn't see much snow — there's not a speck of rust on it. However, the engine eventually locked up, and it met the fate of far too many classic cars: It was pushed into a garage and left inoperable. Many years later, it got a second chance when its next owner — whose grandmother lived next door to the first owner — learned of its existence and purchased it. He brought it back to his home in Illinois and did a light restoration, installing

A hefty Warn winch sits in front of the Omix-ADA CJ front grille. The truck also has JW Speaker dual-projector headlights for more forward visibility.

The Poison Spider rear bumper is equipped with a Warn winch, full-size spare tire, med kit, light bar, and backup camera.

These 40-inch Nitto tires and beadlock wheels allow the Commando to tackle some seriously challenging trails.

Castle Fabrication made the center console and dashboard from scratch, with an iPad Pro front and center. The dash also contains a Rugged Radio and controls for the Vintage Air A/C system.

a 4.3L V6 from a 1990 GMC Jimmy to get it back on the road. It lived on in this condition for a while longer, but eventually made its way back into hibernation in the garage for close to 25 years.

The Jeep's third owners, Tony Durbano and Troy Tertany, would completely revitalize it and ensure it never ended up relegated to a dusty garage again. Together, the duo formed Roamr, a partnership of overlanding enthusiasts that has built several custom Jeeps, including the 1974 J20 "Tomahawk" featured in Issue 7 of our sister publication *CARNIVORE* magazine. They decided to set up the Commando for multi-day trail runs with five passengers and an overland trailer in tow.

Part availability for this model was minimal, so Tony and Troy reached out to their friends at Castle Fabrication for some custom sheetmetal work. Castle Fabrication started by cutting the stock metal roof and modifying it into a removable Bimini top. Next, the hood and front end were replaced with CJ-style parts for a classic look, and custom rockers and rear quarter-panels were fabricated. The interior also received a custom-built aluminum center console and dash, with an iPad Pro for navigation and a SnoMaster mini fridge that doubles as an armrest. Poison Spider bumpers and Metalcloak fenders were installed, and the whole body was finished in durable FDE Rhino Liner. Atop the roof, there's a Rhino Rack for extra gear storage and a row of JW Speaker auxiliary lights.

The old 4.3L V6 was pulled out and replaced with a much more potent BluePrint 383 stroker V8, paired with a 700R4 transmission and Advanced Adapters transfer case. Power is sent through Teraflex Tera60 axles, and a Teraflex big brake kit helps bring the 17-inch TR Beadlock wheels and 40-inch Nitto tires to a stop safely. A Teraflex long-arm suspension kit intended for a newer Jeep JK was modified to fit this application. Castle Fabrication also built a custom 31-gallon aluminum fuel tank behind the rear seats, with one third inside the cabin and the remainder beneath the floor. This provides increased range for multi-day adventures.

Tony and Troy wanted to take the Commando out on the trail with

Roamr uses the Commando to tow this Freespirit trailer with a rooftop tent, awning, water tank, refrigerator, LED lighting, and recovery tools.

134 | OFFGRIDWEB.COM

their family members, so a pair of PRP bucket seats were installed up front, along with a three-person PRP bench seat in the rear. A Rugged Radios mobile radio unit offers intercom communication between the driver and front passenger without forcing them to shout over the noise of the V8, mud tires, and wind. It also provides an option for emergency comms in areas without cellular reception. The Vintage Air A/C system, Dakota Digital gauge cluster, JL Audio stereo, and various USB and 12V power ports throughout the cab make this old Jeep feel more modern. Two SwitchPros controllers include a total of 16 switches for the auxiliary power system, lights, console fridge, and other accessories.

The build was christened "Slantback 6" after the combination of CJ-6 styling and the Commando's slantback rear end. Custom-cut metal badges with this name are attached to the fenders and dash, and the same method was used to make raised Roamr logos for each door panel. Since its unveiling at the SEMA Show in 2018, Tony and Troy have used the Slantback 6 frequently. It's no trailer queen — like Roamr's other creations, this Jeep spends most of its time on the trails.

Roamr's Commando has been outfitted with Teraflex axles, suspension, and brakes for a smoother and safer ride.

Compared to the original AMC straight-6 or the GM 4.3L V6 that previously resided under this hood, the 383 stroker V8 offers far more horsepower and torque.

This door on the side of the trailer opens to reveal a pull-out SnoMaster fridge, powered by the onboard Odyssey batteries.

One side of the trailer includes mounting points for a RotoPax water jug, Maxtrax recovery boards, first aid kit, and pressurized Road Shower.

1973 JEEP COMMANDO

DRIVETRAIN: BluePrint Engines 383ci V8, TH700R4 automatic transmission, Advanced Adapters Atlas transfer case, Teraflex Tera60 axles with Teraflex big brakes, custom Castle Fabrication 31-gallon aluminum fuel tank

SUSPENSION: Custom-modified Teraflex Suspension Jeep JK long arm kit with Falcon shocks

WHEELS & TIRES: 17-inch TR Beadlock wheels, 40x13.50R17 Nitto Trail Grappler M/T tires

BODY MODIFICATIONS: Poison Spider front and rear bumpers with spare tire carrier, Omix-ADA Jeep CJ grille and hood, Metalcloak fenders, Rhino Rack Pioneer Platform roof rack; custom Castle Fabrication rockers, belly pan, and rear quarter-panels; body finished in Rhino Lining matched to the FDE color of an AR-15 Hexmag

ELECTRONICS: JW Speaker headlights, Metalcloak taillights, JW Speaker light bar, Warn 70th Anniversary M8274 front winch and 9.0Rc rear winch, Rugged Radios Race Mobile unit with driver/passenger intercom system, Genesis dual battery system with Odyssey batteries, dual Switch Pros control panels

INTERIOR: PRP Enduro Elite Recliner seats, custom Castle Fabrication aluminum dash and center console with built-in iPad Pro and SnoMaster refrigerator, Dakota Digital gauge cluster, Vintage Air A/C system, JL Audio stereo system, Outer Limit Supply med kit

TRAILER: Freespirit Recreation Overlander trailer, Rhino Rack Pioneer Platform and Batwing Compact awning, Freespirit High Country 80-inch rooftop tent, dual Odyssey batteries, KC Hilites Flex LED lights, dual propane tanks, slide-out SnoMaster fridge with kitchenette, Leitner Designs GearPod XL, RoadShower, Power Tank air tank, Maxtrax mini recovery boards, and RotoPax water tank

OWNERS: Tony Durbano & Troy Tertany

URL: roamr.life

INSTAGRAM: @roamrlife

The Tomahawk

Roamr Turned Back the Clock on Jeep Pickups with its Custom 1974 J-20

By Patrick McCarthy
Photos by John Schwartze

Jeep pickups are a common sight these days as a result of the popularity of the new JT Gladiator. Prior to that model's release in 2020, American Expedition Vehicles offered AEV Brute pickups built from modified Wranglers; before that, there was the 1986-92 Jeep Comanche based on the XJ Cherokee. But the history of Jeep pickup trucks — and the Gladiator name — goes back even further. In 1963, Jeep introduced the first Gladiator, also known as the J-Series. Production of this Wagoneer-based truck would continue for more than 25 years, serving as a testament to consumers' desire for a vehicle blending the off-road prowess of a Jeep with the versatility of a pickup.

Above: In case one of the 40-inch Nitto Trail Grappler tires goes flat, a full-size spare is mounted on the Wilco tailgate for quick access.

A Rhino-Rack on the roof provides storage space for additional gear, as well as a mounting point for eight KC Hilites LED lights.

The J-20's interior has been modernized with a Dakota Digital gauge cluster, upgraded sound system, and electronic controls for the Holley EFI system, lights, and accessories.

One side of the bed rack carries a large Leitner Designs storage pod, a Rotopax gas can, and a Rhino-Rack Sunseeker awning; the other side holds a small storage pod and a Maxtrax recovery device.

The tomahawk theme for this build is represented by its custom hood ornament as well as the grab handle embedded in the tailgate.

Roamr is a partnership between overland vehicle enthusiasts Troy Tertany, Tony Durbano, and Jason Miller. The trio has always been fond of J-Series trucks, so when they found a 1974 J-20 for sale, they immediately decided to restore it. "It was rough," Troy said. "The truck was running, but just barely, and there was a lot of body cancer." The cab, bed, and engine were removed, and all the rust was carefully excised. Then, Castle Fabrication shortened both ends of the frame to reduce its length by a total of 13.5 inches — this would improve the approach and departure angles on trails, and also make it more maneuverable around town.

"We decided early on that this build needed 40-inch tires, should be able to go just about anywhere, and should be prepared for several-day excursions," Troy said. This meant the J-20 would need substantial modifications to the suspension and body. The factory sheetmetal panels were cut to make room for modified Metalcloak fenders; Rugged Ridge bumpers and rocker panel guards were also installed. Castle Fabrication crafted a custom suspension setup based on a Metalcloak 6-inch long-arm kit. This provided enough clearance to install 17-inch B.A.D. beadlock wheels and 40-inch Nitto tires.

The shortened bed received a host of new overland-oriented upgrades, including a Leitner Designs rack and storage pods, Decked drawer system, and a Wilco tailgate with spare tire. A Rhino-Rack on the cab serves as a mounting point for eight KC Hilites LED lights; a Sunseeker awning was also attached to provide shade at campsites.

Up front, Roamr installed JW Speaker projector headlights, a black Rhino grill, and a Warn winch. The unique hood ornament is a physical representation of the truck's "Tomahawk" name; a second ax embedded in the tailgate serves as a handle. To complete the exterior, Miller Collision sprayed a coat of glossy Nardo Grey paint onto the body, and OC Rhino coated the bumpers, fenders, rack, and other accents in durable Rhino liner.

The original 401ci V-8 still resides under the hood of this Jeep, fully rebuilt and upgraded with Holley fuel injection. It sends power through a TH400 automatic transmission, BorgWarner QuadraTrac transfer case, and Tom Wood driveshafts to the Dana 44 front axle and Dana 60 rear axle. Both axles have been upgraded with Warn hubs, Yukon gears and lockers, and BJ's Offroad disc brakes.

Inside the cab, the original power seats and door panels were reupholstered in diamond-stitched leather from Relicate. New black carpet, a plaid headliner, and a leather-wrapped dash were also installed. To bring this '70s Jeep into the 21st century, the Roamr crew added a Dakota Digital gauge cluster, Bluetooth head unit, JL Audio speakers, Holley touchscreen fuel injection controller, and Switch Pros switch panel for the exterior lights and Viair air compressors.

Although Troy says this frame-off J-20 build was a huge challenge, he's extremely proud of how it turned out. "This beast drives straight and smooth with one finger on the wheel at highway speeds," he explained before adding, "But it's frankly dangerous on the freeway because so many passersby veer toward it as they stare." Although it's driven on the road occasionally, it's clearly made for the trail. "We have had it out to Moab twice — that's its natural habitat."

Although Troy says he loves the classic 401ci V-8, he has also considered swapping it out for a turbodiesel motor. The additional torque would be helpful in spinning the big 40-inch tires.

The Decked storage system offers a flat cargo surface and two slide-out, lockable drawers for tools and recovery equipment.

1974 JEEP J-20

ENGINE: Rebuilt AMC 401ci V-8 with Holley Sniper fuel injection, Be Cool radiator and fans

TRANSMISSION: TH400 3-speed automatic

DRIVELINE: 4WD with BorgWarner QuadraTrac 1339 transfer case and part-time 2WD conversion kit, Tom Wood driveshafts

BRAKES: BJ's Offroad disc brake conversion

AXLES AND STEERING: Dana 44 front with truss and chromoly shafts, stock Dana 60 full-float rear, Reid knuckles, Artec steering, PSC hydraulic assist, Yukon gears and lockers, Warn hubs

SUSPENSION: Custom setup by Castle Fabrication based on a heavily modified Metalcloak LJ 6-inch long arm kit, coil spring conversion, Metalcloak 6Pak shocks, Teraflex SpeedBump bump stops

WHEELS AND TIRES: 17x9 B.A.D. beadlock wheels, 40x13.5R17 Nitto Trail Grappler tires

BODY MODIFICATIONS: Rhino grille; heavily modified Metalcloak fenders; Rugged Ridge bumpers, mirrors, and sidesteps; Wilco tire carrier tailgate; Leitner Designs Active Cargo System bed rack; Decked bed storage; Rhino-Rack over-cab rack and awning; bodywork and Nardo Grey paint by Miller Collision

LIGHTING & ELECTRICAL: Genesis Offroad dual battery kit with Odyssey batteries, JW Speaker headlights, KC Hilites light bar, Warn winch with Factor 55 FlatLink, Viair dual air compressors, Power Tank air tank

INTERIOR: Original power seats and door cards reupholstered with Relicate leather, Dakota Digital gauge cluster, full dash restoration, plaid headliner, JL Audio speakers, Switch Pros switches

OWNERS: Troy Tertany & Jason Miller

Roamr
Instagram: @iamroamr
iamroamr.com

SUVs

Bugout Truck
Escape The End Of The World Or Just The Daily Grind
By RECOIL STAFF

hether you're fleeing a natural disaster or an all-out zombie infestation, a properly setup truck can provide the key to survival. When setting up a bug-out vehicle, the important factors to consider include the environment, what you're escaping, who with and where you are going.

Although the needs of someone traversing mountainous regions differ from someone driving through flat, open country, the basis of good transport is a four-wheel-drive truck, no matter where you are or are going. Having four wheels drive your vehicle gives you much more control when navigating everything from debris to boulders. Four-wheel drive is more stable in inclement weather, as well.

Vehicle size is also a factor. Be sure that the truck is large enough to accommodate everyone and everything you will need. Nothing would be worse than having to draw straws to see if you get left behind. Think ahead to where you will have to travel. For example, a large, wide vehicle might not be a good idea if you need to drive over narrow mountain passes.

The vehicle should be weatherproofed and capable of sustaining you and the other occupants for at least the amount of time that it will take you to relocate to a safe zone. It should be reliable and have high enough ground clearance to get over obstacles.

Because there might not be a truck that is perfect for all of these contingencies, modifying one to suit your needs is your best bet. Our friends at *Four Wheeler* magazine recently built up a great example of a bug-out truck, starting with a 2010 Toyota 4Runner Trail Edition. Its fulltime four-wheel-drive system coupled to a 4.0L V6 engine provides an excellent mix of traction, power and fuel efficiency.

To further perfect the Toyota to meet bug-out needs, the *Four Wheeler* staff added a few modifications. They ended up with a truck that can get you home from a rough day at work or a rough day running from mutant brain eaters.

SIDE AUXILIARY ROOF LIGHTING
Extra lighting is essential for seeing what's around. A set of flood lights was mounted to either side on the roof rack of the truck. Floodlights can provide security as well as a good work site in dark areas.
BRAND: KC HiLites
MODEL: 26 Series 2x6-Inch 55W Floodlights
MSRP: $62
URL: www.kchilites.com

ROOFTOP STORAGE
A roof rack can be especially helpful for storing anything that can't be crammed inside. Use it to store extra survival gear, provisions and, in this case, temporary housing.
BRAND: ARB
MODEL: Steel Touring-Style Roof Rack
MSRP: $752
URL: www.arbusa.com

ROOFTOP TENT
Being able to sleep 6 feet above the ground solves many problems. A rooftop tent is easily deployed and keeps your living quarters out of potentially harmful environments. This means no sleeping in the mud or finding a snake in your tent. The higher vantage point is a bonus.
BRAND: ARB
MODEL: Series III Simpson Rooftop Tent
MSRP: $1568
URL: www.arbusa.com

OVERSIZED ALL TERRAIN TIRES
What you need from tires is aggressive traction. All-terrain tires differ from regular road tires in that their wide tread pattern is designed to shed large amounts of water, mud and snow. All-terrain tires usually have stiffer belts and thicker sidewalls that allow for better survivability over rough surfaces.
BRAND: Falken
MODEL: 285/70R17 Wildpeak A/T Tires
MSRP: $229 each
URL: www.falkentire.com

STRONG, LIGHT-WEIGHT WHEELS
Wheels that don't bend or crack are important for fending off rugged terrain. Lightweight wheels can also help you increase the distance you can travel by saving fuel.
BRAND: ATX
MODEL: 17x8 Mohave Cast-Aluminium Wheels with Teflon Coating
MSRP: $174 each
URL: www.atxwheels.com

TRUCK ARMOR
Armor protects your vehicle from obstacles that can potentially destroy the undercarriage. A rock slider is an important piece that protects the doorsills. A pair of rock sliders will ensure that you can open your doors even if the sills are impacted by boulders or ruts.
BRAND: EVO MFG.
MODEL: Rock Sliders
MSRP: $639
URL: www.evomfg.com

SUSPENSION
We can't say enough about a proper suspension setup. A 2- to 3-inch lift over the stock ride height of most trucks allows for ample clearance without sacrificing driving stability. More clearance means better survivability on and off the road. Stiff shocks help with the extra loads the truck may need to carry and allow for better traction.
BRAND: Old Man Emu
MODEL: 3-Inch-Lift Coil Springs Front and Rear; Old Man Emu Nitrocharger Front Struts and Rear Sport Shocks
MSRP: Complete Kit $919
URL: www.arbusa.com

SUVs • BUGOUT TRUCK | 141

① FORWARD AUXILIARY ROOF LIGHTING
Night driving on unpaved roads can be especially hazardous. Safe navigation starts with being able to see far ahead. Having two different-powered lights on the roof rack provides for lighting flexibility that can be chosen for the occasion. Their high mounting position gives the lights farther reach over longer distances.

BRAND: KC HiLites
MODEL: 57 Series 5x7-Inch 100W Long-Range Lights; 57 Series 5x7-Inch 55W Driving Lights
MSRP: Long Range $198; Driving $163
URL: www.kchilites.com

② AUXILIARY BUMPER LIGHTING
Closer to the ground than roof-mounted lights, auxiliary bumper lights are unbeatable at piercing the night during long, dark drives.

BRAND: KC HiLites
MODEL: 6x9-Inch 50W Long-Range HID Lights
MSRP: $1266
URL: www.kchilites.com

③ FRONT UTILITY BUMPER
A robust front bumper capable of mounting a winch is a must. A solid bumper can get you out of trouble in more ways than one. Not only can a winch be used to extract your truck if you ever get stuck, but also it can be used to help other stranded vehicles. If you're traveling alone in the outback, a winch is an absolute necessity.

BRAND: ARB
MODEL: Deluxe Bull Bar
MSRP: $1237
URL: www.arbusa.com

BRAND: Warn Winch
MODEL: XD9000i Premium Series Winch
MSRP: $1259
URL: www.warn.com

EXTRA FUEL
Who knows when your next fill-up will be. In most emergency situations, fuel and other supplies will be hard to come by. Keep a good stash of your own fuel on your vehicle for this possibility.

BRAND: Expedition One
MODEL: Geri Can Fuel Packs
MSRP: $76 each
URL: www.exp-one.com

COMMUNICATIONS
Keep up to date on emergency broadcasts with a communications system. Some choose to go with citizens band (CB) radio and some go amateur radio (ham). Whichever you choose, it's a good idea to have something to communicate with.

BRAND: Firestik
MODEL: Cobra WX ST 75
MSRP: $23
URL: www.firestik.com

REAR UTILITY BUMPER
Like the front bumper, the rear bumper can get you out of a few jams. A good rear bumper can mount additional gear, including your extra fuel tanks and an oversize spare tire.

BRAND: EVO MFG.
MODEL: Rear Tire Carrier
MSRP: Estimated $1400
URL: www.evomfg.com

13-GALLON WATER TANK
Water is a necessity regardless of the situation. Beneath the rear of this vehicle sits a 13-gallon water tank in place of the factory spare. The unit was custom built using marine tank parts and water pump and is fitted with a hose connection.

Ain't No Status Symbol

This Land Rover Discovery Series II Looks Like a Luxury Vehicle, But Can Ride as a Hardcore Off-Road Truck or a Mean Bug-Out Rig

By Patrick Vuong
Photography By Henry Z. De Kuyper

The image of the Land Rover as one of the preeminent off-road rigs has somewhat faded in mainstream American consciousness. Instead of recalling gritty photos of European soldiers driving the Series IIA in war-torn landscapes, or of hunters wheeling the civilian versions on African safaris, most Americans these days think of Land Rover as nothing more than a luxury vehicle. You can thank Victoria Beckham and all those trophy

1 WHEELS

Sturdy and light, these standard steel wheels do their job well at a great price. This set features a custom powdercoat.

MAKE: Atlantic British
MODEL: 16x7 Steel Matte Black
MSRP: $110 each
URL: www.atlanticbritish.com

2 TIRES

Positive traction is everything on and off the road. Climbing over rocks and other obstacles can get slippery and even damage tires, leaving you stuck. Falken WildPeak A/T tires are all-terrain, meaning they can go the distance with confidence over a variety of rocks, dirt, mud, water, and snow.

MAKE: Falken
MODEL: WildPeak A/T
SIZE: LT265/75R16
MSRP: $197 each
URL: www.falkentire.com

3 FRONT BUMPER

ARB's Sahara Bar not only provides protection from off-road elements, but also maintains the OEM look. It accepts the factory airbag sensors, turn signals, and fog lamps.

MAKE: ARB
MODEL: Sahara Bar
MSRP: $1,414
URL: www.arbusa.com

4 AUXILIARY LIGHTING (FRONT BUMPER)

Bugging out won't get you far if you don't have the vision to see where you're going. These forward-mounted driving lamps enhance road visibility in terms of both reach and beam pattern width.

MAKE: PIAA
MODEL: 520 Ion Yellow Driving Halogen Lamp Kit
MSRP: $329
URL: www.piaa.com

5 FOG LAMPS

These lights feature a widespread light pattern that helps light up the surrounding area forward of the truck. This increases peripheral vision when driving in extremely dark areas.

MAKE: PIAA
MODEL: 510 SMR Fog Xtreme White Plus Halogen Lamp Kit
MSRP: $299
URL: www.piaa.com

6 WINCH

This Warn M8000 is rated to pull 8,000 pounds, giving this Land Rover the capability to get unstuck and help others out of trouble in a pinch.

MAKE: Warn
MODEL: M8000
MSRP: $650
URL: www.warn.com

7 WINCH ISOLATOR

This winch isolator keeps the winch hook from rattling.

MAKE: Daystar
MODEL: Winch Isolator, Roller, Red
MSRP: $30
URL: www.daystarweb.com

8 ROOF RACK

This lightweight rack is strong and runs the full length of the roof to maximize storage space. Though this particular model is out of production, a similar rack is now available from a company called Voyager Offroad (www.voyagerracks.com).

MAKE: Safety Devices
MODEL: Series II Highlander High Roof Rack
MSRP: $1,330 (discontinued)
URL: www.safetydevices.com

9 AUXILIARY LIGHTING (ROOF FORWARD)

PIAA's ATP (All Terrain Pattern) lamps project a far-reaching narrow beam pattern for superior visibility at a distance. Having them mounted high on the roof rack provides even more piercing distance.

MAKE: PIAA
MODEL: 510 ATP Intense White ATP Halogen Lamp Kit
MSRP: $329
URL: www.piaa.com

10 DOORSILL GUARD

A harsh landing after climbing an especially treacherous rock could damage your doorsill to the point of the door not being able to open. Rock sliders help protect from that sort of damage.

MAKE: Atlantic British
MODEL: Rock Slider
MSRP: $599.95
URL: www.atlanticbritish.com

11 LIMB RISERS

These cables are used to deflect low-hanging tree branches over your roof to prevent windshield damage. They also make handy clothes lines when drying your gear at the campsite.

MAKE: Bush Cables
MODEL: Stainless Steel Set
MSRP: £40 (about $65)
URL: www.bushcables.com

12 DIFFERENTIAL GUARDS

Tall rocks can dent and even puncture differential casings. A damaged casing could mean being stuck out in the middle of nowhere. The QT Services front and rear guards help protect these essential parts when on the trail.

MAKE: QT Services
MODEL: Diff Guard (front, rear)
MSRP: $120 (front); $120 (rear)
URL: www.lucky8llc.com

1 ROOF TENT

A roof tent makes for a better sleeping environment — it keeps you off the cold (and sometimes wet) ground, while keeping insects and roving animals out. Plus, a higher vantage point helps you see threats approaching from a distance. It takes only minutes to set up and is just as easy to pack up.

MAKE: ARB
MODEL: Series III Simpson Rooftop Tent
MSRP: $1,569
URL: www.arbusa.com

2 AWNING

An awning is a handy thing to have, particularly when the summer sun is harsh or when a rainstorm suddenly hits. It's quick to deploy and doesn't add too much extra weight to your load.

MAKE: ARB
MODEL: Awning 2000
MSRP: $226
URL: www.arbusa.com

3 FUEL CAN

Fuel is liquid gold when you are far from a source. Always keep some extra when wading deep into no man's land.

MAKE: NATO
MODEL: Jerry Can 20L Military Spec.
MSRP: $90
URL: www.amazon.com

4 WATER CAN

Drinking water can be even more valuable than gas. Always have extra on hand for an unexpected emergency.

MAKE: Atlantic British
MODEL: Jerry Can 20L - Metal - Blue
MSRP: $45
URL: www.atlanticbritish.com

5 CAN HOLDER

Cans full of fluids can be tricky to secure. The Expeditionware holders can be bolted to just about anything. In this case, they are attached to the roof rack. The added security of them being lockable is a plus.

MAKE: Expeditionware
MODEL: Single Jerrycan Holder (EW30)
MSRP: $75
URL: www.expeditionexchange.com

INSECT NET
(NOT PICTURED)

Not everyone thinks of insects until, of course, they've nearly been eaten alive. Keep mosquitos and other flying pests at bay by placing this net on the awning.

MAKE: ARB
MODEL: Mosquito Net 2000
MSRP: $165
URL: www.arbusa.com

wives, Hollywood celebrities, and bubblegum pop singers for that.

Well, it's time to take back the brand from all those yuppies, who wouldn't know a leafspring from a coilover if one smacked them upside their heads.

Inspired by the Willys Jeep of World War II, the Land Rover was born as an all-terrain 4x4 meant to tackle harsh conditions. By the mid-20th century, it was widely used by the British Army and various European forces — and even by the U.S. Army to a limited degree. Today, Land Rovers are used around the world by military and police of numerous countries. Though the 2004 Land Rover Discovery Series II you see in these pages will never see combat, it was definitely built to be an off-road workhorse that any soldier or cop would admire.

But perhaps its greatest advantage is that it can easily blend into almost any environment a shooter might find himself in. As a

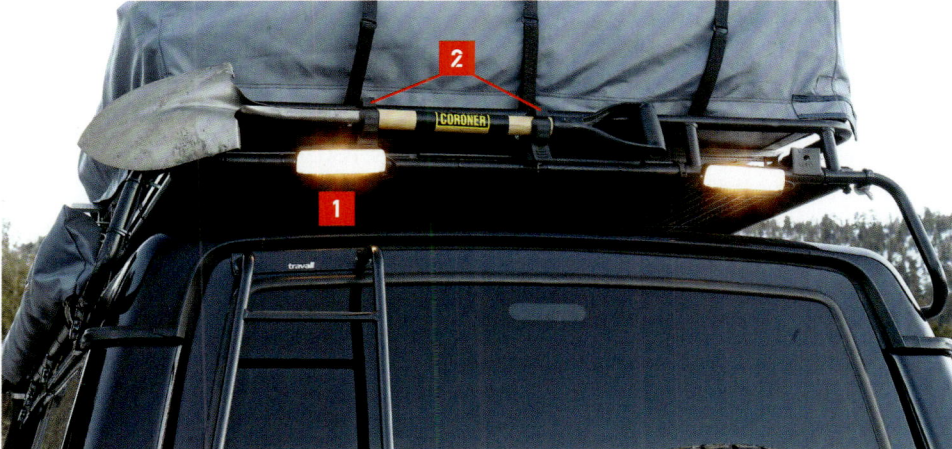

1 AUXILIARY LIGHTING (ROOF REAR)

The rear of the truck features high-mounted lamps, which serve a dual purpose as auxiliary backup lights and as convenient flood lamps for lighting up your campsite or outdoor workspace.

MAKE: PIAA
MODEL: 1500 Back-Up Clear Halogen Lamp Kit
MSRP: $229
URL: www.piaa.com

2 QUICK FIST CLAMPS

Some shooting ranges require you to bring a shovel for fire concerns. Quick Fist Clamps are an easy, secure way to carry a shovel.

MAKE: Quick Fist
MODEL: Original Quick Fist Clamp
MSRP: $11 for two
URL: www.endroad.com

3 REAR BUMPER

Similar to the front bumper, this heavy-duty rear bumper from Terrafirma guards against rocky terrain while incorporating OEM lights. Plus, it comes with sturdy, easy-access recovery points.

MAKE: Terrafirma
MODEL: Heavy Duty Rear Bumper with Swivel Recovery Eyes
MSRP: $888
URL: www.lucky8llc.com

4 CAM CAN TRAIL BOX

You can store recovery straps and other equipment in the Cam Can Trail Box.

MAKE: Daystar
MODEL: Cam Can Trail Box, Complete Kit
MSRP: $130
URL: www.daystarweb.com

5 D-RING ISOLATORS

These inserts keep ¾-inch shackles from tapping against bumpers and other recover points.

MAKE: Daystar
MODEL: D-Ring Isolators, Black
MSRP: $10
URL: www.daystarweb.com

6 EXHAUST

This bolt-on upgrade is said to increase horsepower and torque, in addition to giving the rig a powerful bark.

MAKE: MagnaFlow
MODEL: Stainless Cat-Back System Performance Exhaust
MSRP: $590
URL: www.magnaflow.com

daily driver, this Discovery Series II is discreetly powerful and elegantly clean — like a muscled Daniel Craig in a bespoke fine wool suit. As a 4WD recreational vehicle, it can easily leave the pavement behind to get to an out-of-the-way outdoor range or camping site. And as a bug-out vehicle, there's no doubt it can cut over streams and rocks to get to safer ground when shit hits the fan.

RECOIL readers will be pleased to see a Tuffy Tactical Gear Security Drawer installed in the back. Bolted to the truck's frame, this system safely stows firearms, ammo, accessories, and tools (loose items flying around the cabin can be very dangerous) while simultaneously securing the valuables from desperate thieves with a number combination and a traditional key as backup.

Underneath the hood, this Land Rover has both the power and the handling to be agile on asphalt and dirt alike, thanks to the parts and accessories — all installed and maintained by Gearheinz Power Service in Duarte, California — that help it match form with function. The Discovery II features a 4.6L V-8 engine, Old Man Emu suspension system and steering damper, Falken WildPeak A/T tires, EBC brake pads and rotors, and MagnaFlow performance exhaust. A South Down 4x4 Products snorkel and a K&N air filter ensure the truck only breathes clean, dry air instead of water from crossing a creek or dust from following in a caravan.

If these parts are the guts of the rig, then the body armor is the

1 HARD CASES

Pelican Storm Cases can hold any mission-essential gear that you need on your trip. In the case of this Land Rover, it's camping equipment, shooting-range supplies, and emergency tools.

MAKE:
Pelican

MODEL:
Storm Case (various models)

MSRP:
varies

URL:
www.pelican.com

2 WEAPONS/TOOL STORAGE

Tucked away and safely stowed, guns and ammunition are stored in this locked security drawer. The drawer slides on smooth bearings that can handle substantial weight. The drawer is configurable with inserts to address a multitude of load outs. The system is bolted to the frame of the truck and features a dual lock system that is accessible with a keyed lock as well as a number combination lock. Shown with optional accessories.

MAKE:
Tuffy

MODEL:
Tactical Gear Security Drawer (Ford Escape model)

MSRP:
$1,157 (base price)

URL:
www.tuffyproducts.com

TIRE DEFLATOR
(NOT PICTURED)

When you need get over soft terrain — such as sand, snow, or even tough spots like steep rock faces — this deflator lets you quickly air-down your tires for better traction.

MAKE:
ARB

MODEL:
E-Z Deflator Kit

MSRP:
$41

URL:
www.arbusa.com

PORTABLE AIR COMPRESSOR
(NOT PICTURED)

Heading into the hills means being able to air up and air down your tires for greater tire traction. Keeping this compressor onboard means never being stuck for lack of tire pressure.

MAKE:
ARB

MODEL:
Portable High-Performance 12-Volt Air Compressor

MSRP:
$352

URL:
www.arbusa.com

TIRE REPAIR KIT
(NOT PICTURED)

When taking the road less traveled, a tire puncture is a definite possibility. This tire repair kit is essential to not being stranded. We suggest everyone learn how to use a kit like this before getting that first puncture.

MAKE:
ARB

MODEL:
Speedy Seal Tire Repair Kit

MSRP:
$42

URL:
www.arbusa.com

tough-as-nails skin. Rock-crawling can cause some serious damage to a vehicle's fenders and undercarriage and could even leave one stranded. This Land Rover's rear and front diff guards from QT Services help ward off dents and punctures caused by tall rocks. Likewise, the Atlantic British Rock Slider helps fend off landing damage to your doorsill after climbing steep rocky terrain. Meanwhile, limb risers from Bush Cables help keep low-hanging tree branches from smashing into the windshield.

ARB's Sahara Bar front bumper provides hardcore protection while accepting the factory airbag sensors, turn signals, and fog lamps, which helps maintain the Disco's overall stock look. The Terrafirma Heavy-Duty Rear Bumper with Swivel Recovery Eyes incorporates that OEM aesthetic while offering sturdy, easy-access winching points. And speaking of recovery, the Warn M8000 winch is rated to pull 8,000 pounds, giving the Land Rover the ability to get unstuck and help other vehicles out of precarious positions, as well.

If you're looking to build a bug-out vehicle based on a Land Rover, consider this truck your template. With very little flash, but a whole lot of functionality, this Discovery Series II is prepped for any duty, be it daily driving, four-wheeling, or bugging out. It proves that the Land Rover legacy as a reliably rugged off-road rig still lives — yuppies and their status symbols be damned.

1 AIR INTAKE

A snorkel is a great way to keep the truck running on clean, dry air. The snorkel top can be angled away from especially dusty air when following in a caravan.

MAKE: South Down 4x4 Products Ltd.
MODEL: Discovery 2 Snorkel Unfinished
MSRP: £139 (about $224)
URL: www.southdown4x4.co.uk

AIR FILTER
(NOT PICTURED)

K&N's air filter replaces the OEM filter and allows for more free-flowing air when compared to the stock filter. More clean air means a more efficient engine.

MAKE: K&N
MODEL: Air Filter
MSRP: $51
URL: www.knfilters.com

2 BRAKE PADS

Brakes are only as good as the pads they use. The Yellowstuff compound features a wide temperature range and allows strong bite without having to warm up the pads.

MAKE: EBC
MODEL: Yellowstuff Brake Pads
MSRP: $161 (front); $123 (rear)
URL: www.ebcbrakes.com

3 BRAKE ROTORS

All these added upgrades add significant weight to the truck. The heavier it is, the harder it is to stop with its standard brakes. EBC brake rotors and pads help keep all the extra weight manageable at speed on city roads, as well as on steep mountain trails.

MAKE: EBC
MODEL: USR Series Sport Slotted Rotors
MSRP: $222 (front); $177 (rear)
URL: www.ebcbrakes.com

4 BRAKE LINES

Standard brake lines expand when under braking pressure, leading to less braking power. These steel-braided lines resist expansion so they keep brake pressure optimal. They are also lengthened to account for the raised suspension.

MAKE: Expeditionware
MODEL: Disco2 DOT Brake Hose Kit (front, rear)
MSRP: $70 (front); $70 (rear)
URL: www.expeditionexchange.com

STEERING DAMPER
(NOT PICTURED)

Driving on rough terrain could make your steering jostle about unruly-like. A heavy-duty steering damper helps reduce or eliminate nervous steering, increasing stability on beat-up roads, paved or otherwise.

MAKE: Old Man Emu
MODEL: Steering Damper
MSRP: $87
URL: www.arbusa.com

SUSPENSION: SHOCKS
(NOT PICTURED)

Upgraded shocks means your rig can handle more road abuse, which means there are more places you can go to and get to — and that means more places you can shoot.

MAKE: Old Man Emu
MODEL: Nitrocharger Sport Shock Absorbers
MSRP: $110
URL: www.arbusa.com

SUSPENSION: SPRINGS
(NOT PICTURED)

These springs help lift the truck up a couple of inches in overall ride height. This helps the truck get over obstacles, such as uneven dirt roads, rocks, or road debris.

MAKE: Old Man Emu
MODEL: Medium Load Springs
MSRP: $176
URL: www.arbusa.com

Blue Oval Blitzkrieg

Say Hello to RECOIL's Ballistic Bronco

By John Schwartze
Photography by Kenda Lenseigne

If you've been a longtime reader of RECOIL, you've seen our Transport column run the gamut from mild to wild, practical to outrageous. We get asked periodically, though, what kinds of firearms us staff guys have in our safes or in the vehicles we drive.

Well, this month we're answering one of those questions. Our Grand Poobah Iain Harrison wanted his own tactical vehicle that could be had on an editor's budget, but still have some semblance of practicality, versatility, and style. Since Iain is about as subtle as a Sam Peckinpah movie, you can bet that his mode of transportation would follow suit. That's right, just good ol' fashioned American iron.

The Ford Bronco has been a staple of the 4x4 community since its unveiling in 1966, and many consider the solid-axle '78-'79s as the best of the bunch. If you saw this story and experienced an eight-track flashback, you might be asking if this old horse is even practical. Seriously? That's like asking if Dirty Harry's S&W Model 29 was a sensible choice for stopping criminals. Of course it was. These trucks were made when things were meant to last for decades if maintained properly, instead of the planned obsolescence inherent to many of today's vehicles.

1 LIGHT BAR	**2** BUMPERS	**3** NITRIDING	**4** WHEELS	**5** TIRES	**6** EXTERIOR COVER WRAP
MAKE: 4 Wheel Parts	**MAKE:** Rob Bonney Fabrication	**MAKE:** H&M Metal Processing	**MAKE:** Pro Comp	**MAKE:** Pro Comp	**MAKE:** Fast-Trac Designs
MODEL: Three 8-inch 130-watt halogen	**MODEL:** Custom	**MODEL:** Custom BLACKNITRIDE ferritic nitrocarburizing treatment	**MODEL:** 17-inch	**MODEL:** Xtreme MT2 315/70/17	**URL:** www.fast-tracdesigns.com
URL: www.4wheelparts.com	**PHONE:** (602) 370-7955	**URL:** www.blacknitride.com	**URL:** www.procompusa.com	**URL:** www.procompusa.com	

1979 FORD BRONCO
460CI V-8
C6 AUTOMATIC

1	**MINIGUN**	MAKE: Dillon Aero — MODEL: M134 — URL: www.dillonaero.com
2	**ROLL CAGE**	MAKE: Dillon Aero — MODEL: Custom — URL: www.dillonaero.com
3	**EXHAUST**	MAKE: Gibson Performance — MODEL: Custom — URL: www.gibsonperformance.com
4	**REAR BRAKES**	MAKE: LMC Truck — MODEL: Disc conversion — URL: www.LMCTruck.com

Old-School Is New Again

The aftermarket industry for classic trucks is booming. Though they have the usual hitches older vehicles are known for, go look up the price of a few Broncos or F-100s that have aged some 20-plus years. You might be surprised. Their value continues to climb. Finding replacement parts from companies like LMC Truck is easy, and on many components, the variety of upgrades has boosted the lifespan of these old haulers considerably.

Does this thing guzzle gas? Now that Iain dumped the factory 351 in favor of a 460 that's been topped with a Holley intake and 650-cfm carb, it's as thirsty as a sailor on a liberty pass. Since Iain is a desert dweller familiar with the damage that floods can create, staying above the waterline in a GTFO situation is a must, hence the large 17-inch Pro Comp wheels, black nitrided by H&M Metal Processing. Gibson Performance handled the custom 3.5-inch exhaust, complete with a removable center section to service the factory C6 trans. New Rancho shocks all around, along with a rear disc brake conversion from LMC Truck, help keep this ride stable and stoppable. An LMC Truck fuse block also resides in the engine compartment, at the ready for future electrical accessory updates.

Exterior appointments were kept pretty true to stock, but that didn't stop Iain from making things a bit more interesting. Since this was more go than show, it made sense to pass on a shiny paintjob, so the body was wrapped in beige with some camo components by Fast-Trac Designs in Phoenix. Custom armored bumpers by Rob Bonney Fabrication adorn the stem and stern, along with a Smittybilt XRC winch in front and a light bar with three 8-inch 130-watt halogen spots mounted, courtesy of 4 Wheel Parts.

For the inside, you'll find a pair of Smittybilt bucket seats with G.E.A.R. MOLLE covers. An LMC Truck soundproofing kit and vinyl carpet help keep decibels down (or perhaps

up, when Iain is blaring Motörhead). A pair of TNVC PVS-14 optics for driver and passenger will also make night excursions a bit more exciting.

If this is boring you, and you're asking yourself, "Where are all the guns?" — just look up top, and you'll be pleased to find a muthaf#¢king Dillon Aero minigun mounted atop the cage of the same make. Don't tell us you've never had the urge to put one on your daily driver. A custom BCM rifle also resides in the truck, for when Iain gets bored of going through pallets of ammunition and switches to something smaller. A FLIR marine gimbal is also in the works to sit on the roof for some thermal goodness and additional nocturnal peace of mind.

If you think it all stops here, nothing could be further from the truth. Monthly updates can be seen at RECOILweb.com and at the *Dirt Every Day* channel on YouTube. Look for future additions — including weapons storage, a recovery kit, integrated fuel and water tanks, IR lights, a rooftop tent system, and much more. Yes, it's a work in progress, but with Iain's "this one goes to 11" type of British swagger we really didn't expect anything less.

1 RIFLE
MAKE: BCM
MODEL: Custom 5.56mm: 14.5-inch enhanced upper receiver, 13-inch handguard, Mod4 charging handle, auto bolt carrier group. Mod 1 compensator, Mod 1 grip, folding sights, Geissele Super Dynamic 3 Gun trigger, Magpul enhanced trigger guard, VLTOR A5 system, BCM Gunfigther Stock Mod 0, FLIR RS64
URL: www.bravocompanymfg.com

2 SOUND DEADENING/CARPET
MAKE: LMC Truck
URL: www.LMCTruck.com

3 SEATS
MAKE: Smittybilt
MODEL: Bucket with G.E.A.R. MOLLE cover
URL: www.smittybilt.com

4 CLOTHING
MAKE: 5.11
URL: www.511tactical.com

5 WINCH
MAKE: Smittybilt
MODEL: XRC 12,000-lb
URL: www.smittybilt.com (NOT YET INSTALLED)

6 THERMAL IMAGING
MAKE: FLIR
MODEL: Marine gimbal
URL: www.trvc.com (NOT YET INSTALLED)

But Wait, There's More

Why Minimize When You Can Maximize? Meet Survivor Truck 2.

By John Schwartze
Photos by Iain Harrison

2000 FORD EXCURSION
5.9L CUMMINS 6BT DIESEL
ATS AUTOMATIC
WWW.SURVIVORTRUCK.COM

Back in RECOIL Issue 8 we featured Jim DeLozier's Survivor Truck — a 1980 Chevy C70 kitted up with just about everything a doomsday prepper could want on a vehicle...and then some. We figured it wouldn't be the last time we heard from someone so serious about stayin' alive. Well, guess what? He's at it again; this time with a 2000 Ford Excursion that leaves little, if anything, off the survival gear checklist. Many of you may wonder why he's created another version. A glutton for gear, you might ask? That may be so. But like owning a gun, there's not one that works perfectly for every situation. While you might think having two vehicles this extreme is overkill, Jim considers it practicality.

The first truck is more of an evacuation/gauntlet breaker, but the second iteration could be used as a daily driver. The Excursion is the largest SUV made — packing up gear and five adults that may be wearing body armor, you need all the room available. The stock V-10 gas engine was ditched in favor of a diesel 5.9L '97 Cummins 6BT to get better mileage and, if necessary, run on biodiesel, Jet A, Jet B, or kerosene. Jim selected this engine since it was the last year of non-computerized Cummins engines and it will, theoretically, run after an EMP strike. It's all tied to an ATS diesel transmission with a Five Star Viscous Clutch Drive torque converter and extra deep pan.

With all the equipment and modification on this truck, it's tipping the

1 TIRES
MAKE: Pro Comp
MODEL: MT2, 37-inch
URL: www.procompusa.com

2 WHEELS
MAKE: RBP
MODEL: Fury, 20-inch
URL: www.rollingbigpower.com

3 JACK
MAKE: Cequent Performance Products
MODEL: Bulldog SWL 190 DL-BTSMQ
URL: www.bulldogproducts.net

4 LIGHT
MAKE: Light Force
MODEL: XGT Xenon 100-watt w/clear, red, green, IR filters
URL: www.lightforce.com

5 LIGHT
MAKE: Go Light
MODEL: Stryker LED
URL: www.golight.com

6 LIGHT BAR
MAKE: Pro Comp
MODEL: 50-inch dual row LED combo beam
URL: www.procompusa.com

7 FOOTLOCKERS, COOLERS
MAKE: Pelican, Engel USA
URL:
www.pelican.com
www.engelcoolers.com

8 SUPPLIES
MAKE: Watershed Drybag with United Tactical SPEEDS Kit, CBRN gear, and Scott Safety SCBA
URL:
www.drybags.com
www.unitedtacticalsupply.com
www.scottsafety.com

9 FLUID STORAGE
MAKE: Rotopax
URL: www.rotopax.com

10 AWNING
MAKE: Smittybilt
MODEL: Overlander
URL: www.smittybilt.com

11 CAMERAS
MAKE: VDO
URL: www.vdo-gauges.com

12 ANTENNAS
MAKE: Firestik CB antenna, Mobile Mark 3G/4G/LTE
URL:
www.firestik.com
www.mobilemark.com

Although not armored, the exterior was coated with Rhino Linings and given a custom 1.75x.120-wall DOM tubing exoskeleton, courtesy of Nichols AutoFab in Prescott, Arizona. Smittybilt accessories abound, including two 12,000-pound winches, as well as their Defender roof rack, canopy, trail jacks, shovel and axe mount, and traction ramps. 928 Solutions treated the windows with their low-glare vinyl wrap. And there's certainly no shortage of lighting with ProComp Explorer LED light bars, Whelen emergency, Lightforce xenon, and Golight 360-degree pan units.

Of course security is part of survival, so optical surveillance comes from eight VDO force protection cameras, an Avigilon 5 megapixel minidome in a Dotworkz bulletproof housing, and Samsung HD day/night cameras — all working in conjunction with motion detectors, microphones, an Optex perimeter laser scanner system, and a Helios thermal imaging system to provide a virtual fence out to 1,500 meters while stationary. The platform is kept stable using a Cequent Products Bulldog Jacks external load stabilizing system. Three VDO and two Tote Vision monitors let you keep an eye on things from inside the cab, while a Viper alarm keeps occupants from being snuck up on.

The interior (or command center, rather) is a cross between what originally came from the factory and something that resembles a police cruiser. Communications consist of Harris communications handheld radios and radiohead, a Cobra CB, Yaesu handheld HAM radio, Panasonic Toughbook / Toughpad in Havis docking stations, Havis center console with Blue Sea switches, Cradlepoint router, Mobile Mark and Firestik antennas, and Wamar Technologies network and signal extenders. The seats have Wet Okole

scales at around 11,500 pounds, so the suspension had to be robust. The front was given a Pro Comp BMX 8.5-inch lift with dual-reservoir shocks and an AGR Performance RockRam hydraulic-assist steering module. The rear consists of a Firestone Ride-Rite system, custom tuned leaf springs, and single-reservoir shocks. t's all rolling on RBP Fury wheels rated at 3,500 pounds and Pro Comp 37-inch MT2 rubber that are brought to a stop by SSBC eight-piston calipers and slotted rotors all around.

1 TENT
MAKE: Cascadia Vehicle Tents
MODEL: Mt. Hood
URL: www.cascadiatents.com

2 LAPTOP
MAKE: Panasonic
MODEL: CF-31 Toughbook
URL: shop.panasonic.com

3 MAP LIGHT
MAKE: Havis
URL: www.havis.com

4 SEAT COVERS
MAKE: Wet Okole
MODEL: custom with MOLLE webbing
URL: www.wetokole.com

seat covers with MOLLE webbing and Tuff Products MOLLE nylon gear, with Husky Liners protecting the floor. An Engel-USA refrigerator/freezer and coolers keep food cold, while a Shurflo pump and Everpure water purification system keep all inhabitants hydrated.

So how do you power all this shit? Juice comes via eight Odyssey batteries with an American Power Systems high-output alternator, Blue Sea ACR smart charge relays and circuit breakers, Renogy solar panels, and Smittybilt generator. The rest of the gear on the truck includes just about everything you can imagine: firearms, rappelling hardware, tools, rations, first-aid, Cascadia rooftop tent, Miller mig/tig/stick welder, personal lighting, and search-and-

1 REFRIGERATOR/ FREEZER
MAKE:
Engel
MODEL:
in Tembo Tusk LoadSpotter slide
URL:
www.engelcoolers.com
www.tembotusk.com

2 REAR WINCH
MAKE:
Smittybilt
MODEL:
"Black Box" with Smittybilt X20 12,000-pound winch
URL:
www.smittybilt.com

3 SAFE
MAKE:
Truck Vault
URL:
www.truckvault.com

4 WHITE BOARD
MAKE:
WriteyBoard
URL:
www.writeyboards.com

5 RIFLE
MAKE:
Remington
MODEL:
700P w/Boyd's Laminate stock
URL:
www.remington.com
www.boydsgunstocks.com

6 SHOTGUN
MAKE:
Remington
MODEL:
Vang Comp 870 w/Choate folding stock
URL:
www.vangcomp.com
www.remington.com
www.riflestock.com

7 SHOTGUN
MAKE:
Remington
MODEL:
Vang Comp 870 Magnum w/Ace folding stock
URL:
www.vangcomp.com
www.remington.com
www.riflestock.com

8 RIFLE
MAKE:
Colt carbine upper w/J&J Armory lower
MODEL:
M4 w/ Ace stock
URL:
www.colt.com
www.riflestocks.com

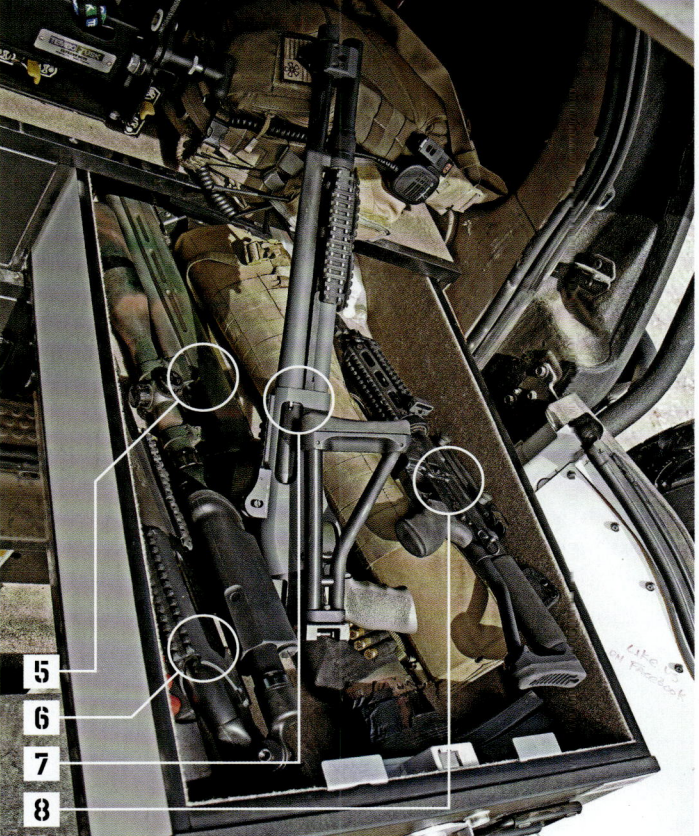

rescue and decontamination gear with fixed and removable storage to handle it all. The onboard Viair air compressor, Roto-Pax and EZ-Pack spare fuel containers, Tank Depot water tank, and Hexagon Ragasco propane cylinders will ensure this thing stays self-sufficient for quite a while. Is your head spinning yet?

As before, DeLozier plans to make Survivor Trucks available to the public, be it the Ford Excursion platform or any vehicle that satisfies the requirements of his clientele. Like us, you're probably wondering if he plans on doing yet another version in the future; the answer is yes. Keep your eye out for a covert Survivor Truck on a smaller vehicle to appear sometime in the future. In the meantime, we'll be looking through our medicine cabinet for something to treat the carpal tunnel we're suffering from after typing out everything that's on this truck.

Ballistic Bronco Bulletin

How has RECOIL's Trusty Steed Held Up to 12 months of Abuse? Read on.

By Iain Harrison
Photos by Kenda Lenseigne

It's been a year since we pressed the Ballistic Bronco into service, so we thought this might be a good time to update y'all on its progress. It's hauled steel targets and ammo to the range, an occasional trailer, and our sorry asses into the desert and back on several four-wheeling trips. Throughout its travels, it's averaged a whopping 7, yes 7, mpg of regular unleaded -- a figure that makes hippies weep.

We're not sure exactly how many of them there torques a mildly built 460 big-block turns out, but it's evidently sufficient to contribute significantly to global warming and twist a driveshaft completely off the transfer case yoke. One of the first jobs we wrenched on this year was to replace and upgrade the factory unit, which gave out on a trip from Cowtown. Fortunately, we'd already completed the range session and had another couple of vehicles along for the ride, otherwise it would have been a long wait for recovery.

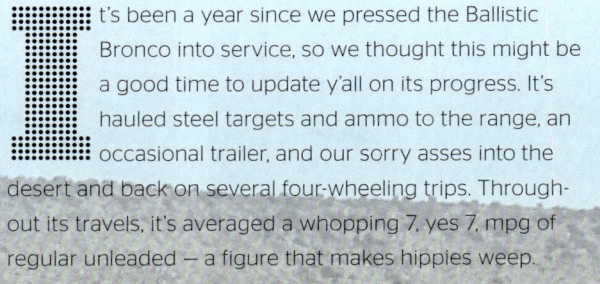

We're not sure whether the driveline failure had anything to do with shredding the tranny's rear seal, but about a month after we took possession of a shiny new driveshaft, the usual few drops of various automotive fluids normally found under old trucks became a small puddle. Evidently, the Bronco was becoming incontinent. We'd be inclined to ignore the problem and write it off as just another symptom of advancing years (look on the bright side, it does its own transmission service), but when we wound up having to add fluid every time we hit the gas pump, we knew it was time to do something about it.

One addition we made in fairly short order was an ARB compressor to handle the chore of airing up tires before rejoining pavement. Hard mounted to the engine side of the firewall, it provides enough air to run power tools and was originally developed for military applications, so it's probably going to last as long as we need it to. We stuffed the small collector tank under the dash, allowing us to hit all four corners of the vehicle without having to pop the hood.

If you live in the desert, you quickly learn to appreciate the value of a cold beverage. We'd toyed with the idea of installing a center console between the driver and passenger seats in order to increase the Bronco's available storage area, but in the end decided that hydration was more important. Hence the installation of a Smittybilt fridge/freezer, which proved to be more versatile that we thought. Able to run on both household and ve-

hicle power, we discovered another use for it on a recent dove hunting trip when it was tasked with chilling freshly killed birds.

When you're dragging a few thousand bucks worth of high-end death machines around in an open-top vehicle, you can either post a guard every time you walk away from it, or invest in a little security. We bolted up an Adventure Box from 4 Wheel Parts, which gives a couple of lock- able storage compartments for both handguns and long guns, as well as swallowing up a range bag or two. It's not quite as convenient as a slide-out locker, but it's also about one third of the cost, which means more money for ammo. And we like that.

All told, the Ballistic Bronco has been a fun project and one that's likely to spawn others. 2016 might just see us going a little bigger on the next build — don't touch that dial, kids ...

Poaching Rhinos

We Rode the Rhino GX Hard, Put it Away Wet, and Were Admittedly Swooning Afterward

By John Schwartze
Photos by Jorge Nuñez

hen given a chance to get behind the wheel of a recent entry into the exotic vehicle market, we'll be honest — we had low expectations, because luxury SUVs are a strange breed. They ride the line between practicality and bling, but often sacrifice the former for lots of the latter — maybe too much.

Remember the Lamborghini LM002? Seemed like a good idea at the time, but we think the one belonging to Uday Hussein that the U.S. military blew up probably had a bigger audience than the 328 that were produced. How about the Hummer? After years of mixed reviews, a struggling economy, and GM's failure to sell the brand, it too went the way of the LaserDisc.

Here's the rub — we walked away from our experience remembering why someone might buy a Cabot Black Diamond Deluxe 1911 over a much cheaper version. It's cool, they can afford it, and they want to belong to that elite group who can say they have one. We know you guys are out there too, so perhaps you should look at the Rhino GX instead of that Unimog you might be eyeballing. Your sh*t-eating grin might look like ours after driving it.

We came across the Rhino GX made by U.S. Specialty Vehicles (USSV) while at the 2015 SEMA Show, and since its California home base was close to the RECOIL HQ, we hit up the owners about getting a chance to drive this behemoth for ourselves. The company started out building limos, and their Chinese clientele requested a prototype of a larger SUV to fill the void left by the Hummer — still in huge demand over there. USSV created a version called the G Patton, and it became an overseas sensation. Next stop, the American market.

First impressions? It's big. To give you an idea, a new Escalade is about 7,000 pounds and change, while the Rhino weighs in around 10,000, but it's duty rated for a 14,000-pound load. A new Escalade is 80.5 inches wide by 74.4 inches high, with a 116-inch wheelbase. The Rhino GX is 96 by 88 inches with a 140.8-inch wheelbase. It's built on a Ford F-450 Super Duty chassis offered with either Ford's 6.8L V-10 or 6.7L diesel V-8 and a five-speed automatic. All

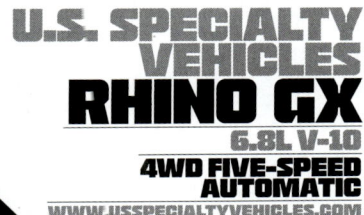

U.S. SPECIALTY VEHICLES RHINO GX
6.8L V-10
4WD FIVE-SPEED AUTOMATIC
WWW.USSPECIALTYVEHICLES.COM

1 BODY
MAKE:
U.S. Specialty Vehicles
MODEL:
Dual-layer 20-gauge steel
URL:
www.usspecialtyvehicles.com

2 TIRES
MAKE:
Mickey Thompson
MODEL:
38x15.5R20 Baja MTZ Radial
URL:
www.mickeythompsontires.com

3 WHEELS
MAKE:
20x10 custom
COLOR:
10-lug cast aluminum
URL:
www.usspecialtyvehicles.com

4 ROOF LIGHTS
MAKE:
Tuff LED Lights
MODEL:
Square LED Work Light — 5-inch 40-Watt
URL:
www.tuffledlights.com

5 MOTOR
MAKE:
Ford
MODEL:
6.8L V-10
URL:
www.usspecialtyvehicles.com

are four-wheel drive, and the gas version gets around 8 to 10 mpg, with diesel being slightly better — all from a 40-gallon tank. We assume if you can afford the Rhino GX, gas mileage isn't a major concern of yours.

The previous leaf-spring setup is ditched in favor of a three-mode, self-leveling hydraulic system and solid twin-coil monobeam Bilstein shocks in front. While hauling arse down the interstate, it was a smoother and quieter ride than we expected with such meaty tires. The interior is hella spacious and comfy with eight-way seats that are Ford frames reshaped and upholstered in leather by USSV. You can even have a third row of seats as one of the options they offer. Front and rear cameras, Alpine electronics, exotic wood accents, telescopic side mirrors, a Securilock Passive Anti-Theft system, and a litany of other high-tech doodads round out the electronics, but a host of other options are available.

The body is virtually all proprietary dual-layer, 20-gauge steel. You'll feel how thick it is when you tap it with your knuckle and compare that sound (or lack thereof) to the panels on standard cars and trucks. B6 body armor can be outsourced, and we're told would add another 1,800 pounds without encroaching on interior space. The hood, fender flares, and rear bumper are fiberglass. Although this one is black, you can pick from a few other matte colors, with gloss becoming available soon.

As the pictures show, we were given the chance to open it up a bit

on some steep inclines and do some donuts. It'd rained the day before, so the ground was nice and muddy. The rep from USSV told us to "have fun with it." We weren't sure he knew what he was telling us, as we fully intended to put the wood to it. That's just what we did, to the point of getting it stuck in the mud. We removed the wheelcaps, put the front hubs into 4WD mode, and crawled out of it as easily as we got into it. The other company rep who accompanied us while we drove around like joyriding teenagers even decided to make a quick exit before we continued. We think we may have frightened her a bit.

Any time we publish something that's priced higher than someone's means to buy it, we get grief from some readers. But many of those who say that something's "too expensive" do so only if *they* can't afford it, rather than if said item's cost exceeds its true value. We RECOIL guys don't exactly have money falling out of our arses either, so we understand the need for gear that's not exclusive to the Forbes 500 tax bracket. However ….

Our initial expectation was that we'd be invited to drive the Rhino politely on some surface streets, very carefully photograph it in the mud to make it look tough, and then be quickly pointed the way back to our office. Well, we were wrong and slogged a $200,000 truck througwh the muck and some off-road trails without any performance issues or resistance from the staff. Any company who stands behind a vehicle this expensive with that much confidence, well … try requesting those same test conditions next time you're kicking tires on a new 4x4. They'll laugh you off the lot before they allow you to do what USSV cordially gave us the chance to do. There's something to be said for that — it embodies the spirit of American-made vehicles.

2015 TOYOTA 4RUNNER TRD PRO
4L V-6
FIVE-SPEED AUTOMATIC
WWW.LAWNDARTDESIGN.COM

Everyday Overlander

From Stock 4Runner to Full Off-Road Dream Rig

By Isaac Marchionna

Vision. It'd be easy to say in hindsight there was a clear, start-to-finish vision for this truck. But, like many project builds, getting from stock to upgraded was an ever-evolving path. For me, a professional filmmaker and pixel pusher, it was about treading the line between daily driver and overlanding. I wanted something that could serve as a utility vehicle for carrying precious cargo comfortably and safely into remote locations.

The project began with an inferno-colored 2015 4Runner TRD Pro and the balance of its on-road performance and off-road handling. The 4Runner is based on the tough-as-nails, body-on-frame, Toyota Prado 150 platform with a manual transfer case and bombproof reliability because … Toyota. The TRD Pro from the factory was seemingly everything originally desired as a base platform, with factory skidplates, larger Nitto Terra Grappler A/T's, larger Bilstein shocks, and aggressive, retro styling. That was all that was needed, or so I thought.

The entire upgrade process was a back-and-forth facilitated by 503 Motoring. Iain Gordon, 503 Motoring's shop manager, served as the conduit, offering sensible design choices, suggestions, and alternative executions. As a shop that routinely handles supercars, the 4Runner provided an interesting change of pace for its staff, mostly patrons of pavement.

Upon delivery from Japan, I immediately began altering the 4Runner for more overland-specific use. I first added a Gobi Stealth model with a rear ladder to carry more gear and expand the vehicle's capability. facing is a 40-inch Rigid E2 combination flood and spotlight LED lightbar, while work lights are a pair of top-mounted Rigid D2 white LED flood lights. An ARB 2,000mm awning was mounted to the driver side of the vehicle's rack to ward off the ever-present Pacific Northwest rain and provide protection from the sun during trips to shinier climes.

The 4Runner stayed untouched for a total of three weeks before I decided it needed a winch. Given that WARN Industries is a local Oregon company, there was no debate about brand. I chose the ZEON 8-S, with synthetic line, to provide 8,000 pounds of pulling power. I was reticent to give up the styling of the OEM front end, which admittedly was what attracted me to the original vehicle in its base form. The solution was to use a hidden winch mounting system from Pelfreybilt, requiring the removal of the original aluminum crush bumper assembly, and installing the steel winch plate in its place. With this system, once the front bumper valence is trimmed, you have a winch that hides neatly behind the bumper.

Unfortunately, if you live in a two-plate state, finding a good solution for a license plate is a challenge. The solution came from Cascadia 4x4

SUVS • EVERYDAY OVERLANDER | **169**

1 PLATE FLIPPER
MAKE: Cascadia 4x4
MODEL: Flipster V1 (Hawse Fairlead)
URL: www.cascadia4x4.com

2 AMBER LIGHTS
MAKE: Rigid Industries
MODEL: D2 Wide Single
URL: www.rigidindustries.com

3 FRONT BUMPER
MAKE: Pelfreybilt
MODEL: Aluminum Front Plate Bumper
URL: www.pelfreybilt.com

4 SNORKEL
MAKE: Safari Automotive Technology
MODEL: 5th Gen Prototype Snorkel
URL: www.safarisnorkel.com

5 TOP LIGHTBAR
MAKE: Rigid Industries
MODEL: 40-inch E2 Combo Spot/Flood Lightbar
URL: www.rigidindustries.com

6 AWNING
MAKE: ARB
MODEL: Awning (2,000 mm)
URL: store.arbusa.com

7 ROCK RAILS/SLIDERS
MAKE: Pelfreybilt
MODEL: Bolt On Tapered Kickout Sliders
URL: www.pelfreybilt.com

8 ENGINE LIGHTS
MAKE: Anti-Dark
MODEL: Universal Engine Light
URL: anti-dark.com

in Vancouver, British Columbia, Canada, with its Flipster license plate system. It works with either the Hawse or roller fairleads by placing a bracket behind and over the fairlead, allowing the license plate to swing up and out of the way when winching. Sandwiched between that is the Factor55 Flatlink and Hawse Fairlead, both extremely low-profile solutions. The Flatlink replaces the traditional hook, making for a safer and more visually attractive option for using a winch. Great, it's done, right? Not even close.

The vehicle looked good with its added carrying capacity and self-recovery abilities. But all that weight had a rather adverse affect on the stance of the vehicle. So, I decided

1 ROOF RACK
MAKE: Gobi
MODEL: Stealth Roof Rack (with rear ladder)
URL: www.gobiracks.com

2 RECOVERY BOARDS
MAKE: Maxtrax
MODEL: MKII FJ Red
URL: us.maxtrax.com.au

3 DRAWER SYSTEM
MAKE: Goose Gear
MODEL: SUV Module 2 Drawer 1/3-2/3 Split
URL: www.goose-gear.com

4 FRIDGE
MAKE: ARB
MODEL: 50-Quart Fridge/Freezer
URL: store.arbusa.com

5 FRIDGE SLIDE
MAKE: TemboTusk
MODEL: LoadSpotter Levitating Fridge Slider
URL: tembotusk.flyingcart.com

6 REAR BUMPER
MAKE: CBI Offroad
MODEL: 5th Gen 4Runner Rear Bumper (with Swing Away Tire Carrier, Double Jerry Can Holder)
URL: www.cbioffroadfab.com

7 TIRES
MAKE: Nitto
MODEL: Trail Grappler M/Ts (285/70/17)
URL: www.nittotire.com

the next goal would be to tackle the suspension and tires.

I opted for the Icon Vehicle Dynamics Stage 2 suspension and Nitto Trail Grappler 33-inch tires, while still maintaining the original factory TRD rims; I didn't want to give up their strength and visual appeal. But, before I could get anything installed I had reverse buyer's remorse, and changed the suspension from the Icon Stage 2 to the Stage 5, which gained remote reservoirs on all shocks, upgraded lower trailing arms, and tubular upper control arms.

The Nitto Mud Terrain tires were selected from past experience, as they present a good balance between off-road performance, with minimal impact to on-road noise and handling. The Nitto's have an excep-

SUVS • EVERYDAY OVERLANDER | 171

tionally aggressive sidewall tread, giving them a beefier side profile without resorting to the use of wheel spacers.

Toyota designs their vehicles to use a 265/70 as their largest factory equipped tire. As a result, some alteration was required here and there. Being that the factory spare (already undersized by comparison to the TRD Pro's original 31.5-inch tire) would not be ideal in an emergency with the new 33-inch tires, the solution was a rather dramatic one, and would require the first major alteration of the vehicle's body through the use of power tools and sparks, lots of sparks.

The simplest solution for carrying a spare tire is on the roof. Does this work for most people? Absolutely. However you're most likely not changing a spare tire under ideal conditions to begin with, and trying to haul 85-plus pounds of wheel from your roof is a serious pain in the ass. Combined with raising the vehicle's center of gravity, a roof-mounted spare was out of the question.

The solution instead was through the CBI Offroad rear steel bumper. To say this bumper is well built would be a comedic understatement; it's absolutely a tank, made entirely of steel. God help whoever rear-ends that bumper. In preparation the rear springs were swapped with Old Man Emu 2898 440-pound springs to handle the increased constant rear load. The CBI rear bumper provides a tire carrier on a steel locking swing arm, while also allowing provisions for dual jerry cans, HiLift jack mount, and cutouts for rear bumper lights (because, why not more lumens!).

In the pursuit of self-sufficiency an ARB twin compressor was installed, allowing for in-the-field airing up of tires or for cleaning off camera gear or other equipment. The main battery was also swapped out with an Odyssey Group 31 battery, the weight of which is akin to that of a dying neutron star. However, the added capacity helps ensure power when you need it. The vehicle can also be powered from the Overland Solar panel array that can easily top off the battery while at a campsite.

The original intent was to keep the vehicle's front end as stock looking as possible. However, after a trip to the Oregon desert, where many jackrabbits sacrificed themselves on the front bumper, I decided it was only a matter of time before the plastic front end would suffer a cruel fate. You've got a lot of options with the 4Runner in regards to front bumpers. Mostly it comes down to your particular tastes.

Since the vehicle lives downtown in a rather dense city, making the vehicle longer is undesirable. The CBI rear bumper already increases the overall length of the vehicle by 1 or 2 feet due to the jerry cans and rear tire, and a large front step bumper would be both heavy, and increase the vehicle's length further. It's a challenge to balance out what works great off-road with what has to be practical on-road, especially in an urban landscape.

The solution, again, came from Pelfreybilt, which had just begun offering

an aluminum frontend. Its frontend mimicked the general profile and shape of the OEM frontend and is a complete drop-in front replacement, no cutting required. Because it was aluminum it was also a staggeringly light 62 pounds. This meant when the steel winch plate was removed the net gain was only 6 pounds due to the addition of the Rigid Combo 30-inch single-row lightbar.

The advantages of the bumper were better articulation off-road, quicker access to the winch's mechanical controls, provisions for amber Rigid D2 foglights, and, of course, added defense against front impacts. As more and more OEM components fell by the wayside, they were replaced by additional components such as the ARB steel skidplates, which integrate perfectly with the Pelfreybilt frontend. Other components were either gusseted or additionally armored to protect from trail damage.

The next upgrade, while not for the squeamish, was an amazing opportunity as the vehicle was selected to serve as a test mule for the upcoming Safari/ARB ARMAX snorkel for the fifth-gen 4Runner. What you see on the vehicle is actually a 3D printed prototype, which should inspire a bit of awe when you consider how big the printer must be to accommodate such a large end result. The ARMAX snorkel, besides providing cleaner air in the desert, and fording capabilities, also increases horsepower and benefits in increased engine efficiency, seeing a noticeable boost in miles per gallon.

Internally the 4Runner TRD Pro (based on the Trail Edition Premium) comes incredibly well setup from the factory. So the goal was to make the vehicle as livable as possible, using a full drawer system from Goose Gear. This provides full-length lockable drawers in the rear and a mounting platform for the ARB 47-quart fridge mounted on the TemboTusk LoadSpotter fridge slide.

Other major additions were fire extinguishers, medical kits from Dark Angel Medical, cargo organizers from Blue Ridge Overland, and navigational aids. For navigation the vehicle uses its onboard GPS, Garmin Montana GPS, and an iPad with Bluetooth GPS module in a RAM mount for backcountry navigation. In addition, the vehicle is wired with a HAM radio for long-distance communication in the desert, along with a C.B. and Delorme InReach.

Ultimately this is a snapshot of the vehicle as it currently stands. It would be a boldfaced lie to say it's done. The vehicle has and continues to outperform our expectations. Not just in how it looks, but the terrain it can tackle safely. While treading dangerously close to serving as a background vehicle along the trails of Fury Road, it still serves admirably as an obnoxiously fun daily driver.

1 JACK
MAKE:
Hi-Lift
MODEL:
Jack X-Treme (with JackCover)
URL:
www.hi-lift.com

2 WATER CANS
MAKE:
Rotopax
MODEL:
2-gallon water
URL:
rotopax.com

Self Preservation

Who Says the Old Family SUV Can't Become the Perfect Bug-Out Rig?

By John Schwartze
Photos by Mountain Motion Media

here was a time when cars (and many other things) were built to last as long as you maintained them. Unfortunately it seems as if planned obsolescence has become the manufacturing industry's purview and buyers are brainwashed into believing that "new" is synonymous with "better." Things are pretty disposable now. The general paradigm has gone from repair to replacement, depriving people of any willingness to fix what's broken or modify an aging piece of equipment.

So what does this outta sight/outta mind mentality say about people who never learned how to repair anything? Their lack of resourcefulness, coping skills, and self-reliance is as obvious as Quentin Tarantino's foot fetish. Think about how they'll react if things break down on a Great Depression-type scale once again. I'm talking all-out chaos with no power, no food, and no cell phones to post selfies every 10 minutes. Those same people will get desperate and look to strip the well prepared of everything they have. Time to start planning contingencies.

While many might think this 1994 Land Cruiser has passed its vehicular shelf life, owner Joe Galt is a dedicated prepper who doesn't subscribe to the instant gratification mindset. This passionate family man stays up to snuff on the latest survival trends, studies the works of James Wesley Rawles, and wanted to turn his aging family SUV into a viable bug-out rig. Whether it's bad weather, war, EMPs, or if the latest crop of Evergreen State College students ever get anywhere near a job on Capitol Hill, Joe has already planned his disaster response accordingly.

There are several reasons Galt felt a Land Cruiser of this ilk made for the perfect SHTF vehicle. It's vintage, yes, but as previously stated, sometimes you're better off that way. "The 1994 is a specific year I was looking for. I wanted the least amount of electronics possible," he says. "I also wanted it because it had front and rear floating axles, front and rear coil spring suspension, front and rear disc brakes, ABS, and factory electronic lockers, which is a combination of components that, to this day, I think there's very few produced today that have every one of those elements on it."

1994 TOYOTA
LAND CRUISER FJ80
5.9L CUMMINS DIESEL
4WD, MODIFIED ORIGINAL AISIN TRANSMISSION

WWW.SLEEOFFROAD.COM; WWW.REVIVA.COM;
WWW.DIESELCONVERSION.COM; WWW.3D-OFFROAD.COM;
WWW.CRUISEROUTFITTERS.COM;
WWW.DOUGLASCOUNTYDIESEL.COM

1	**BUMPERS**
MAKE:	ARB
MODEL:	Deluxe (front) Dual Carrier (rear)
URL:	www.sleeoffroad.com

2	**TIRES**
MAKE:	Toyo
MODEL:	315/75R16 MT
URL:	www.toyotires.com

3	**WINCH**
MAKE:	Warn
MODEL:	12k
URL:	www.warn.com

4	**FOGLIGHTS**
MAKE:	PIAA
MODEL:	9-inch
URL:	www.piaa.com

5	**ROOF RACK**
MAKE:	Front Runner
MODEL:	Slimline II Land Cruiser 80
URL:	www.sleeoffroad.com

6	**MOTOR**
MAKE:	Cummins
MODEL:	6BT
URL:	www.reviva.com dieselconversion.com

Galt has actually owned several Land Cruisers over the years. This FJ80 version was picked up at a used car lot in remarkably good shape, and became the family SUV for many years. After clocking a total of about 250,000 miles and becoming increasingly concerned about disaster events, Joe reached the point where he decided to breathe some new life into a platform that already had a lot going for it. He wanted something nimble, easy to work on, reliable, and the right size to carry both family and gear safely out of his hometown of Denver if something went awry.

"Whether it's winter storms, a volcanic ash event that could come from Yellowstone, or an EMP, I wanted to be prepared for anything that might make driving hard," Galt says. "The Land Cruiser fit that bill so well that, even in today's market, trying to find another vehicle like it is almost impossible. If I bought a new one, I could end up spending a hundred grand. As a kid I lived through the Mount St. Helens explosion and seeing what that did to people and communities was kind of devastating. It's an unlikely event, but it's an event that eventually will occur again."

The stock inline-six is a notoriously sluggish (and thirsty) powerplant. Switching to a Euro or Japanese diesel wasn't practical when it came to maintenance and parts accessibility. Joe went with the venerable Cummins in the form of a '93 5.9L 6BT from Reviva in Minneapolis. The motor was brand new with zero miles, completely remanufactured, and dimensionally similar to the original 4.5L 1FZE. It was adapted to the vehicle courtesy of Diesel Conversion Specialists in Montana. Bringing the specs to roughly 240 hp and 420 lb-ft of torque was a huge improvement. It all breathes through a Safari snorkel.

Next was pairing it with to the transmission. Here's where things get interesting. "In the '93 and '94 FZ platform, Toyota used the Aisin A442F transmission, which was designed for commercial use, and adapted to the Land Cruiser. Cummins has now adopted Aisin as its

1 RIFLE
MAKE: Sako
MODEL: TRG 42 .338 Lapua
URL: www.sako.fi/rifles

2 GUN CASES
MAKE: 5.11 Tactical
MODEL: 50-inch Hard Case, 50-inch Urban Sniper bag, 36-inch shock rifle case
URL: www.511tactical.com

3 STORAGE
MAKE: Slee Off-Road
MODEL: Outback Drawer system
URL: www.sleeoffroad.com

transmission producer, so there's a natural bearing between engine and trans, but using a conversion kit mates it very nicely to the stock transmission, transfer case, and entire driveline." The torque converter was rebuilt and provides flawless power and integration.

Suspension work was next on the list. Slee Off-Road, who specializes in aftermarket Toyota components, provided a 6-inch lift kit, rear springs, and a number of other suspension upgrades. Old Man Emu front heavy-duty coil springs and shocks were added to compensate for the increased weight of the Cummins. Tom Wood's double cardan driveshafts round out the underpinnings to account for the lift. ARB slotted brakes were added to improve the existing system.

A Uniden CB radio and portable Baofeng HAM radio keep communications in order, and much of the electronic work can be credited to 3D-Offroad. An Outback drawer system keeps extra supplies organized and locked up. Slee Off-Road skid plates and rock sliders help traverse rocky terrain without getting banged up. "I never go anywhere without my poncho, my Cabela's sleeping bag, and my Kelly Kettle," Galt says.

"I also carry first aid, firearms, extra ammo, tow straps, tools, lubricants, spare parts, and a full complement of Western U.S. maps."

An auxiliary battery system stays disconnected and can be used in the event of an EMP. Part of the beauty of a vehicle of this age is that no electronics are needed (except the

1 BACKPACKS
MAKE:
Kifaru
MODEL:
Nomad 2
URL:
www.kifaru.net

starter) to run the motor or transmission. It can all be run mechanically, which may be outdated, but is a superior design to modern systems if you're in a dire situation and need to make repairs in the field.

Overall, there's probably another $55,000 sunk into the vehicle, but that's still cheaper than a new Land Cruiser, and more practical. "You can go down the road at 90 mph with the 4.10 gears I have and it rides as nice as my ¾-ton Dodge Ram," Galt says. Although it weighs roughly 7,000 pounds (over a ton more than stock), the diesel manages about 15 to 19 mph versus the original 8 to 9 mph. It's already been on a 1,200-mile trip after its completion and gets a 400-mile workout on an average weekend. Just goes to show you that old doesn't mean obsolete.

Hidden Agenda

The Peter Gun Theme Comes to Mind When You Delve into What's Lurking Beneath the Surface of AddArmor's Executive Protection Escalade

By John Schwartze
Photos by Mark Saint

Many of you might remember a 1980s arcade game called Spy Hunter, in which you'd use a machine-gun-equipped sports car to take out enemy vehicles that'd shoot at you, try to spike your tires, or run you off the road. Your car would also rendezvous with a semi truck that'd upgrade your weapons with smoke screens, oil slicks, and missiles to thwart and destroy the other vehicles. Although much of this was a mishmash of stuff seen in James Bond movies and Knight Rider, it certainly made that coin-dispensing kid pine away over owning a vehicle with these capabilities one day.

Not only has AddArmor provided an answer to that fantasy, they've redefined the term "armored vehicle" into "mobile safe room." As mentioned in the "What if Your Vehicle is Attacked by an Angry Mob?" article in Issue 27 of RECOIL OFFGRID magazine, your car may be the only thing protecting you from grave injury or death from active shootings/bombings, car-jackings, smash-and-grabs, and blockades. From the outside it looks like a mildly modified Escalade, but there's actually much more going on than the unsuspecting eye might catch ... and that's the idea.

First a little background on the company. AddArmor President Jeff Engen had always been intrigued by the luxury armored vehicle segment. With his background in law enforcement, he paired up with former Delta Force commander Pete Blaber, who serves as CEO. They decided to develop the best armor they could and apply that technology to any vehicle. The Escalade ESV fit the criteria of not only being one of the best luxury vehicles out there, but also having a chassis large enough to keep it from feeling cramped with the addition of other amenities and armor. "We wanted to make it as luxurious as we possibly could, kind of like the interior of a private jet, and at the same time, add armor to it so a dignitary, actor who might be concerned about stalkers, or any high net-worth people could feel totally safe," Engen says.

Unlike most armored vehicles that are designed with more of a defensive mindset, you could say that AddArmor has also given the owner offensive capabilities. "If you've spent any time in armored cars, they tell you never to open the doors, so you can't fight back. I was hearing stories of areas where they'd box in armored cars and pour in gasoline to burn out the occupants. One reason why most of our armored cars have gun ports is that, if someone blocks you in, you have the option to return fire with standard or less-lethal munitions," Engen says. The gun ports are hidden so it's not obvious to the outside threat.

Optional pepper spray dispensers, barrier-busting bumpers, and electrified door handles are also just some of the other options to protect passengers. A loud speaker/siren/sound cannon provides a way to disperse crowds through non-lethal means. Although restricted to government agencies, tear gas canister dispensers can be added as well. You might be thinking that gas dispensers could also compromise anyone riding inside. Although this isn't a concern with liquid pepper spray, an overpressure system and gas masks can also be installed to help protect passengers against any deliberate or inadvertent gas exposure directed at the vehicle. Sniffing units that detect explosive gas from mines detonated in its proximity is another feature owners can add.

AddArmor's namesake comes from their armoring options, which can run from NIJ-level B4 to B7 ballistic protection. The armor technology is a proprietary composite that, according to AddAmor, is 10 times stronger than steel, 60-percent lighter, and tested by an independent laboratory. All body panels are armored, as well as the glass, floors, and engine compartment. To give you an idea, the B6 armor on the vehicle seen here adds approximately an additional 1,250 pounds of weight. The suspension is reinforced with heavy-duty springs, shocks, sway bars, and larger brakes. You can even request a supercharger be installed. A dual-battery system allows for auxiliary power, or both can be run tandem.

The vehicle's more opulent appointments include a raised roof for more headroom, fridge, custom-made heating and A/C, a 4k high-def TV system with surround sound, a bar, and reclining heated/cooled seats with massage settings.

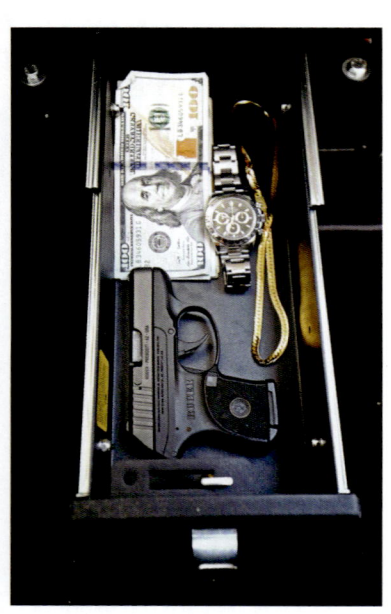

The glass is multilayered lead/polycarbonate offered with the same choice of protection levels as the exterior.

"The most memorable experience with the vehicle was shooting it with a Daniel Defense MK18 5.56 rifle. We have an extensive testing process, and the only way to really know how the vehicle will stand up in an attack is to attack it with live weapons. After shooting the glass several times with the 5.56, we shot it eight more times with a .45 caliber Colt. There was no penetration. You can see the video at https://youtu.be/i-iXkl12qIk," Engen says.

Optional communications systems consist of Iridium sat phones for coverage anywhere in the world as well as a secondary system using a satellite beacon mounted in the car. When activated via a switch in the car or an app on your cell phone, it goes to a command center staffed by former intelligence officers, first responders, and military veterans to display your location and prompt a response to a designated cell number, which (if preauthorized) activates your camera phone to get a voice imprint and visual to assess the situation.

There you have it. State-of-the-art security, comfort, and offensive capabilities all in one package. Cost for an Escalade like this hovers around $300,000, and build time is approximately nine months. You can purchase the vehicle directly from AddArmor or bring in your own to have modified. They also offer Sprinter vans as part of their fleet and even recently armored a 200-mph Audi RS 7. And yes, they do other vehicles if you'd like to indulge your need for preferential treatment. Whether it's your VW bug, Land Rover, plane, or helicopter, you can kit it out with ballistic protection and other accouterments ... and yes, a smoke screen is one of them.

ADDARMOR EXECUTIVE PROTECTION ESCALADE

MAKE:
Cadillac

MODEL:
Escalade ESV

DRIVETRAIN:
6.2L V-8 with 8-speed transmission

URL:
www.addarmor.com

OPTIONS:
- Sound cannon with PA
- Run-flat tires
- Hidden gun ports
- 360-degree night vision camera system with cameras in front, sides, and rear
- Red/blue police lights
- Outside microphones for enhanced listening
- Electric shock handles
- Airtight seals and DM71 explosive/landmine protection
- Bomb blankets
- Pepper spray dispenser activated via toggle switch
- CS tear gas canisters launched via a switch in the cockpit (available for government agencies only)
- Military-grade anti-jamming satellite communication system
- Multi-gas detection system (with gas masks for passengers)
- Biometric gun racks
- Interior lock boxes
- Blinding high-intensity aircraft-grade lights installed in the bumpers
- Smoke screen
- 24/7 global satellite 911 system connected via satellite (and doesn't need a cell phone signal to work). It also comes with an app for your cell phone that works everywhere in the world.
- Signal/cell phone jammer to protect against remotely activated detonations (available for government agencies only)
- "Barrier busting" bumpers
- Partition between passengers and front cockpit

Back by Popular Demand

The Ballistic Bronco Redux

By John Schwartze
Photos by Kenda Lenseigne

1979 FORD BRONCO
ENGINE: 460ci V-8
TRANSMISSION: C6 automatic
URL: @recoilboss

Appealing to nostalgia can be a tricky proposition in the automotive business. While models like the Chevy Suburban have been around continuously since the 1930s, not many manage to last that long. Occasionally, companies reintroduce names previously thought to be extinct in an effort to make people want to relive their past and possibly win over some new fans.

VW dusted off the Beetle for another go-around, but after a respectable second act, it was ultimately retired again not long ago. Ford attempted to revive the Thunderbird and appeal to baby boomers with a design reminiscent of its 1955 inception, yet three years later they called it quits. Well, OK boomer! As e-cars become increasingly popular, an electric version of the Hummer is set to go on sale in 2021. What's the over-under this green new deal develops a reputation beyond bro-dozer for hipsters? Place your bets.

The Blue Oval announced some time ago that it was rereleasing the Bronco this September after being shelved back in 1996. While we've seen some "revealed" images of the new design (that looks suspiciously like a glorified Explorer), it's too soon to tell if this homage will manage to top its initial 30-year run. Back in Issue 17, we showed you our editor-in-chief's '79 Bronco, affectionately known as the Ballistic Bronco. Since then it's had some upgrades, and we felt the timing couldn't be better to help spur the sentimentality some of our readers may feel about a model that's now seeing a revamp. So here's what's new with Harrison's Ford.

The builder, Dominic Janeway, had marching orders to make it look dark and mean. Cosmetically, it had previously been wrapped in vinyl, which was covering a rattle-can enamel paintjob. Needless to say, the metal fatigue and dings that had accumulated over 40 years could no longer be ignored. It took about two weeks of prep work in order to get it ready for paint. The body was hammered out and resurfaced to give it a proper foundation for its new coat of stealth, low-gloss gunmetal gray. Holes where trim originally resided were filled in to keep with the sleek new look.

The original C6 transmission was retained, rebuilt, and fitted with a Monster Transmission low-stall torque converter. Skyjacker generously donated one of its 4-inch lift kits with Black MAX shocks as well as spacers to account for change in driveshaft-to-pinion gear angle. This required the addition of a dropped Pitman arm and modified suspension towers up front to make room for an extra pair of shocks, which were added in order to stiffen up the front end, as extended control arms necessitated removal of the sway bar. Bronco aficionados are undoubtedly familiar with Duff Tuff, which provided extended radial arms modified to fit the truck. Anyone familiar with this generation of Broncos knows the original brakes sucked, and adding bigger tires make them suck more. Since Iain replaced the original engine with a 460 big-block some time ago, upgrading the stopping power was a no-brainer. Accoutrements came courtesy of Wild Horses Four Wheel Drive in the way of new stainless steel plumbing and a larger master cylinder.

Bumpers were cut down a bit and repainted black. The old-school halogen illumination was upgraded with a set of LED trail and infrared lighting from Rigid Industries on the front bumper and on top of the cab, which when lit up give the appearance of a second sun. Brake and side

Being an Arizona truck meant that the chassis and body were corrosion-free, so adding extended control arms was easy.

Secure storage and gun racks give a clue as to what the truck's job entails.

Although this is a work, rather than show, truck, the black accents and matte gray body always get attention in the parking lot. Note IR driving lights for stealth mode.

marker lights were given some translucent black lenses to keep with the stealthy dress code. The increased demand for current now meant more power was needed to operate the new electronics, so rewiring the stock dash was the next order of business. A Tuffy Products steel-locking center console was installed in the cab for obvious reasons, and gun mounts from Blac-Rac bolted to the internal roll cage. New upholstery from 4 Wheel Parts completed the cab, while the cargo area was treated to sliding drawers, outlined in RECOIL Issue 43.

Nowadays, this horse is finally looking a little more like a stud and a little less like it was rode hard and put away wet. Like any good project, you never really finish it, you just start on another area. Although originally this was a two-year-only body design, thankfully the aftermarket parts supply for these Broncos is fairly forgiving if you want to have a go at rebuilding one yourself. Hard to believe that just a few years ago trucks of this era were regarded by many as gas-guzzling pigs. Nowadays, older Broncos command sums of money that make you wish you'd held onto them when they had that reputation. They're only going up in value.

It's easy to look at this no-frills build and understand why these trucks still have a loyal following. You don't need to do much to make them look good. They're simple, rugged, and still stylish all these years later. If we had to choose between fixing this one up and purchasing one of the impending revamps, it's not hard to figure out why we'd open our wallets for the older bottle of wine. Forty years from now, we doubt we'll see anyone restoring the Broncos soon to hit dealerships.

PARTS SOURCES

WILD HORSES >	www.wildhorses4x4.com
RIGID INDUSTRIES >	www.rigidindustries.com
MONSTER TRANSMISSION >	www.monstertransmission.com
4 WHEEL PARTS >	www.4wheelparts.com
TUFFY PRODUCTS >	www.tuffyproducts.com
DUFF TUFF >	www.dufftuff.com
SKYJACKER SUSPENSION >	skyjacker.com
DOMINIC'S CUSTOM RIDES >	dominicscustomrides.simpl.com

Bug-Out Bronco

Brandon Barton's 1978 Ford Bronco "Lucille" Was Built as a Low-Tech Way to Get Off the Grid

By Patrick McCarthy
Photos by Brennan King

Anyone who has owned a classic car or truck knows that they come with some trade-offs. On the plus side, they tend to be astonishingly simple, at least by modern standards. Instead of a digital engine control module with tendrils woven into the ignition, fuel injection, transmission, brakes, and other critical systems, you get a distributor and a carburetor — systems that can be maintained in a driveway with basic handtools. However, these aging vehicles can also be more temperamental than their modern counterparts, so occasional tinkering comes with the territory.

When Brandon Barton started shopping for a classic 4x4, he was well aware of these pros and cons. "I have always loved having an extraneous 'fun' car, but until I found my Bronco, they had been sports cars or the occasional sportbike. As I have gotten older, doing 0-60 in 4 seconds has become less important. I started thinking about the practicality of an older vehicle after reading William R. Forstchen's *One Second After*." That novel tells the story of the aftermath of an electromagnetic pulse (EMP) attack within the United States, which fried the sensitive electronics in newer vehicles, but left classic cars relatively unharmed. Barton admitted that's an unlikely event, but liked the idea of a low-tech, easy-to-maintain vehicle that could survive a wide range of catastrophes.

After looking at a few Jeeps and International Scouts, Barton found this 1978 Ford Bronco: "She ticked all the boxes: mechanically sound, four-wheel-drive, pre-1980s tech with new tires and a lift to boot." After taking the Bronco home, he decided to call it Lucille. He says he's often asked if this name came from *The Walking Dead*, but it's actually a reference to Kenny Rogers' 1977 country song of the same name. "Old vehicles and Murphy's Law being what they are, I figured if I were ever in a pinch, that would be when the ordinarily reliable old truck would 'pick a fine time to leave me' as

RENEWABLE ENERGY

With about $400 and a few hours of work, Barton assembled this solar power bank system. It includes 12V outlets and USB ports so he can keep his tools and small electronics running wherever he goes, without running the engine or draining the battery under the hood of his Bronco. You can read Part One of his DIY guide at offgridweb.com/?p=10962, and Part Two at offgridweb.com/?p=11296.

A salvaged '78 Ford F-100 bed with a camper shell was converted into a trailer, complete with matching paint, wheels, and tires.

Barton's Doberman is his canine copilot. He can often be found in the passenger seat with his tongue flapping in the breeze.

the song said." Despite the tongue-in-cheek name, Barton started building this truck into a rig he could use for camping, off-roading, or getting out of town quickly in an emergency.

Lucille's original 351M V-8 engine and four-speed manual transmission were still going strong, so Barton chose to leave them as-is. It also had a new 4-inch suspension lift, 15-inch Bart Wheels, and 32-inch BFGoodrich tires. However, the torn interior upholstery was patched with duct tape, and the exterior sheetmetal was showing signs of rust. Barton cleaned up the interior with some Saddle Blanket seat covers, and took the truck to Creative Colors in Clinton, Oklahoma, for some much-needed bodywork. There, the rusted fender edges were cut out and replaced with Bushwacker fender flares, and the body was repainted in Lead Foot Gray, a color offered on the late-model Ford F-150. For visual flair and improved durability, the lower body, bumpers, grille surround, fiberglass bed cover, and part of the hood were coated in Rhino bedliner.

In order to enhance the truck's off-grid capabilities, Barton decided to add an onboard emergency power source. He started with a DIY power bank built from a deep-cycle marine battery, MinnKota trolling motor power center, and Peak mobile power outlet with USB ports. The whole setup cost him roughly $200, but its specifications are comparable to a $1,000 Goal Zero Yeti 1250. For another $200, he hooked up a 20-amp solar charge controller and a 100-watt monocrystalline solar panel to passively replenish the battery anywhere the sun shines. The panel is mounted on an inexpensive roof rack he found on Craigslist, along with a shovel and ax for vehicle recovery or road-clearing.

With the power bank, full-size spare tire, winch, and other survival gear, the small bed of the Bronco fills up quickly. Barton came up with a clever way to expand its capacity and add a comfortable, weather-proof sleeping quarters for camping and overland adventures. He bought the remains of a scrapped 1978 Ford F-100 pickup, and adapted its 8-foot-long bed into a custom trailer with matching paint, fender flares, wheels and tires, and a camper shell.

Barton says his Bronco has been at the center of many good memories. He taught his 16-year-old daughter to drive stick in it — unfortunately, she accidentally revved the engine too high, panicked, and popped the clutch, causing the driveshaft U-joint to shatter. They limped the truck home in front-wheel-drive, but it's a day they can look back on and laugh

The 43-year-old carbureted V-8 under the hood might not be pretty, but it has stood the test of time and always been easy to maintain.

about now. Lucille has also been a source of bonding with his stepson, through camping trips and car show attendance together. And it wouldn't exist in its current form without assistance from Barton's father, who "provided inspiration, guidance, help, and funding when I was short of all four."

Like many classic car projects, Lucille is never quite finished. "At the end of the day, she's nothing fancy or advanced, just a cool old truck that hopefully will run in the improbable event of an EMP. She still doesn't have a radio," he said with a laugh.

1978 FORD BRONCO

ENGINE: 351M 5.8L V8
TRANSMISSION: BorgWarner T-18 four-speed manual
DRIVELINE: 4x4 with two-speed transfer case
SUSPENSION: 4-inch lift kit with new coil springs, add-a-leaf springs, and shocks
WHEELS & TIRES: 15x8-inch Bart Wheels Super Trucker with 32x11.5R15 BFGoodrich All-Terrain T/A
TRAILER: Modified 1978 Ford F-100 8-foot truck frame and bed with camper shell
PAINT: Ford Lead Foot Gray with black Rhino liner accents

A Dying Breed

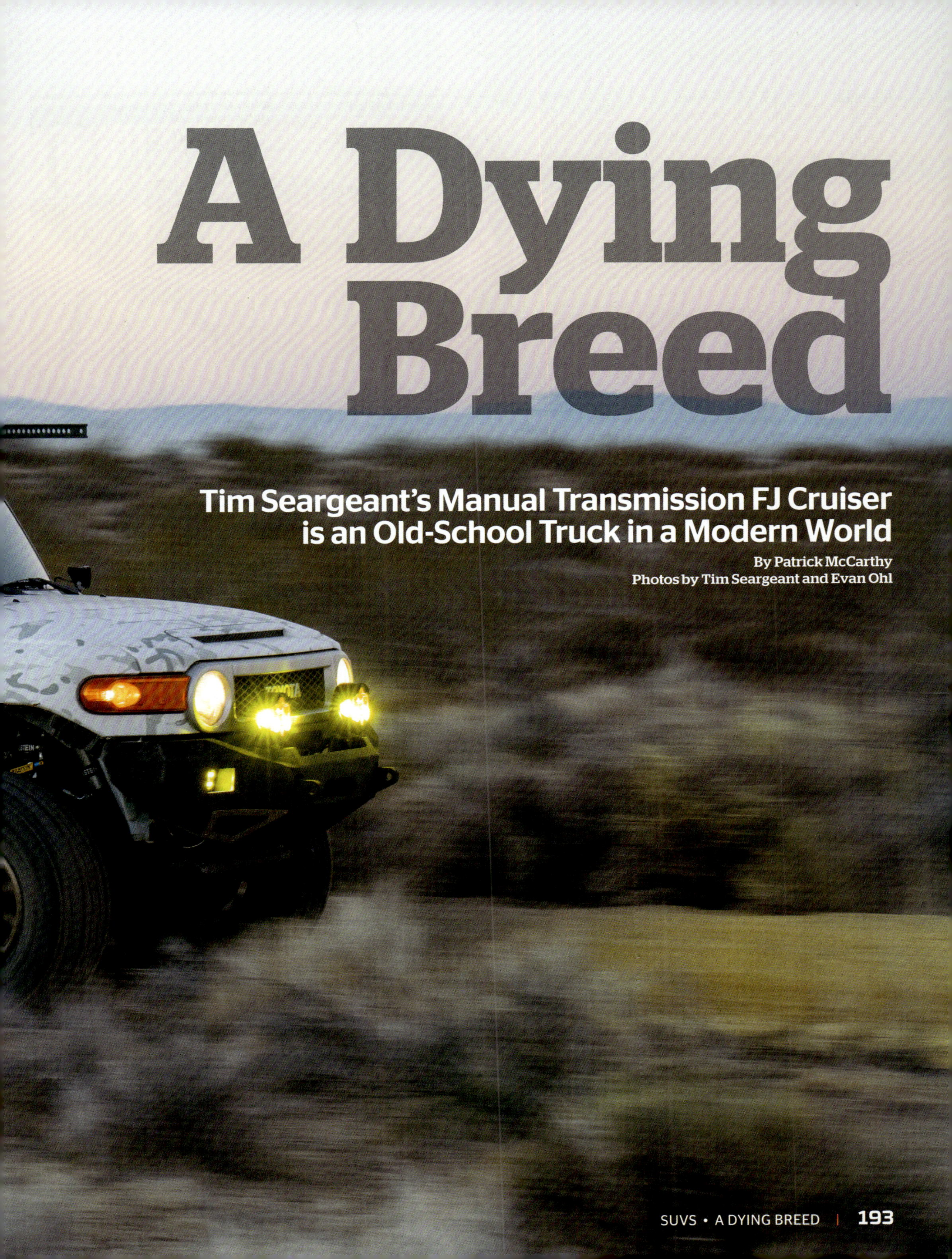

Tim Seargeant's Manual Transmission FJ Cruiser is an Old-School Truck in a Modern World

By Patrick McCarthy
Photos by Tim Seargeant and Evan Ohl

Like it or not, the manual transmission is going the way of the dodo, at least when it comes to new vehicles. According to a study by CarMax, only 2 percent of the vehicles sold by the company in 2020 had manual transmissions, a number that has plummeted from 27 percent in 1995. For most drivers, it's less hassle to simply press the gas pedal and let a computer do the shifting, but for those who enjoy modulating the clutch and smoothly changing gears, this extinction feels tragic. Tim Seargeant, a lifelong sports car enthusiast who has never owned a vehicle with anything but a manual transmission, is firmly in the latter category. When Tim decided to purchase a truck, he knew it had to have a six-speed, but he also wanted something relatively new and reliable enough for long road trips with the family.

After plugging in the requisite filters on AutoTrader, Tim soon learned that the Toyota FJ Cruiser fit the bill and found roughly 40 manual-equipped FJs that fit his criteria in the United States. Luckily, one of them was only a short drive from his home in Southern California. Five hours later, he drove away with a new truck, already thinking about modifications to make it more capable on- and off-road. The next week, the build began.

The first phone call was made to Tim's friend, the founder of Titan7 wheels. Although the company primarily makes lightweight forged wheels for motorsport applications, they offer one model for off-roaders. Tim wrapped the 17-inch Titan7 T-AK1 wheels in 34-inch Nitto Terra Grappler G2 tires. These were paired with Bilstein coilovers and upper control arms in front, as well as Bilstein shocks and leaf springs in the rear.

At this point, Tim wanted a more distinctive look, so he decided to enlist the help of a friend and cover the original silver paint with Multi-Cam Alpine vinyl. Next, a Front Runner roof rack was installed, along with a retractable awning, mount for the Smittybilt jack, stowable folding table, and even a rack-mounted bottle opener. To protect the FJ from damage on the trails, the front bumper was replaced with a Smitty-bilt M1 metal bumper, and a set of DeMello Offroad rock sliders were installed.

According to Tim, he knew he wanted to upgrade the truck's light output, but he intentionally put this off. He wrote, "Wiring, electronics, splicing, and soldering intimidates

Right: The Pioneer NEX stereo head unit offers wireless Apple CarPlay and Android Auto compatibility, which make it more convenient to navigate on long road trips.

A BOSS StrongBox drawer, Tactical Walls VMod door panel, and Refined Cycle window MOLLE panels offer plenty of storage for guns, recovery gear, and camping supplies.

me … it was the most challenging part of the build." After talking with more experienced friends and putting himself through "YouTube University," he was able to successfully install an array of Baja Designs lights, including LP6 Pro driving lights on the front bumper, Squadron fog lights and ditch lights, and S2 auxiliary lights around the perimeter of the roof rack. Everything is wired to CH4x4 push switches that match the amber interior lighting. A Pioneer touchscreen stereo with Apple CarPlay, speakers, and a secondary backup camera were also added to modernize the truck.

Since he works in the gun industry, Tim wanted a secure way to carry guns and gear, so he ordered a 40x22x10-inch locking drawer system from BOSS StrongBox and bolted it to the floor. Additional storage options come by way of a pair of Refined Cycle rear window MOLLE panels and a Tactical Walls VMod rear panel. These hold an Urban Medical Gear trauma kit, recovery tools, and other accessories, many of which are attached to Vanquest Gear hook-and-loop panels for quick tear-away access.

Tim says he has had many memorable experiences with this FJ Cruiser, including a recent trip with his wife and sons to Utah. During that trip, they hauled all their guns and gear to a Fieldcraft Survival course, tackled some challenging rock crawls in "Little Moab," and even fired up the Baja Designs lights to drive through an abandoned train tunnel carved into the mountains. Knowing that the days of new manual transmission vehicles — not to mention fossil-fuel-powered vehicles in general — are likely numbered, Tim takes every opportunity to row through the gears and enjoy the old-school ruggedness of his truck. He'd like to thank his friends Gene Y., Randall T., Don N., Josh E., Kento K., Michael E., Mark H., and Chris F. for donating their time and expertise to help him complete the build.

Although Tim was intimidated by the prospect of learning how to wire these Baja Designs lights, the results were well worth the effort.

2012 TOYOTA FJ CRUISER

DRIVETRAIN: 4.0L V-6 with 6-speed manual transmission

SUSPENSION: Bilstein B8 8112 front coilover shocks, upper control arms, 8100 rear shocks, and B12 1.5-inch lift rear leaf springs

WHEELS & TIRES: 17x8.5 Titan7 T-AK1 wheels (-8 offset) and 305/70R17 Nitto Terra Grappler G2 tires

BODY MODIFICATIONS: Front Runner Outfitters Slimline roof rack, 2m awning, jack mount, and stainless steel folding table with under-rack mount; Smittybilt M1 front bumper and Trail Jack, DeMello Offroad rock sliders, MultiCam Alpine vinyl wrap

ELECTRONICS & LIGHTING: Pioneer NEX 7600 stereo head unit, 6x9 speakers, and backup camera; Baja Designs LP6 driving lights, Squadron SAE fog lights, Squadron Pro ditch lights, and S2 Pro side and rear auxiliary lights; CH4x4 push-button switches, Blue Sea 12-circuit fuse block

INTERIOR MODIFICATIONS: BOSS StrongBox 7126-7611 gun safe drawer, Tactical Walls VMod rear door panel, Refined Cycle RM3 and RM4 rear window MOLLE panels, Vanquest Gear MOHL-AIR tear-away panels with Urban Medical Gear TRK-1 IFAK and other MOLLE accessories

These forged 17-inch Titan7 wheels are significantly lighter than the FJ's factory wheels, so it retains most of its acceleration and braking performance, even with larger 34-inch all-terrain tires.

Off-Grid Rig

When the World Goes to Hell in a Hand Basket, Let's Hope You Have a Bug-Out Vehicle Like this Toyota Land Cruiser

By Patrick Vuong
Photography by Jorge Nuñez

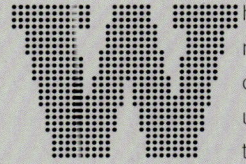

When crap meets fan, the most common response city folks have will be to use their cars to get out of the proverbial toilet. But if you think you're going to pack your go-bags and your family into a PT Cruiser and evade the incoming catastrophe on the highway, you're seriously mistaken. History has proven that when wide-scale emergencies strike unexpectedly, freeways become giant parking lots. City streets get jammed like strawberries with panicked people hoping to get out of Dodge. And short of flagging a rescue helicopter or utilizing a DeLorean to jump space and time, you'll be stuck to ride out the calamity wherever you happen to be — unless you have a bug-out vehicle.

For urbanites, bugging out (or evacuating when danger is imminent) is possible only in a vehicle that can handle the terrain when the pavement ends and the backcountry begins. And that's just the start. So, even a stock pickup truck won't cut it, let alone a family sedan.

Clayton York understood this concept well. As an import-car enthusiast, he knew his way around an engine bay, which also meant he knew the inherent limitations of using, say, a lowered Subaru Impreza WRX in a SHTF scenario. So, applying his knowledge as a car nut, York set out to build a truck that could serve as both a camping mule and a hardcore off-grid rig. He accomplished his goal of building this Toyota Land Cruiser after two years, more than $30,000, and a lot of assistance from friends — such as his former employer Adventure Trailers and ex-coworkers David and James Argust, who helped with custom coatings and some woodwork.

Whether you're looking to soup up your commuter for some outdoor adventures or you've already begun building your own Landmaster for a *Damnation Alley*-style dystopian future, read on. You're sure to pick up a few prepper pointers.

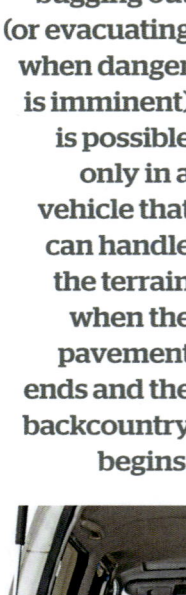

For urbanites, bugging out (or evacuating when danger is imminent) is possible only in a vehicle that can handle the terrain when the pavement ends and the backcountry begins.

Make and Model

Let's be clear: there's not one be-all, end-all automobile to start with when building a rig for the end of the world as we know it (TEOTWAWKI). Car, truck, SUV, or ATV? Everyone's situation is different, so the make and model of your vehicle is highly dependent on your needs, driving skills, surrounding environment, and (perhaps most significantly) the size of your wallet.

Money's no object? Then consider an overland expedition vehicle. Some combine the luxuries of a high-dollar RV with the powerful capabilities of a heavy-duty work truck, such as the EarthRoamer XV-LT (www.earthroamer.com). Others, like the Survivor Truck (www.survivortruck.com) featured in Issue 8 of RECOIL magazine, are geared more toward security and surveillance — it is resistant to electromagnetic pulse attacks, after all. Maybe you're good on two wheels and plan to face the apocalypse solo? Consider a dual-sport bike, which can easily slip through traffic jams and handle wooded or desert terrain with ease (see RECOIL Issue 10 for proof).

York needed a rig that would be affordable and versatile. He looked for an SUV that could work as a daily driver, a camper, and a SHTF rig. While other preppers like to use Ford Raptors, Jeep Wranglers, or Toyota Tundras as the base for their "bug-out-mobiles," York sought out an 80-series Toyota Land Cruiser and found a 1994 model that fit the bill for just $2,200.

Engine

Why an older Land Cruiser instead of, say, a brand-new Corolla? Well, aside from the lack of cargo space, the sedan has a 1.8L engine, which is a puny. Think about it this way: a 2-liter soda bottle holds more volume. An off-road vehicle, and specifically a bug-out rig, needs to have a powerful motor to meet the brutal demands Mother Earth will put on it.

With four-wheel drive and a 4.5L six-cylinder engine, the Land Cruiser had the heart and the legs to grow into an off-road beast. York had just one problem with the Land Cruiser he found: it had a blown engine. That didn't faze the car nut, who replaced the motor and related parts at an additional cost of $2,800. He also added a Safari Snorkel system with an air ram that can rotate, ensuring that the engine not only gets cool, clean air, but is also protected from precipitation — whether he's driving over a small creek or through a snow storm.

Suspension

Very rarely does a factory suspension system come even remotely close to meeting the demands of off-road driving.

Encounter a TEOTWAWKI scenario? Forget about it! A stock truck will just get stuck in a ditch or hung up on some rocks.

So, York had Nichols Autofab in Prescott, Arizona, replace the worn suspension with brand-new OEM heavy-duty shocks and springs, as well as 30mm polyurethane rear-spring spacers — all of which help the Land Cruiser absorb hard landings, whether they come from driving down from higher elevations or from evading danger over bumpy terrain. The Land Cruiser also has a 3-inch lift kit with adjustment brackets so that it can better clear obstacles, such as road debris, fallen trees, or downed power lines. He also installed new OEM lockers with a center differential lock switch, which provides extra traction by forcing both wheels to turn in unison.

Wheels and Tires

Some people think that all they need to drive off-road is a powerful 4WD truck with hardcore suspension. What they fail to realize is that without complementary wheels and tires, they'll be going nowhere fast. If the wheels aren't strong enough, they can actually deform under all that torque and compression delivered to it by the axle and the force of gravity. Low-quality tires can easily disintegrate once driven off asphalt, while the wrong type of traction could send your vehicle spinning into a rock face or careening into a ditch.

York installed powdercoated OEM wheels because they're reliable and time-tested, rather than go with flashy aftermarket wheels that can crack. He swapped out the tires for a set of Toyo Tires Open Country A/T II. These "meats" have an aggressive, wear-resistant tread design with deep groves, tough sidewalls, zigzag sipes, and stone-ejecting blocks — all of which help to maintain traction in dirt, mud, and snow. Being all-terrains, the Open Country provides a relatively quiet ride on asphalt compared to chunkier mud-terrain tires without sacrificing any noticeable performance on or off-road. This versatility will serve York during a widespread emergency, considering he wouldn't want to waste valuable minutes mounting not one, but four tires.

The Land Cruiser also has a 4-pound air tank mounted in the front bumper. Because you need to air down the psi of your tires for certain off-road terrain, the air compressor is handy to pump up your meats when it's time to return to pavement or to work pneumatic tools.

Body Armor

If you're heading off-grid, you'll need protection and so will your vehicle. While regular bumpers are meant to absorb the impact of a traffic collision, a bug-out truck won't likely get into any fender-benders in the backcountry. Instead, it'll need body armor to deflect hazards like rocks and tree branches.

> **Some people think that all they need to drive off-road is a powerful 4WD truck with hardcore suspension. What they fail to realize is that without complementary wheels and tires, they'll be going nowhere fast.**

York elected to remove the factory bumper and install an ARB Bull Bar, which provides superior protection while integrating mounts for lights, antenna, tow points, and limb risers. Speaking of limb risers, these are essentially taunt steel wires that run from the Bull Bar to the roof rack to prevent thick tree limbs from smashing the windshield. Outback Proven out of Las Vegas, Nevada, supplied York with a Kaymar bar that not only reinforces the rear, but also contains carriers for a spare tire and a fuel can.

Recovery Tools

It's nearly impossible to drive in remote areas and not get stuck, whether it's hitting a patch of soft sand, getting caught in deep snow, or finding yourself "high-centered" on a rocky cliff. To stay off-grid but unstuck, you'll need the tools to extricate yourself (or your friends and loved ones) from a tough spot.

The Land Cruiser features a Factor 55 ProLink attached to the synthetic rope of a Warn V10000 winch that's integrated into the front Bull Bar. This winching system can pull the SUV out of most jams and help to free up any traveling companions. Outback Proven also helped York with a set of MAXTRAX MKII extraction devices, which are essentially two planks made of reinforced polymer with cleats that sink into both the tire treads and the terrain. This design prevents the vehicle from slipping back into the precarious spot, allowing for a faster vehicle recovery. While they were made in Australia and proven on the sands of the outback, MAXTRAX work just as effectively in mud, dirt, or snow, and can even be used as shovels when turned upside down.

Lights

For most drivers, stock headlights suffice because city street lamps make up for their deficiencies. But when you're roaming through BFE (AKA the middle of nowhere), those deficiencies can lead to disaster. Visibility is cut short and peripheral vision is nonexistent in the backwoods. So, the Land Cruiser can light up the night with numerous additional lighting sources, including a 21-inch LED bar mounted on the front bumper and two 18-watt LED flood lights. Inside in the rear, York even installed a Hella LED map light for when you're stopped and need to find your bearings in the darkness.

Batteries

With an array of additional lights, a Yaesu FT-8800R shortwave radio, and state-of-the art electronics (like a Kenwood touchscreen radio and Boston Acoustics and Kicker speakers), the Land Cruiser's electrical system would no doubt fry if they all ran on the original battery. So, York installed a dual-battery system with an Optima Red Top power plant running the alternator and winch and another feeding

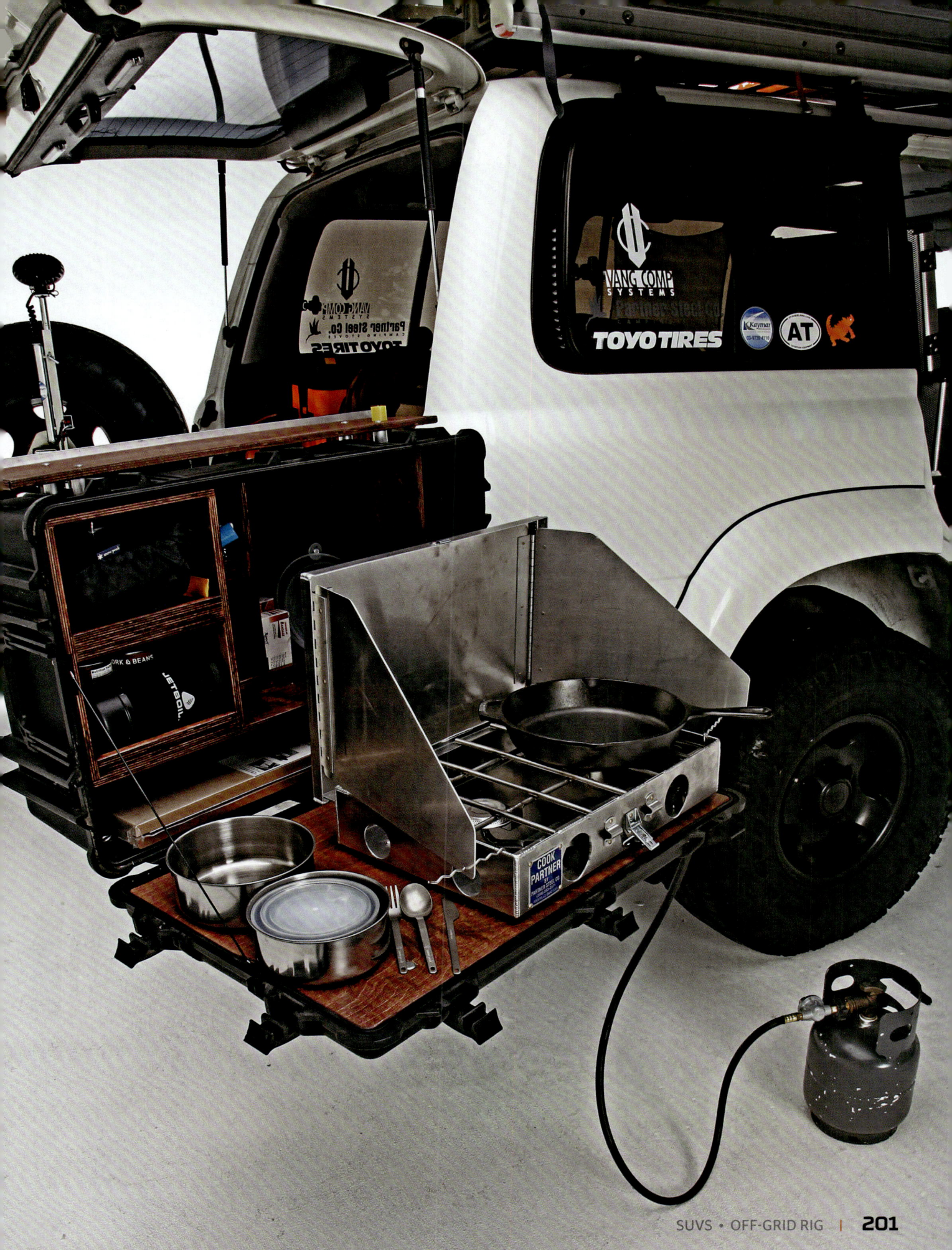

the auxiliary functions, like the electronics and radio. And as a backup, he fitted a 15-watt solar-charging panel to the roof.

Fuel and Food

A bug-out vehicle has to be more than just a mode of transportation. It must utilize every square inch for specific tasks or to house vital supplies. Why? Because when a calamity strikes, your vehicle might become your bedroom, kitchen, and warehouse for God knows how long. No wasted space allowed, so York maximized every compartment of his Land Cruiser.

In the event of a Mad Max scenario in which fuel is gold, York has his petrol needs covered — at least for some time. His rig has an auxiliary 44-gallon fuel tank, which more than doubles his travel range to about 700 miles. Inside, there's a mounted National Luna fridge for storing food and drinks. Connected to the Kaymar rear bumper is a Pelican chuck box that hides an onboard kitchenette. No joke. It holds a 5-pound propane tank, an 18-inch Partner Steel two-burner stove, and various pots and pans. This one-off kitchenette was the result of some fine craftsmanship by Nichols Autofab and the Argust brothers at Adventure Trailers.

And if that weren't enough, York installed a 27-gallon shower system with a hot/cold mixer and water pump.

Survival Storage

No off-grid rig would be complete without self-defense tools. Under the dash on the driver's side, there's a mount for a tanto blade. Behind the driver's seat is a custom-made stand for an AR-15 rifle that York fashioned from a fishing-pole mount. In the back, an Adventure Trailers Drawer System conveniently and safely secures his ammo and other firearms, including a badass Remington 870 that's been kitted-out by the shotgun gurus at Vang Comp Systems.

Topside, there's a BajaRack EXP roof rack that greatly increases the Land Cruiser's cargo-carrying capacity and where he keeps other survival gear. Other important supplies securely stowed include a shovel, a medical kit, and an SPA fire extinguisher.

At the Ready

The make and model of a bug-out vehicle isn't nearly as important as what you're prepping it for, how practical its setup will be in relation to your individual circumstance, and how well you know its capabilities and shortcomings.

With this vehicle, York has proven that with thorough research, proper craftsmanship, and a lot of help from friends, you can build an SUV for getting groceries, going camping, and facing the end of days. The Land Cruiser is a pavement pounder that can head for the hills at a moment's notice, making it the ideal off-grid rig.

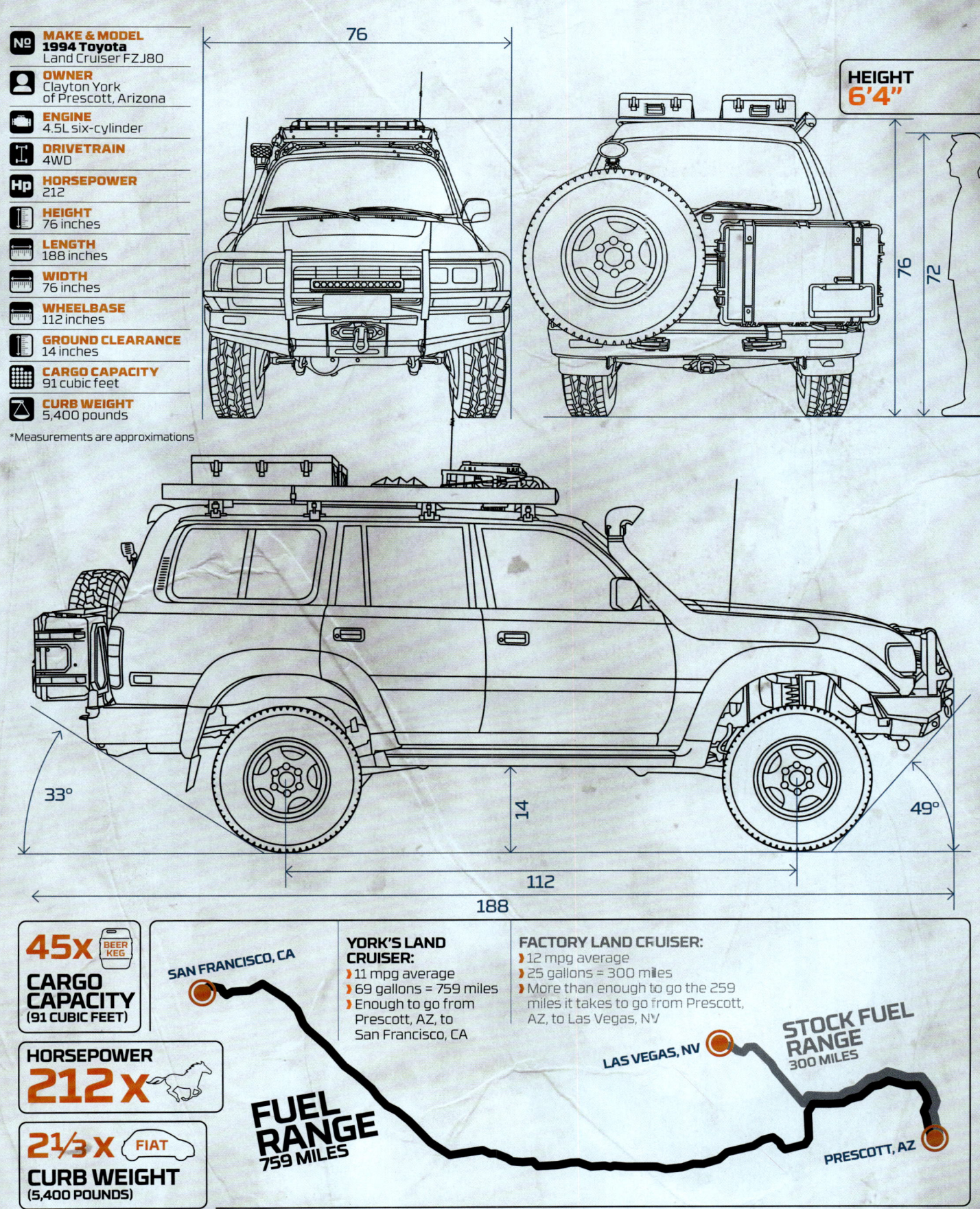

4 Motorcycles & UTVs

Christini AWD 300
Technical Knockout

By Chris Denison
Photography by Adam Booth

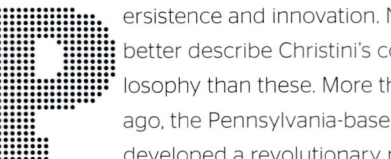

Persistence and innovation. No two words better describe Christini's corporate philosophy than these. More than five years ago, the Pennsylvania-based company developed a revolutionary non-hydraulic all-wheel-drive system that simultaneously created and dominated a new segment of the off-road market. A consistent race effort and a dedicated customer base both helped improve performance and raise awareness of Christini technology, but when the economy tanked, the brand failed to explode in popularity like everyone predicted. Still, Christini kept pushing. The AWD system began finding a successful niche in military applications, though Christini's dream of selling an all-wheel-drive stock motorcycle through one of the major OEMs struggled to gain traction but remained alive. As a result, Christini did what any like-minded entrepreneurial brand would do: It built its own bike.

The all-new Christini AWD 300 is just that: a Christini. This complete machine is not a Honda or a KTM but rather a blend of components that make the bike uniquely Christini-like. Sure, the AWD uses a 300cc Gas Gas two-stroke engine, but that doesn't mean it has much in common with anything you've seen on dealer floors. A hydraulic clutch, Paioli front suspension, six-speed transmission, and optional electric start are some of the main features of the AWD 300, not to mention the fact that power is delivered to the front wheel when the rear loses traction via an all-mechanical system.

If you haven't ridden the AWD setup before, here's a bit of background: The Christini system feels very different on the trail compared to a rear-wheel-drive bike. Due to the unfamiliar handling, some riders click with the Christini, while others struggle to get used to it. We think it is awesome off road, so long as you know how to ride it and don't fight the front end. The biggest downside we notice is that the Christini's front wheel will try to crawl out of ruts when the shoulder knobs of the tire grab traction, and this

1 Twin Spar Aluminum Frame

2 Gas Gas 300cc Liquid-Cooled Two-Stroke

3 Kick Start (Electronic Start Optional for $600)

4 Hydraulic Clutch

5 Paioli Open Chamber Front Suspension

6 CSR Single Shock with Linkage and High Speed, Low Speed and Rebound Adjustability

7 Suspension: 305 mm (12-inch) Front & Rear

8 Front Tire: 21-inch Kings Tire Tube Type

9 Tank: 9.8L (2.6-gallon)

— along with a feeling of the front end "pulling" — means the bike will sometimes just go where it wants, much like how a traditional rear-drive bike feels in sand. Minor unweighting of the front end and continually bringing it back down with the wheel slightly cocked are responsible for a huge part of this sensation. This is not a big deal on a traditional bike but can be very consequential on the AWD, since the front will grab and send you off in whatever direction the handlebar is pointing. Additionally, the added weight of the AWD components make it more difficult to get the front wheel off the ground, which leads to a tendency to slam into obstacles rather than pop over them.

With that said, the benefits of the system far outweigh the negatives. In loose rocks, tough hills, and overall nasty terrain, the Christini is magic. It truly is like having a motivated minder pulling you over obstacles with a tugger strap. You need to be aware of how you're modulating the power and the clutch in order to find the best blend of traction and rpm, but overall the Christini does an excellent job of hooking up and getting going.

If there is one thing about the AWD 300 that makes it stand above other iterations of the Christini, it's that the frame is not at all rigid and promotes a balanced overall handling feel. The chassis obviously carries the extra weight of the system near the front of the frame, but it doesn't feel like this weight is in front of the stem, like one of those awkwardly heavy auxiliary number plate fuel tanks. Instead, the weight feels forward

10 AWD Engagement Switch

11 FMF Pipe and Silencer with Spark Arrestor

12 Six-Speed Wide-Ratio Transmission

AWD Drive Ratio: 0.64:1 (9:16 tooth)

Final Drive Ratio: 13:48 tooth

13 Black Anodized Rims and Billet Hubs

14 Ground Clearance: 356 mm (14-inch)

15 Wheelbase: 1,478mm (58.2-inch)

16 Rear Tire: 18-inch Kings Tire Tube Type

17 Front and Rear Brake: Single-Disc 240mm (9.4-inch)

18 Seat Height: 952 mm (37.5-inches)

but lower than expected, and there aren't any odd leaning or turning issues, except for those mentioned above. Even with a bulkier fuel tank to accommodate the internal gears of the AWD, the ergonomics were comfortable and easy to get used to.

As an avid two-stroke lover, this author found the 300cc Gas Gas powerplant to be a great complement to the function of the AWD. Easy to roll on and packed with torque, the engine does best in the low-to-mid rpm range and can easily be short-shifted to maintain great traction.

The biggest downside we felt was that vibration got a bit heavy when the revs went too high. Starting and jetting were both where they needed to be, and the exhaust was not overly noisy. Of course, four-stroke lovers can also get a taste of Christini technology through the new AWD 450, which features an engine that is similar in appearance to a 450cc Honda.

Perhaps the coolest part of the AWD 300 is the price, which is $8,995 for the complete bike. Most riders are under the impression that a Christini costs an arm and a leg, but the reality is that riders can now get a hard enduro-ready All Wheel Drive 300 for less than the cost of a new KTM. The AWD 450 is even cheaper at an astonishing $6,895. For something this advanced, the complete package is great. For a trail bike, the AWD 300 is a very awesome option for the average rider. It used to be that riders would buy Christinis as a second bike, but given how far the technology has come, this bike definitely deserves consideration as a primary machine.

MAKE: Christini
MODEL: AWD 300
SEAT HEIGHT: 37.5 in
CLAIMED DRY WEIGHT: 239 lbs
GROUND CLEARANCE: 14.0 in
FUEL CAPACITY: 2.6 gal
MSRP: $8,995 includes one-year AWD warranty
URL: www.christini.com

Dirty Deeds

From Desert Dunes to Asphalt Jungles, the Tomcar Proves that Big Things Come in Small Packages

By John Schwartze
Photography By Henry Z. De Kuyper

If at first blush you thought this was just another sandrail, dune buggy, or UTV, we regret to inform you that you couldn't be more wrong. While it could be used to haul coolers and ditzy girls while you're hanging out at Glamis listening to Crazy Town, bro, the Tomcar is a military-grade off-road vehicle that's the culmination of progressive engineering and practical accessorizing.

MAKE: Tomcar
MODEL: TM5
YEAR: 2009
ENGINE: 1.4L Diesel
DRIVETRAIN: 2WD
WHEELBASE: 101 inches

In other words, when shit gets hairy in the field, the guys at Tomcar have anticipated the contingencies and designed the vehicle around them. While the Tomcar is available to the public, the TM5 model we're showing you is an example of one created as part of a fleet that was deployed in South Asia and outfitted with several non-standard features for that type of environment.

A major problem currently faced in designing a vehicle for combat is the IED threat. A vehicle is already a moving target, and while the obvious reaction to increase armor might make sense on paper, in battle conditions it's often proved to make vehicles larger and slower moving targets, which are obliged to run on predictable routes. The Tomcar's designers took a different approach creating a vehicle that is evasive, agile, and carries a very high payload for its size. It's hard (but not impossible) to hit a target that's small, quick, and can go off the map to avoid IEDs altogether. Initially conceived as an infantry mule, the Tomcar is resilient and powerful enough to carry men and supplies to the front line, and carry wounded out — something larger vehicles can't do in certain situations.

One of its most unique features is its frame. This is no bolt-together Erector Set deal. Over 300 pieces have been seamlessly welded together. Several different grades of steel are used throughout the frame's construction for increased durability at stress points. Lighter varieties are used in other areas to keep the overall weight down and maintain a low center of gravity for balance. The side steps that extend beyond the width of the cab also serve to protect occupants during a rollover.

With 15 inches of ground clearance and a standard 1,200-pound payload for the diesel engine (shown), the Tomcar TM5 is built to traverse rough terrain, especially when hauling a heavy load. An

FUN FACT: The Brits use the TM5 in Afghanistan to pick up air-dropped 1-ton pallets by running the winch cable over the cab, hooking the load, and pulling it up a ramp into the bed.

aircraft-grade, full-length aluminum skidplate under the belly helps prevent debris from slowing the momentum of the vehicle during travel.

The rear swing arms and longer-than-average chromoly A-arms in the front allow for 13 inches of suspension travel. You might be asking yourself, "Why chromoly? That's soft." Exactly. It's meant to absorb any impact energy so you can keep going. A bent A-arm will help you GTFO. A broken one will leave you stranded. The final drive is part of the rear swing arm system, which allows for a greater degree of movement than a typical rear A-arm system — plus it's encased in a sealed oil bath.

One of the most vital occurrences in the field with vehicles is maintenance. Things break, but the Tomcar is meant to keep going even if they do. In combat situations, the less time spent making repairs, the more time you're in the fight. Ease of accessibility with Tomcar's components keeps downtime to a minimum. An exposed beltdrive, various symmetrical parts that can be interchanged on either side, and rebuildable parts where just the affected item can be replaced (rather than having to replace the entire unit), such as ball joints and coilover shocks, help keep driver and passengers on the road longer.

You've probably wondered what's powering the TM5. A four-stroke 1-liter four-cylinder gas engine or four-stroke 1.4-liter diesel engine is connected to a high-low transmission. You might think that's a weak combo, but remember, keeping things light is also what keeps this

1 WHEELS/TIRES

Reinforced steel wheels with aftermarket tires for sand, mud, and snow (shown). Standard are aluminum wheels with 25x8-12 6-ply, front; 26x12-12 10-ply, rear.

2 HEADLIGHTS

MAKE:
KC

MODEL:
Pro Sport HID 6-inch Driving Lights

MSRP:
$547

URL:
www.kchilites.com

3 FRONT PACKS

MAKE:
Cabela's

MODEL:
Trail Tamer Gear Molded Fender Bag

MSRP:
$45

URL:
www.cabelas.com

4 LED LIGHT BAR

MAKE:
KC

MODEL:
LZR LED — 40-inch Bar Combo Spot/Flood - Black - 240 watt

MSRP:
$1,211

URL:
www.kchilites.com

5 SIDE PACKS

MAKE:
CamelBak

MODEL:
Squadbak

MSRP:
$243

URL:
www.camelbak.com

6 RESTRAINTS

Four-point safety harnesses (standard).

URL:
www.tomcar.com

7 FUEL TANK

Seven-gallon standard. Second tank with selector also available (same capacity).

MSRP:
$1,100

URL:
www.tomcar.com

1 REAR SHOCKS

Reinforced (shown). Dual coilover gas hydraulic shocks, with accumulator to keep shock oil cool to prevent fade (standard).
URL: www.tomcar.com

2 BELTDRIVE SYSTEM

Standard. Easily accessible for maintenance.
URL: www.tomcar.com

3 GUN MOUNT

MAKE: Lone Star Field Products
MODEL: Spec Rest Quad Pod
MSRP: $650
URL: www.lonestarfieldproducts.com

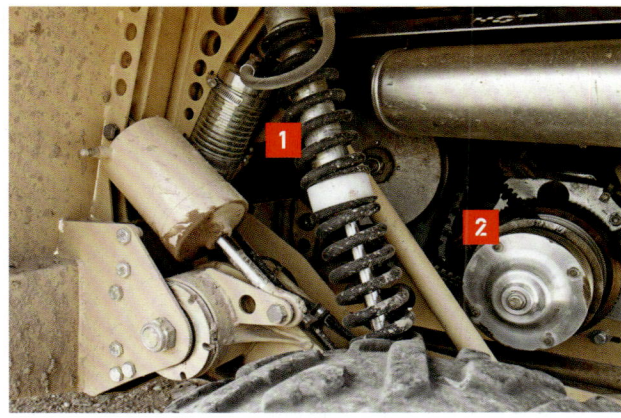

4 GUN

MAKE: HK
MODEL: SP89 Clone with Gemtech Raptor suppressor
CALIBER: 9mm

5 CARGO BOX

66x53 inches
URL: www.tomcar.com

6 MOTOR

1.4L naturally aspirated four-cylinder diesel engine, liquid cooled.
URL: www.tomcar.com

7 FRAME

Fully welded roll cage and frame.
URL: www.tomcar.com

8 FINAL DRIVE SYSTEM

Double roller chains in oil bath encased in armored steel. Part of rear swing arm suspension system.
URL: www.tomcar.com

MOTORCYCLES & UTVS • DIRTY DEEDS

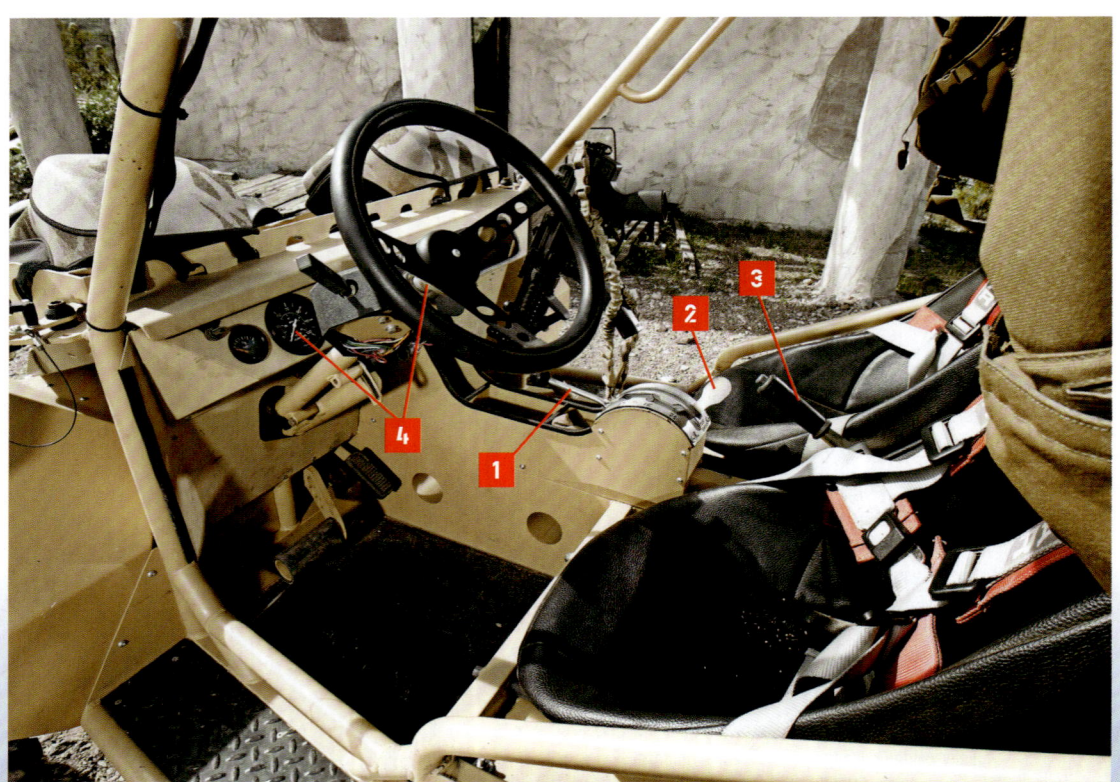

1 TRANSMISSION

High-Low with reverse. To be shifted while at idle or stationary.

URL:
www.tomcar.com

2 DIFFERENTIAL LOCK

Standard. Can be activated at any time while driving to turn both rear wheels.

URL:
www.tomcar.com

3 EMERGENCY BRAKE

Standard.

URL:
www.tomcar.com

4 INSTRUMENTATION AND STEERING

Speedometer, odometer, voltmeter, fuel, temperature. Rack and pinion steering, adjustable column.

URL:
www.tomcar.com

little devil quick and allows it to tow approximately 1,800 pounds.

The Tomcar is not four-wheel drive, which adds to its fuel economy, traction, and power-to-weight ratio. A locking differential that can be manually engaged acts as a positraction to turn both rear wheels to get out of tough spots or operate one wheel should there be a loss of power to the other. An optional second 7-gallon fuel tank is also available, doubling the range to 200-300 miles, depending on road conditions. Like the symmetrical components, these redundancies are meant to keep you moving. Four-wheel power assisted disk brakes are another feature that'll give you plenty of stopping power.

With a base price of around $20,000, we think you'll get a lot of bang for your buck with the Tomcar, as well as a long service life. It continues to see action in combat theaters rigged up for everything from an unmanned ground vehicle to a troop and supply transport. If NATO, the British Army, and Israeli Army see fit to add it to their arsenal, we think you'll be plenty satisfied with how well it performs in rough conditions, whether it's as a rugged commercial vehicle or a fun off-roader for vacations.

5 WINCH

This model no longer available as standard Tomcar option.

MAKE:
Ramsey

MODEL:
Honcho 5000

MSRP:
$744

URL:
www.ramsey.com

6 SIDE CARGO BOXES

Lockable compartments on either side of the vehicle.

URL:
www.tomcar.com

Little Big Rig
Eat Your Heart Out, A-Team

By John Schwartze
Photography By Troy Kruger

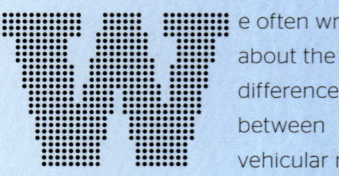e often write about the difference between vehicular necessity versus preference. The point being that none of us have unlimited budgets. In a perfect world, we'd love to outfit our bug-out vehicle with every piece of kit and performance upgrade imaginable. Since that isn't practical for all of us, we like to show you alternatives that may help spur some ideas you hadn't considered or just plain didn't know were possible. Some of you may even have fabrication skills to your credit. If that's the case, you may want to resist the temptation to buy all that great aftermarket stuff, and instead fire up the acetylene torch, pretend you're John Hannibal Smith, and customize something that'll fit your needs and financial constraints.

Take Tony Ashwill's Suzuki Carry, for instance. You may have already glanced at these photos and rolled your eyes. But before you write this vehicle off as some hopped-up truck that a custodian on a college campus would use, read on a bit further. Start thinking about a nationwide calamity, how you would react, and if your discretionary income will enable you to accomplish your pie-in-the-sky transportation plans.

While some may opt to get as far away as possible using standard highways, some others may choose to bug in and want something feasible to navigate narrow rural roadways common to the surrounding area — either to hunt, hide out, or reconnoiter for impending danger. Can this be accomplished with a full-size truck tipping the scales near 6,000 pounds even before being loaded down with people and supplies? While it may work on paper, when you think about the possibility of getting stuck or having roughly 12 mpg fuel consumption, bugging out may suddenly become bugging nearby.

While it may be small in stature, this rig still has a lot of the stuff a standard truck would have, but an ATV or side-by-side may not. Think four-wheel drive, a full cab, heater, and (although not on this particular truck) air conditioning. Because it has fully functional highway lights, depending on where you live, this truck may also qualify as street legal. So what was the impetus for this pint-sized hauler? As a Minnesota native, Tony would often go out on one of the many ATV-based roads with friends to camp, but be limited in range by the low fuel capacity of ATVs and side-by-sides. There'd also be times that one of the aforementioned vehicles would experience a flat tire or broken tie rod end and have to be towed out — not easily done by a standard vehicle or tow truck too large to fit down a narrow path.

So he started pondering what the ultimate off-road vehicle would be with a range that would enable him to stay out and about for a while, the space to pack up a bit of gear or extra passengers, and the power to possibly tow a friend's off-road

vehicle back if it got stuck. Since a standard full-size truck was too big for many of these trails and didn't get the mileage he wanted, Tony began considering mini trucks. What he found came via a pair of mini-trucks — the Suzuki and a 1993 Daihatsu Hijet at a local dealer. He was offered a better price if he bought both, so he shelled out $7,500 and took possession. Since the Daihatsu had a few features he didn't care for, he made a few mods and quickly sold it. Now, onto the Suzuki.

With a background in metal fabrication and mechanics, Tony had the eye for engineering and requisite skills to make many of the modifications himself. Since aftermarket items for these kinds of trucks are limited at best, that worked out just fine. The entire roof rack, windshield guard, taillight guards, fender flares, skid plate, and bumper guards were all custom made by Tony. Due to the uneven weight distribution, Tony added .125-inch deck plate throughout the box and tailgate to strengthen it and make the rear a bit heavier.

Storage boxes were also added to the sides, one of which houses tools and controls for the front and rear winches, and the other a standard and auxiliary battery. Seats from a Kawasaki Teryx are mounted to a removable fixture that hovers above the box and attaches to the rack. An air compressor in the bed also serves to repair flats if need be. Numerous LED and HID lights mounted front and rear take care of illuminating the backcountry when out on patrol at night. He shod the whole thing in desert tan CARC paint, and covered the interior in MultiCam synthetic material to continue the military theme.

One of the most unusual features of the truck is a custom tow bar Tony built, in case

the truck needs to serve as a mobile recovery vehicle. With a high/low transfer case and locking rear differential, this little beast has the juice to play some serious tug of war. Having drug a 1,200-pound Polaris RZR out of the sticks, this truck has proven it offers respectable payload that most people probably overlook. The tow bar can also be broken down and stored on the truck.

The suspension features some custom tweaks to make it more off-road worthy and give it an additional 2 to 3 inches of lift. The control arms were boxed for extra torsional strength. Modified car shocks were added to the front and the stock coils replaced with rear coils from a Polaris RZR, adapted with custom mounting plates. The rear has springs that have been given additional leaves, and Tony fabbed up some custom shackles to increase the ride height and keep the weight of the box from rubbing on the rear tires.

Now for those wheels. As you may have suspected, they've been improved. The original aluminum wheels were swapped out for steel ones, modified to fit the 4x115mm bolt pattern. Since that left extra holes, Tony decided to have a bit of fun with it and created faux lugs, though only four of the eight actually fasten the wheels to the hubs. To give them a three-piece beadlock look, he cut ¼-inch steel rings to fit down inside the rim, with another ring set into the outer bead of the wheel. Twenty stud holes per rim were cut to give it the look he was after. One-inch spacers were

1 FRONT AND REAR HID LIGHTS	2 FRONT LED LIGHT BAR	3 FRONT AND REAR LED VISOR LIGHTS	4 FRONT AND REAR WINCHES	5 BUMPER GUARDS	6 SKID PLATE
MAKE: 50 Caliber Racing	**MAKE:** 50 Caliber Racing	**MAKE:** Maxxima	**MAKE:** Viper Max Winch	**MAKE:** Ashwill Industries	**MAKE:** Ashwill Industries
MODEL: 4-inch	**MODEL:** 24-inch	**MODEL:** Oval LED 6-inch Reverse Lights	**MODEL:** 4,500 pound	**MODEL:** Custom	**MODEL:** Custom
URL: www.50caliberracing.com	**URL:** www.50caliberracing.com	**URL:** www.maxxima.com	**URL:** www.motoalliance.com	**EMAIL:** ashwillindustries@gmail.com	**EMAIL:** ashwillindustries@gmail.com

dass appearance. Definitely works of art.

You may be wondering about parts for these kinds of vehicles. Internet and mail order are no problem, but when going to your local parts store, don't expect to find much more than the standard replacement items readily available: coolant, spark plugs, oil, and filter. That, and being right-hand drive with a manual transmission, seems to be the only drawbacks of this truck. But we must say they don't really feel like deal breakers in the grand scheme of things.

We hope we got your creativity fired up with this out-of-the-box take on a tactical bug-out vehicle. So if you are a DIY guy and have the tools and know-how for projects like this, start humming *The A-Team* theme, get out in your garage, and see if you can drum up something similar that may save you tons of money in the long run. Tony estimates a 300-mile range with this little truck — and with extra fuel cans on the back, probably a lot more than that. So when loaded down with people and supplies, and able to bug out into some unforgiving terrain that only certain vehicles can access, this all makes a lot of sense.

added to keep the wheels from rubbing. And he didn't stop there. He welded caps to pieces of pipe, which were in turn welded to the spacers to give it a full-floating axle look. Additional studs were added to the caps to add some more oomph to the ba-

7 AIR COMPRESSOR
MAKE: Puma
MODEL: PD1006
URL: www.pumaairusa.com

8 BED RACK
MAKE: Ashwill Industries
MODEL: Custom
EMAIL: ashwillindustries@gmail.com

9 INTERIOR FABRIC
MAKE: Synthetic
MODEL: MultiCam
URL: www.atomictarp.com

10 WHEELS
MAKE: ITP
MODEL: Delta Steel
SIZE: 12x8, modified to fit 4x115mm flange
URL: www.itptires.com

11 TIRES
MAKE: Carlisle
MODEL: All Trails
SIZE: 23x8x12
URL: www.carlisletransportationproducts.com

12 TOW BAR
MAKE: Ashwill Industries
MODEL: Custom
EMAIL: ashwillindustries@gmail.com

Blade Runner

This Polaris RZR is a Sharp Addition to Your Bug-Out Kit

By John Schwartze
Photography By Yoshi Andrego

2014 POLARIS RZR FOUR-STROKE 1,000CC
AUTOMATIC PVT 2WD & 4WD

Since we know there's no one-size-fits-all tactical vehicle out there, this month we bring you another "category" to further jostle your imagination as to what exactly you might need. Whether you call it a UTV, ATV, or side-by-side, this type of four-wheeled off-roader is definitely gaining in popularity, and as described in previous articles, they can go places that a fully loaded four-wheel-drive truck just can't. In many states, these vehicles can be outfitted with horns, turn signals, mirrors, and other accessories to make them street legal — furthering their level of practicality. And since quite a few of them boast four-stroke motors, you can run straight off pump gas. How wild can you really get with these? Well, if you're Hans Luenger, putting limits on a build is not in your vocabulary.

As owner of HMF Racing, a builder of aftermarket race components for off-road vehicles, Hans is no stranger to the industry. He chose a 2014 Polaris RZR 1000 for its versatility, and because maintenance and component accessibility was comparatively easy. What initially began as a race-type vehicle eventually snowballed into a more tactical, apocalyptic theme. You can see by the pictures that this decked-out UTV should probably be using the acronym WTF instead. So if you've only thought something

1 SEATS
MAKE: Mastercraft
MODEL: 3G
URL: www.hmfracing.com

2 LIGHT BAR
MAKE: Race Parts Online
MODEL: 38-inch
URL: www.rpopowersports.com

3 CAMO WRAP
MAKE: Avery Dennison
URL: www.averydennison.com

4 NERF BARS
MAKE: HMF/IQ
URL: www.hmfracing.com

5 HID LIGHTS
MAKE: Baja Designs
MODEL: (1) Spot / (1) Pencil Beam
URL: www.bajadesigns.com

6 WINCH
MAKE: Superwinch
MODEL: 4,500-pound w/ synthetic rope
URL: www.superwinch.com

of the full-size pickup persuasion could be kitted out with some serious trimmings, think again.

Powering this nimble little ride is the factory 1,000cc engine that Hans upgraded with his proprietary HMF Dual Full exhaust package to lower weight and increase horsepower, as well as one of their Optimizer engine management systems to control the fuel curve. A UMP air filter was added to handle dusty conditions that could decrease aspiration. The stock CVT drivetrain, which can switch between 2WD and 4WD, was also given a racier TEAM clutch and Gates belts. Hans cut down the factory cage and redid it himself for a sleeker look and to add more room for roof racks, equipment, and the two solar panels that can charge both batteries in five hours with direct sunlight.

To carry additional gear, suspension duties were modified courtesy of HCR dual A-arms, Walker Evans 2.5-inch shocks, and PAC springs. What additional gear, you ask? For illumination there's not only two Baja Designs HID lights but also a 38-inch LED light bar up top. A 1,000-watt Yamaha generator in the rear and 4,500-pound Superwinch in the front with synthetic rope are also handy tools to have when needed. The Hi-Lift jackstand mounted on the side can help with extrication or any sudden repairs. Custom front and rear racks provide additional storage space, while the front rack doubles as a protective cage and the rear folds down for a table, perfect for your portable stove to sit on.

A rear-mounted camera gives the driver eyes in the back of his head and is viewed through a Pyle LCD screen inside the cockpit. Doors were converted from suicide style to standard and have integrated netting for protection. The factory center panel was replaced by a custom switch panel to operate the lights, auxiliary fan, and interior LEDs. Add to that a PCI helmet cam system so driver and passenger can hear each other, and you have one pretty dialed-in duo.

Don't worry, we didn't forget about the guns. If you saw the RPG rocket sitting on top, we regret to inform you that it's a demilled unit — but at least it's a cool conversation piece and

1 SPRINGS
MAKE: PAC Racing Springs
URL: racingsprings.com

2 SHOCKS
MAKE: Walker Evans
MODEL: 2.5-inch
URL: walkerevansracing.com

3 REAR STORAGE RACK
MAKE: HMF Racing
MODEL: custom
URL: www.hmfracing.com

4 EXHAUST
MAKE: HMF Racing
MODEL: Polaris RZR XP 1000 Dual Full System
URL: www.hmfracing.com

5 TRAILING ARMS
MAKE: HCR Racing
URL: www.hcrracing.com

6 TIRES
MAKE: Maxxis
MODEL: Bighorn 30-inch
URL: www.maxxis.com

7 WHEELS
MAKE: OMF
MODEL: 15x7-inch
URL: www.omfperformance.com

could work to bludgeon someone to death if you had nothing else for protection. Although not pictured, Hans has been known to keep a front-mounted Slide Fire BFR-556A, which will make short work of oncoming "traffic." Behind the fireproof Mastercraft 3G seats resides a Mossberg 500 12-gauge, and the driver's door holds a .45 ACP 1911 for extra peace of mind. If you just so happen to run out of ammo on all those, you can always reach for the United Cutlery M48 tomahawk, spare machete, or one of the CRKT knives in the cab. Lastly, the Avery Dennison camo wrap will help keep you incognito. In other words, you have more safety measures than Ralph Nader could've dreamed up in his wildest hallucinations.

Hans estimates a range of about 180 miles with the stock tank and a couple spare cans of fuel. He's already had it out on some long treks, such as the Hatfield McCoy trails in West Virginia. As you can see, his Northern Ohio home sees some pretty heavy snowfall, and while your daily-driver hybrid might freeze up on the way out of town, it's just another day at the office for the RZR. Is this vehicle right for you? Only you can answer that, of course, by assessing what your surrounding area would allow in terms of a bug out. If something like this is up your alley, this is a prime example of what can be done to outfit an off-road vehicle with some hardcore kit that'd still keep it practical enough for a light, quick escape plan.

1 SOLAR PANELS
MAKE: Battery Tender
MODEL: (2) 10-watt 16x24-inch
URL: www.batterytender.com

2 CAGE / FRONT STORAGE
MAKE: HMF Racing
MODEL: custom
URL: www.hmfracing.com

3 A-ARMS
MAKE: HCR Racing
URL: www.hcrracing.com

4 PISTOL
MAKE: Taurus
MODEL: Custom ceramic-coated 1911 with G10 grips
URL: www.taurususa.com

5 CAMERA/MONITOR
MAKE: Pyle
URL: www.pyleaudio.com

6 RIFLE
MAKE: Colt
MODEL: AR-15 with EOTech 557 AR223 holographic sight and G33 magnifier
URL: www.colt.com
www.eotechinc.com

2016 YAMAHA
TAILGUNNER DILLON AERO M134X INTERCEPTOR
1,000CC INLINE-FOUR WITH A TWIN NITROUS OXIDE SYSTEM
SIX-SPEED
WWW.TAILGUNNEREXHAUST.COM

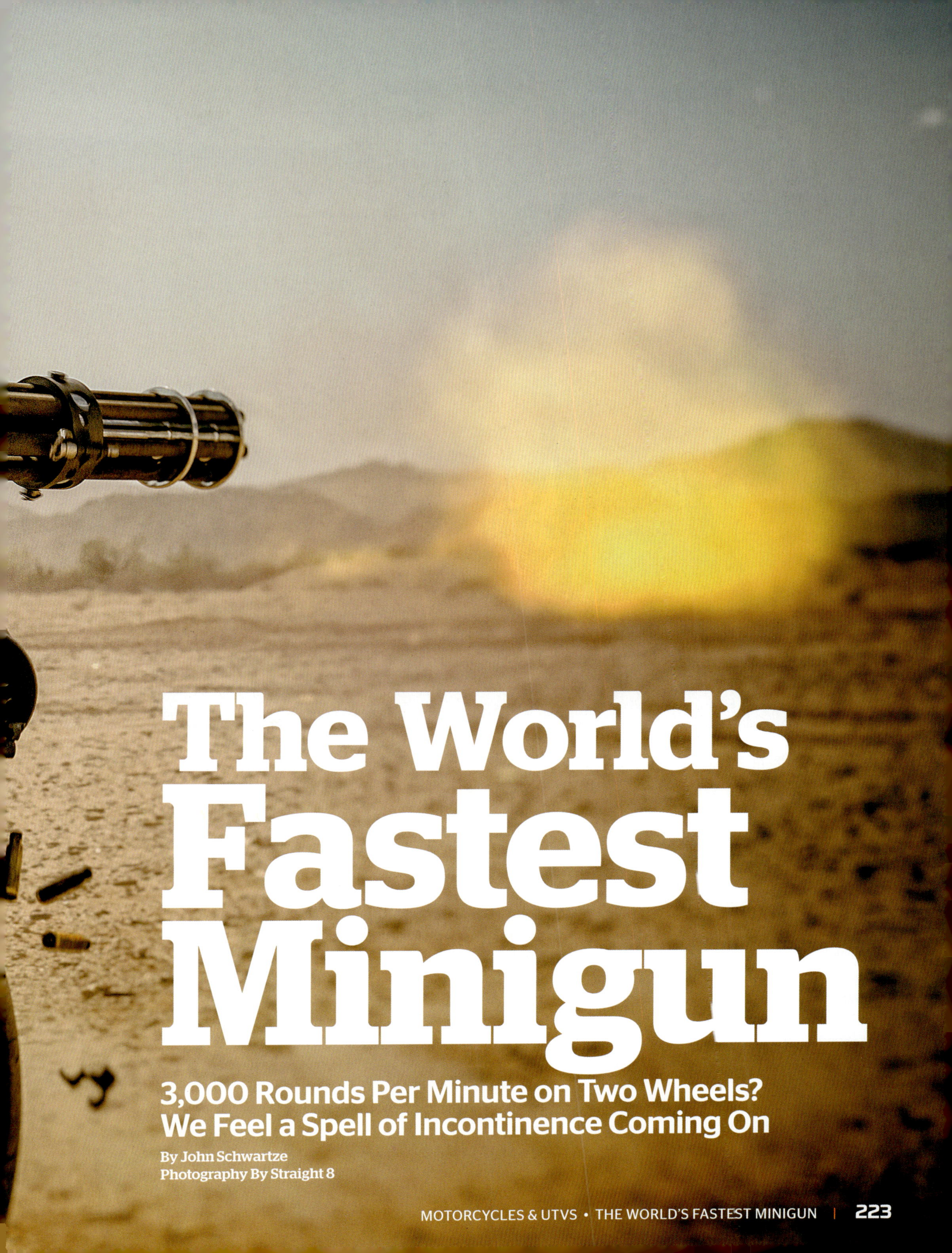

The World's Fastest Minigun

3,000 Rounds Per Minute on Two Wheels? We Feel a Spell of Incontinence Coming On

By John Schwartze
Photography By Straight 8

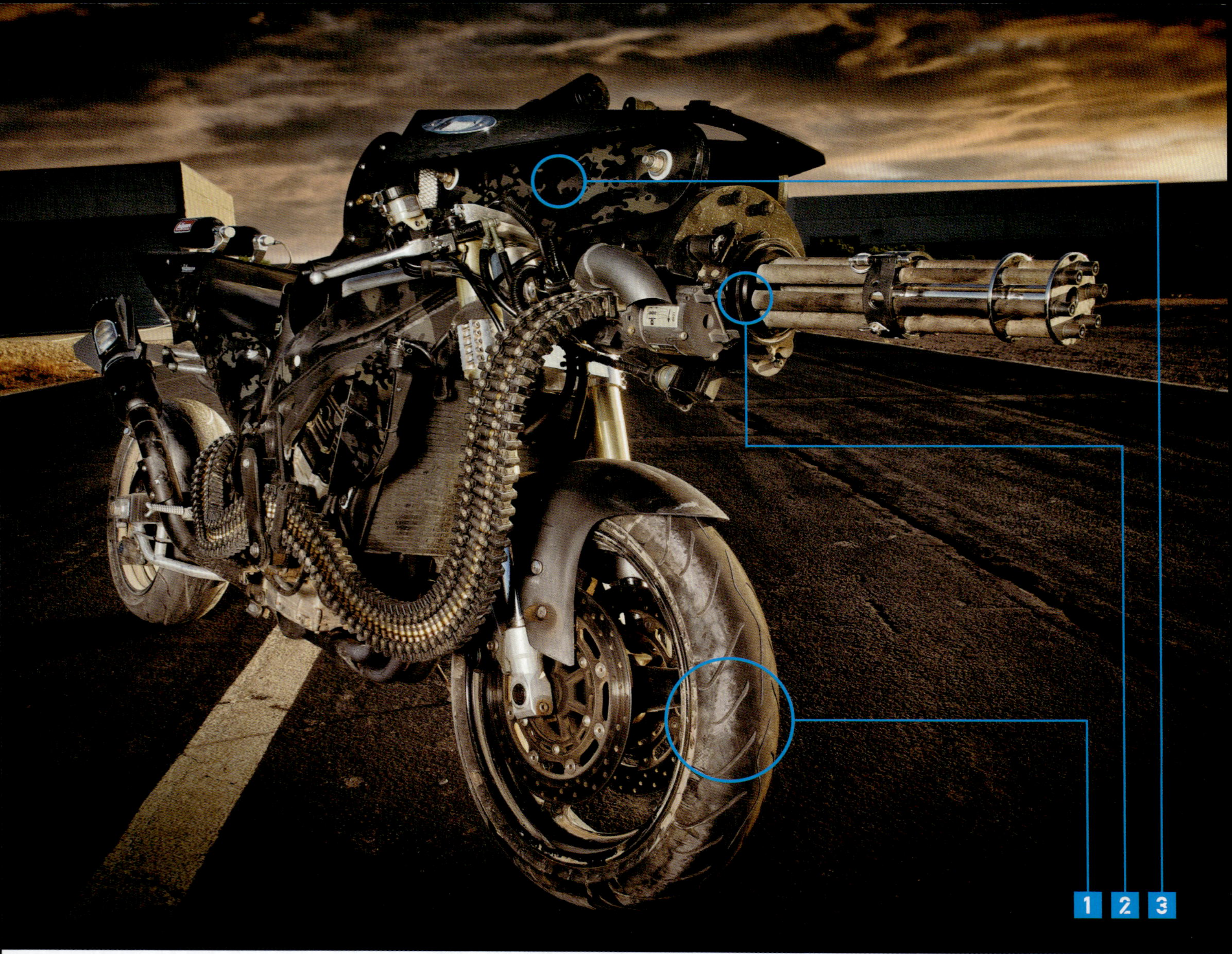

We would've loved to have been a fly on the wall when someone walked into a room and said, "You know what the world needs more of? Motorcycles with miniguns on them!" Did the people blessed with this kind of wisdom previously work as Sonny Barger's life coach? It certainly seems like every 1-percenter's wet dream. Were they perhaps former department of corrections employees who were fired over suggesting that electric chairs be replaced with electric bleachers? Perhaps they once pitched an ad-campaign slogan to Honda along the lines of, "You meet the nicest people on a motorcycle with a cannon."

Wherever the idea came from, it apparently didn't fall on deaf ears. What was once only possible in movies has finally been brought to life, and RECOIL was privileged to see it in action. Lane splitting just took on a whole new meaning.

Brainstorming sessions between Dillon Aero and Tailgunner Exhaust led to something that looks like the bastard son of Blue Thunder. The Tailgunner Dillon Aero M134X Interceptor, as it's called, found its way to our email inbox — so we sent our editor, Iain Knievel, out to investigate the situation further. We were all curious to see if this thing was intended for anything other than a potential reboot of *Street Hawk* (congrats if you even remember that show).

Our research revealed that the M134X was truly an engineering masterpiece. That's because the brains behind it really know their craft. You may have seen the work of brothers Cal and Charlie Giordano, proprietors of Tailgunner Exhaust, not only in their Gatling gun-inspired exhaust systems, but creations such as a handmade submarine that have appeared in episodes of *Modern Marvels*. They decided to approach the minigun gurus at Dillon Aero about creating a promotional conceptual bike. Unlike many concept vehicles that are all show and no go, this one was engineered to be fully functional

1 TIRES
MAKE: Metzeler
MODEL: 120/70-ZR17, front; 190/50-ZR17, back
URL: metzeler.com/site/us/

2 MINIGUN
MAKE: Dillon Aero
MODEL: M134D, 7.62x51mm NATO
URL: www.dillonaero.com

3 VINYL WRAP
MAKE: Crye Precision
MODEL: Multicam
URL: cryeprecision.com

and designed for the average rider to operate.

To our knowledge, mounting a functioning minigun to a motorcycle chassis was never attempted until now. The 300 pounds of recoil generated by the 7.62 NATO-caliber M134 was enough to make people believe that such a feat defied the laws of physics and begged too many unanswerable questions. Even if it could be fired while riding, how long would it take before the frame began to tear? Could it be aimed with any degree of accuracy? Was the driver guaranteed a Darwin Award?

The bike was built not only to defy the naysayers of minigun versatility, but also as a way to deploy the weapon system to the field quickly or to catch a fast-moving vehicle. In order to create a bike that drove and handled well enough to do all this, they chose the proven Yamaha R1 Superbike chassis as the platform. Its aluminum frame and high power-to-weight ratio enables the package to be light on its feet.

To disperse the load, Tailgunner created an aluminum cantilever mount for the gun that attaches where the custom extended swing-arm connects. The linear actuator enables the gun to be moved up and down by a switch located where the turn signal formerly resided. The custom fuel tanks were moved to the rear of the bike for better balance. Heavy-duty billet aluminum steering yokes were also specially made for the project. Body panels are all fabricated from aircraft-grade aluminum and covered in MultiCam wrap by Crye Precision. Believe it or not, the whole bike only weighs about 500 pounds.

An air intake was built into the mount and two external air filters

Minigun Musings

Don't think the fun stops there. Cal made this super shorty Timemachinist AR-M134X to complement the Tailgunner Dillon Aero M134X project. It's an all-billet build based on a Sharps lower and a custom-made Timemachinist/Tailgunner Gatling-style upper. Since the motorcycle itself and miniguns are nearly unobtainable to the public, you might be seeing AR Gatling Gun-inspired full-float tubes for sale in the future if the interest is there. The barrels don't spin, but this pistol version has a Noveske 7.5 Diplomat barrel inside it. While the AR-M134X was designed to look like a minigun barrel assembly, it was engineered to function as a high-performance handguard. Check out more of Cal's work, such as his custom watches, at **www.timemachinistwatches.com**.

were mounted up high to allow for better filtration and easy maintenance. The bike is powered by a Yamaha 1,000cc inline-four with a twin nitrous oxide system. It's all mated to the six-speed Yamaha transmission. The electronics are powered by a 12-volt battery that runs the motorcycle, with a separate 24-volt battery mounted inside the swingarm to operate the gun. A large Samsung smartphone in front of the driver serves as instrumentation to keep it simple.

The motorcycle doesn't have to be running to fire. The gun can be armed with a switch on the console in front of the driver. The trigger is very appropriately located where the horn button was. Aiming is accomplished by moving the cantilever up or down and steering the bike right or left. Although that's really dead reckoning in terms of accuracy, a laser sight and gun-mounted camera may be added in the future, with reticles appearing on the smartphone.

After two years of trial and error, a finished bike finally met the standards of all parties involved. The M134X will be put up for sale when its promotional duties are completed, and it is, in fact, street legal (without the gun, of course, unless you have the proper permits). Tailgunner could even create a replica if the money's there. Civilian and law enforcement versions are already in the works.

Not only have the minds involved disproven the notion that mounting a minigun on a motorcycle was impossible, but they showed that it could be done in a practical way. Who knows, maybe we'll see M134Xs roaming the battlefield one day with additions such as smoke screens, oil slicks, or caltrops. It seems the fellas at Tailgunner figured out a way to channel the spirits of Richard Gatling and Burt Munro. Nice to know guys who can come up with things like this are on our side. Check out the full videos on RECOILtv at www.recoilweb.com to see the M134X in action.

1 BODY PANELS

MAKE:
Custom

MODEL:
Aircraft-grade aluminum

URL:
www.tailgunnerexhaust.com

2 EXHAUST

MAKE:
Tailgunner Exhaust

MODEL:
Custom

URL:
www.tailgunnerexhaust.com

Unbroken

We Tried to Break the Yamaha Wolverine X4, But it May Very Well Be the Vehicular Version of Louie Zamperini

By John Schwartze
Photography By Iain Harrison

ur staff takes pride in testing manufacturer claims. Whenever companies want to take a chance on us trying out their products, especially the four-wheel kind, there's a ravenous anticipation among the staff akin to that of wolves finding stray deer. Given the chance to try out Yamaha's new Wolverine X4 was something we welcomed with open arms and a heavy right foot. We were ready to treat it like the BATFE treats Branch Davidians, but our inability to snap, burn out, blow up, or otherwise return the vehicle to Yamaha in pieces with a heartfelt "oops" and shrugged shoulders earned this UTV some well-deserved respect.

You may remember our coverage of the Minigun Motorcycle in Issue 30, which was built on a Yamaha R1 Superbike chassis. Since its builders chose the aforementioned platform to create that monstrosity around, we knew breaking the Wolverine would be a challenge. Yamaha already had the benefit of the doubt because of its reputation for quality. But first a little history on this model to provide some context. Its ability to suit a variety of tasks was an eyebrow raiser.

The Wolverine has been a part of Yamaha's fleet for a while and evolved to incorporate the beefier benefits of a utility chassis, but in a sportier package. With the recent addition of the X4 four-passenger version with sliding/folding rear seats, it's got more room for passengers and gear. Want a solid trail explorer? Check. Looking for a vehicle that'll perform ranching or agricultural tasks and also double for recreational use? Good to go. Need to haul up to 2,000 pounds worth of trailered ancillaries? You see where we're going with this.

One of the common misconceptions buyers often have when kicking tires is engine size. They have their heart set on a displacement or horsepower amount that's quite a far cry from real-world practicality. As the saying goes: Horsepower sells cars; torque wins races. Sure, the Wolverine X4 might not keep up with other models intended for pedal mashing across flat desert, but we wouldn't be racing the Mint 400 with it. When it comes to the needs of the firearms crowd, it checks off the proverbial dance card nicely with a good equilibrium of power, balance, handling, and storage capacity.

To get a little granular for the gearheads, here's what you get in terms of drivetrain. The engine is a four-stroke 847cc liquid-

2018 YAMAHA
WOLVERINE X4 SE
847CC
ULTRAMATIC V-BELT WITH ALL-WHEEL ENGINE BRAKING
WWW.YAMAHAMOTORSPORTS.COM

cooled twin-cylinder that's surprisingly quiet. It's all hooked to an Ultramatic V-belt drive trans with low, high, neutral, and reverse gearing. An on-command locking differential gives the driver 2WD, 4WD, and full diff-lock 4WD capabilities, rather than the sensing version seen on some other UTVs that's automatically activated when the vehicle thinks it needs to come on.

We plotted our route from Phoenix to Prescott, Arizona, and back via old mining roads, as we felt the topography and landscape would more than adequately test how much damage the Wolverine would or wouldn't withstand. Although it may not have the speed some of its contemporaries do, when we were out on the open road with it, it had more than enough power to get where we needed to go and carry what we needed to carry.

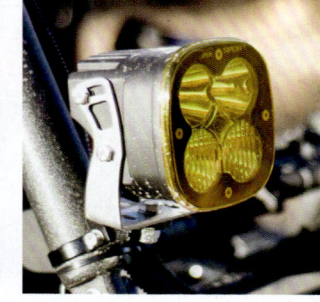

1 GIMBAL
MAKE: FLIR
MODEL: M324
URL: www.flir.com

2 LIGHTBAR
MAKE: OnX6
MODEL: 10" LED Lightbar
URL: www.bajadesigns.com

3 LIGHTS
MAKE: Baja Designs
MODEL: XL Sport LED
URL: www.bajadesigns.com

4 GUN SCABBARD
MAKE: Condition Zero Mounts
MODEL: Rackbone Clamp
URL: conditionzeromounts.com

Independent rear suspension with self-leveling shocks provide for a pretty comfortable ride. You certainly won't get this kind of comfort from a Jeep Rubicon used in the same environment without modifying the hell out of the suspension. With the amount of travel the Wolverine offers, it gives damn near a Trophy Truck level of stability and responsiveness. The power steering doesn't overcompensate to the point where the vehicle is controlling you, rather than you controlling it. Although some might think it's not responsive enough, we think the Wolverine lets the driver sense the feedback and adjust to the road conditions. Since it's meant to haul multiple passengers as well as cargo, we think that's just fine.

Like a good AR, the freedom to accessorize to your personal preference is another benefit this package has going for it. Adding a winch or snowplow, upgrading to a heated and enclosed cab version to go hunting with a few guys in the dead of winter, or adding a stereo are just some of the in-house options, and that doesn't even scratch the surface of what aftermarket companies have out there.

Our journey through the rocky desert landscape was in no way meant to be polite. We traversed some areas that looked like something meant for the Mars Rover at wide-open throttle. There may have even been some shouts of "ramming speed!" said among the occupants. We encountered plenty of ravines and boulders in our path that we negotiated without a problem.

There were deliberate and occasional "bangs" that came from the frame and suspension components hitting things that were even enough to startle us into getting out for a quick inspection. Despite the alarming sounds of our aggressive driving, we never got a flat, started leaking fluid, or experienced a breakage that sidelined the vehicle ... so we kept right on going until the gas tank dried up.

So what does all this equate to? Compared to its contemporaries, it's cheaper than a Polaris General, has more room than a Honda Pioneer, and offers more power than a Kawasaki Teryx. So if you're in the market to purchase a UTV, you may want to kick tires or take one out for a spin to get a feel for our experience with it. We wished we had more time with it. Not only because it was fun, but we really, really wanted to break it. Although we failed in that mission, our conclusion is that it's a sound investment.

1 STORAGE
MAKE: Daystar
MODEL: Cam Cans
URL: 4wheelparts.com

Overland Toy-Hauler

Tactical Application Vehicles' Supercharged, Long-Travel Tundra is Not Your Average Tow Rig

By Patrick McCarthy

Traditionally, the term "toy-hauler" refers to a fifth-wheel trailer with a loading ramp and enough interior space for motorcycles, ATVs, or UTVs. It's a convenient way to travel to the lake, sand dunes, or mountains — when you arrive at your destination, the family piles out of the truck, the toys are backed out of the portable garage, and the trailer is converted into sleeping arrangements. It's a tried-and-true formula ... but what if there were a better way? Walt Wagner, founder of Tactical Application Vehicles, believes he has found one. He and his team at the TAV workshop in Albuquerque built this 2018 Toyota Tundra into his concept of the ultimate overland toy-hauler. It blends the go-anywhere versatility of an overland camper, the practicality of a tow rig, and the high-speed performance of an off-road race truck.

The project began with a stock Cement gray Tundra 4x4 Double Cab. Much like TAV's first project truck, the 2009 "Ranger Goat" Tacoma we wrote about in Issue 6 of CARNIVORE magazine, this Tundra is equipped with a full long-travel suspension setup. This enables the truck to fly down washboard fire roads and soak up bumps, even when it's loaded down with passengers, cargo, and fuel. The suspension consists of a Total Chaos Fabrication long-travel kit with secondary shock hoops, King coilovers and bypass shocks, Alcan leaf springs, and King air bumpstops. For optimal ride quality and smoothness, TAV special-ordered custom shock valving and spring rates for the Tundra.

Since this truck is used for towing, Walt added a Magnuson supercharger to the 5.7L V-8 and installed higher-ratio 5.29 Nitro Gear ring and pinion sets in both differentials. This provides improved torque and low-end acceleration, helping to get the 17-inch Method Race Wheels and 37-inch Toyo mud tires up to highway speeds faster. Front and rear ARB air lockers allow the Tundra to crawl up steep inclines when it's not on tow duty. A 46-gallon fuel tank from LRA makes gas station stops a rarity.

The Tundra's most notable feature is its FiftyTen Full-Size Camping System, which replaces the entire bed with an assemblage of angular sheet metal. This German com-

MOTORCYCLES & UTVS • OVERLAND TOY-HAULER | 233

The Tundra and Can-Am make a perfect pair, with one vehicle for high-speed trail fun and one to serve as an off-grid basecamp.

pany has been manufacturing overland campers since 2017, but only recently entered the North American market; the TAV Tundra was one of the first vehicles in the U.S. equipped with this setup.

Its lower flatbed portion includes locking storage compartments and a slide-out rear drawer; the upper camper portion opens on three sides and pops up to reveal a spacious rooftop tent. Between the camper and cab, there's a slot for a full-size spare tire. Walt also liked that the camper shell is removable, so the Tundra can be used in flatbed configuration as a work truck. But with a base price of $38,400, this system requires deep pockets.

Image Craft printed a custom MultiCam Black vinyl wrap for the FiftyTen camper, which was installed by Revive Wraps. The Tundra's hood was also wrapped in matching material. Other exterior mods include wide fiberglass fenders from McNeil Racing, a Prinsu roof rack with Zarges aluminum storage case, a C4 Fabrication front bumper, and an array of Baja Designs LED lights.

As if this truck build wasn't impressive enough on its own, Walt paired it with a customized 2019 Can-Am Maverick X3. This 172-horsepower UTV was quick in stock form, but Walt added a Stage 1 tune, clutch weights, and a drive belt from EVP to make it even quicker. It also received a list of suspension mods just as extensive as the Tundra's — Geiser Performance arms, TMW bulkhead gussets, ZRP billet spindles, ZRP radius rods and dog bone supports, a Shock Therapy billet steering rack, and much more. All this rides on a set of 15-inch Method Race Wheels 401 Beadlocks wrapped in 32-inch STI Chicane RX tires.

The TMW front bumper is outfitted with more Baja Designs LED lights and a winch, while the Geiser

MultiCam Black vinyl on the camper and hood contrasts nicely with the Tundra's Cement gray paint.

Doors on all three sides of the FiftyTen camper offer easy access to gear within. If more space is needed, the camper shell can be removed entirely, leaving a versatile flatbed.

234 | OFFGRIDWEB.COM

The cockpit is equipped with a powerful Rockford Fosgate sound system, a VHF/UHF radio with intercom headsets, and an sPOD controller for the auxiliary lights.

With a spare tire carrier, tire extinguishers, jerry cans of fuel, two winches, and much more, this UTV is prepared for almost any emergency — day or night.

TAV STAGE 3 2018 TOYOTA TUNDRA

DRIVETRAIN: 5.7L V-8 with Magnuson supercharger, six-speed automatic transmission, Nitro Gear 5.29 ring and pinion, ARB front and rear air locking differentials, LRA 46-gallon fuel tank

FRONT SUSPENSION: Total Chaos Fabrication 2.5-inch long-travel system with secondary shock hoops, King 2.5-inch Performance adjustable coilovers, King 3.0-inch triple-bypass secondary shocks

REAR SUSPENSION: TAV-spec Alcan progressive-rate leaf springs, Total Chaos Fabrication rear shock relocation kit, TAV-spec King 3.0-inch internal-bypass shocks, King 2.0-inch Air Bumpstops

WHEELS & TIRES: 17x8.5 Method Race Wheels 704 Trail Series, 37x12.5R17 Toyo Open Country M/T

BODY MODIFICATIONS: C4 Fabrication Overlander Series front bumper, ComeUp Seal Gen2 12.5RS winch, RCI skid plates, McNeil Racing fiberglass fenders, Prinsu roof rack, Baja Designs LED lights

FLATBED CAMPER: FiftyTen Full-Size Camping System with Image Craft / Revive Wraps MultiCam Black vinyl wrap

IN TOW: TAV modified 2019 Can-Am Maverick X3 X rc Turbo R

URL: tavllc.com

Performance rear bumper holds a full-size spare tire. The X3 also has a Geiser Performance custom cage with windshield, SDR Motorsports doors wrapped in MultiCam Black, and a Front Runner roof rack that TAV modified to fit the UTV. Inside, Walt and his copilot — usually his daughter — can settle into the TMW Triple X bucket seats, crank up the Rockford Fosgate Stage 4 stereo, and communicate at speed via intercom headsets hooked up to the Rugged

Radios VHF/UHF system. Recovery equipment and other emergency gear is stashed in the TMW rear storage bag and Zarges hard case.

This combination of truck and UTV gives Walt the best of both worlds — a platform for comfortable long-distance travel with the whole family, and the thrills of a high-speed trail vehicle. He drives the Tundra on a daily basis, using it to haul parts for the shop. On the weekends, he can lower the camper onto the bed, strap the Can-Am to the trailer, and escape civilization at a moment's notice.

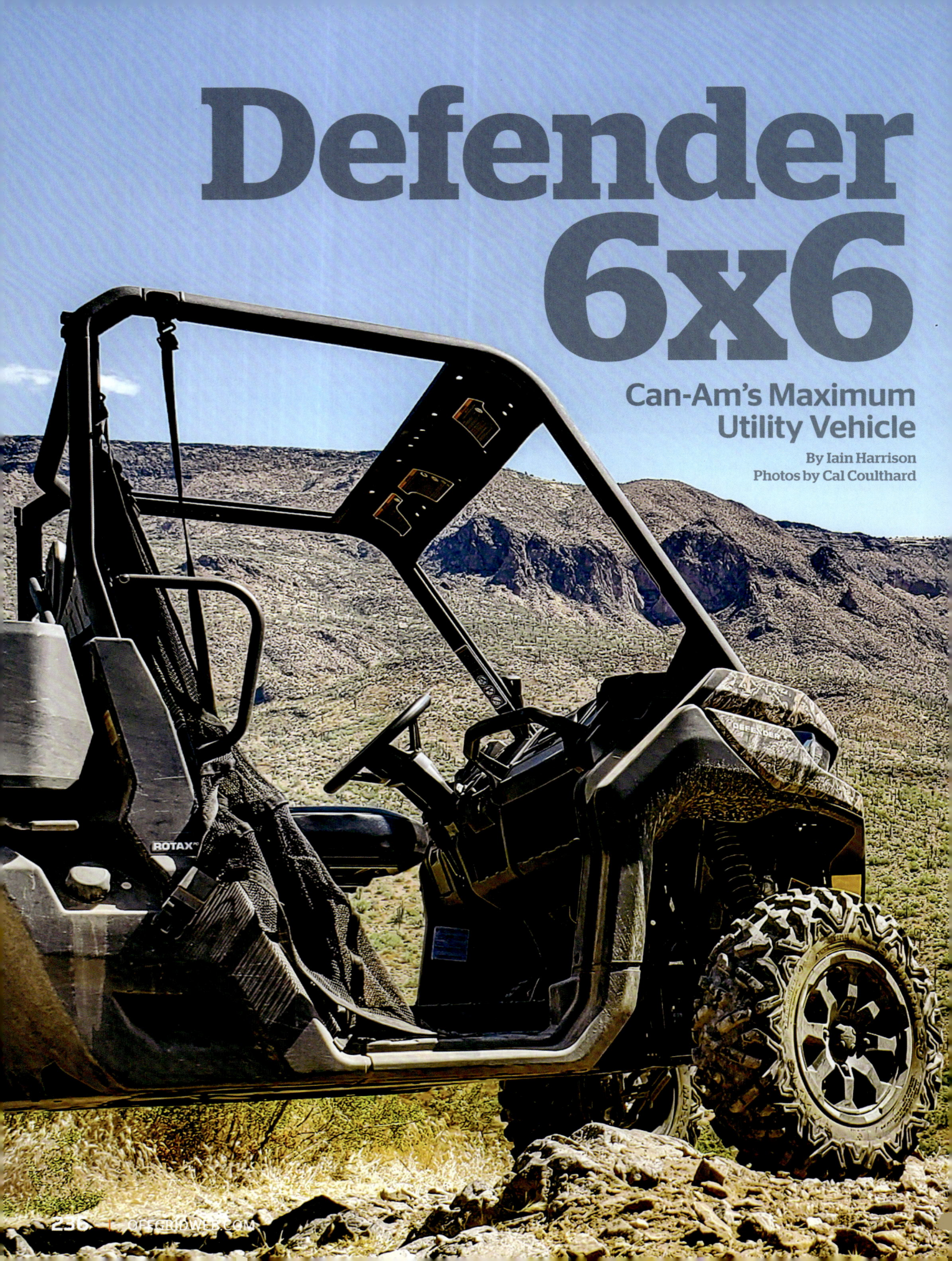

Defender 6x6

Can-Am's Maximum Utility Vehicle

By Iain Harrison
Photos by Cal Coulthard

When it comes to real-world performance, raw numbers rarely tell the full story. So in order to dig a little deeper we spent two months using and abusing Can-Am's Defender 6x6 for everything from high-country camping trips, to moving material, to hucking it over jumps, and thrashing it through off-road obstacles that make lifted-and-locked Rubicons shudder. And despite its homely looks and lack of 37-inch tires, it performs way better than you'd imagine.

Powered by a 976cc Rotax twin-cylinder mill, producing 82 ponies and 69 lb-ft of torque, this utility machine has plenty of low-geared power to climb the steepest terrain, and climb it does. We nicknamed it "the goat," due to its performance on a particularly steep and loose test climb that has bested several of its competitors — about two thirds of the way up a half-mile-long ascent comprised of broken, fist-sized rocks, there's an 18-inch-high ledge that catches the left tire of most UTVs and causes them to lose traction. At which point, you have no choice but to slap it in reverse and back down for another attempt. In the Defender, we climbed it empty, we climbed it with a passenger, and we climbed it with two passengers, five bales of hay, and a pair of dogs perched on top. Each time, it chugged away as if nothing was out of the ordinary and this was just another day at the office.

It's equipped with a tipping bed that measures 72 by 54.5 by 10 inches, and this was the first feature we wanted to test. Figuring that anyone buying this is going to want to load it down with a ton of crap, we loaded it down with a ton of crap. Well, to be entirely accurate: 1,000 pounds or thereabouts of well-rotted horse manure from the pile behind the barn. The single gas strut that serves to tilt the bed is completely overwhelmed when asked to lift a load like this, so you'll wind up dropping the tailgate, accelerating to around 10 mph in reverse, and then slamming on the

Left: Engine braking from the one-liter twin makes for controlled descents, but the lack of a windshield on the base model means you're going to need a wet suit.

Below: 27x11-inch tires provide plenty of grip. When they're in contact.

411 Check out the full video at Recoil.tv to see the defender in action.

Above: Propelled by 82 horsepower from its liquid-cooled parallel twin, the Defender's top speed is limited to 65 mph and takes a while to get there.

Right: Arched A-arms give plenty of clearance and 11 inches of suspension travel, damped by coilovers on all six wheels. You'll want to dial in some preload on the fronts — trust us.

anchors to shift some weight to the rear, but the rest of the vehicle handles a maximum payload without protest. We also put it to work carting tools and materials around a jobsite, and it plays the part of a mini pickup just fine.

For those of us who chase elk around the western states, the Defender's combination of payload and agility means that single-person recovery of an animal is an appealing possibility. Our test vehicle was a bare-bones, bottom-spec version, but we could see that with the addition of a winch, it wouldn't take much to pass the cable over the steel ROPS cab, hook up your wapiti, and winch it into the bed. Anyone who's tried manhandling a corner at a time into a pickup truck knows what a struggle this can be, even with two people. One other option we'd be inclined to add would be a windshield, as the engineers at Can-Am are evidently possessed of a wry sense of humor. Why else would they design the front of the vehicle in such a way that the smallest of water crossings results in the entire bow wave ending up in the driver's lap? Now, we could possibly roll through the wet stuff at a more sedate pace, but that wouldn't be anywhere near as much fun.

It's not until you start asking the Defender to do things it wasn't designed for, that you start bumping up against some limitations. If you compare its specs to sport UTVs of just a decade ago, you might reach the conclusion that it can hang with an older Polaris

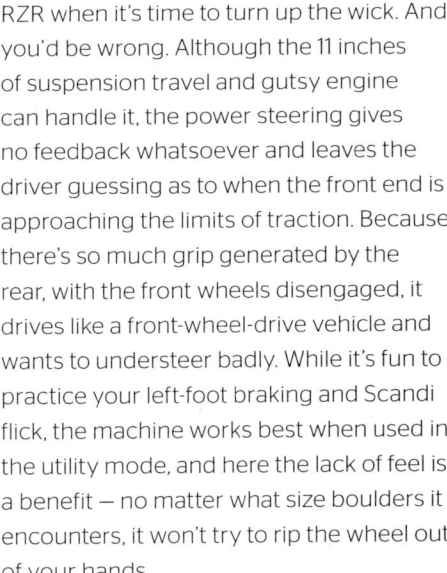

CAN-AM DEFENDER 6X6 DPS HD10

COLOR: Mossy Oak
LENGTH/WIDTH/HEIGHT: 154.1 by 64 by 78 inches
WHEELBASE: 115.5 inches
GROUND CLEARANCE: 13 inches
DRY WEIGHT: 1,945 pounds
MOTOR: Rotax 976cc V-twin
WHEELS: 14-inch
PRICE: $18,699
URL: can-am.brp.com

Far left: Fourteen-inch alloy wheels are shod with aggressive Maxxis Bighorn tires, though six-wheel drive means you'd still get enough traction if they were made of Jell-O.

Left: Look, this must be the hunting model 'cos it's got some camo on it. We wonder how long it'll take this to turn purple in the Arizona sun.

Left: Gear selector is notchy, but straightforward to use. Drive to the front wheels is engaged by means of a toggle switch on the dash.

RZR when it's time to turn up the wick. And you'd be wrong. Although the 11 inches of suspension travel and gutsy engine can handle it, the power steering gives no feedback whatsoever and leaves the driver guessing as to when the front end is approaching the limits of traction. Because there's so much grip generated by the rear, with the front wheels disengaged, it drives like a front-wheel-drive vehicle and wants to understeer badly. While it's fun to practice your left-foot braking and Scandi flick, the machine works best when used in the utility mode, and here the lack of feel is a benefit — no matter what size boulders it encounters, it won't try to rip the wheel out of your hands.

To say we came away impressed after our 60-day evaluation would be an understatement. Despite our best efforts, we couldn't find a job around the ranch or jobsite it couldn't do, and it wasn't until we really heaped on the abuse that we found it wanting. As equipped, the base model could use a couple of upgrades and at 18 grand it's not exactly cheap, but as a tool, it's as versatile as a Swiss Army knife and tough as a hammer. Check out our episode on the Can-Am Defender at www.recoil.tv.

Two-Wheel Torque

We Get Hands-On With the Rokon, a Motorcycle That Needs No Roads

By David H. Martin

ith one twist of its throttle, the stout Rokon motorcycle can transform from a rubber-burning all-terrain vehicle to a gravity-defying projectile that can down an incoming enemy helicopter, sacrificing its own life to heroically save your entire team from a deadly strafing run. Naturally, this can only be done if you're Sylvester Stallone, your team includes Jason Statham, and the helo is a prop in *Expendables 2*.

Artistic license aside, its movie-star turn serves to illustrate what its loyalists have believed for nearly 50 years: the Rokon is not only America's best kept secret weapon, but also the ultimate transporter that can practically roll on, over, and through almost everything.

The modern-day Rokon stakes its claim as the second-oldest U.S. motorcycle in constant production. Remaining true to its heritage, today's Rokon closely resembles the simple schematics that inventor Charles Henry Fehn first submitted with his patent applications in 1958 when he called it the Trail-Breaker. The patent was granted in 1966, and even today's models are instantly recognizable as offshoots of the original version, what with the MIG-welded steel frames and tractor-like 8x12x25 Titan tire treads over hollow aluminum drum wheels. In fact, the sealable drum wheels hold 2.6 gallons each of water or fuel, so you could almost triple the amount of fuel available on board from the standard 2.69-gallon fuel tank. Its four-stroke, fan-cooled 7hp Kohler 208cc engine is mated to a three-speed automatic torque-converter transmission.

With a burn rate of ¼ gallon per hour, and with a running speed of, say, 30 mph, your bug-out-route range will approach 330 miles on one 2.69-gallon tank before you tap into the wheel reservoirs for two additional fill-ups for a total range of over 900 miles. And if things get to *Mad Max: Fury Road* levels of desperation, you can always sling another tank on the back.

And, OK, the Rokon does not fly. But when each wheel drum is left empty, the 218-pound Rokon may be laid on its side and floated across open water, carburetor up. "What good is a floating bike?" you might ask. What if your bug-out route brings you to a deep creek or river and a roadblock is set up at the only bridge crossing for 200 miles? Try wading chest deep with your dual-sport bike or ATV.

A pair of Rokons relied upon by the U.S. Forest Service to hit the trails inaccessible to ATVs and quads.

"Rock and Row"

From his 1915 birth in San Bernardino to his passing in 1972, Fehn lived in Southern California with a penchant for invention and seeking investors, demo-ing the Trail-Breaker in steep sand dunes or by driving over the dropped tailgate and into the bed of his El Camino. Through development of an innovative clutch, front and rear chain-driven wheels, and gearing system, Fehn's ideas enabled the rider to maneuver in tight turns without grounding — a system that has since undergone considerable refinement.

Early bikes were sold in kit form or from various distributors, the most successful being Orla Larsen. Larsen named his distributorship company Rokon, after his Vermont ski lodge that he called "On The Rocks." While some die-hards still pronounce the motorcycle name "Rock-on," the universal pronunciation is "Row-con."

Today the company is enjoying a resurgence as Rokon International, Inc., based in Rochester, New Hampshire, with 29 dealers in the U.S. and eight overseas. Factory-direct custom order sales are strong with Rokons arriving at dealers and doorsteps around the country, said President Tom Blais.

If the Internet's latest "ultimate" bug-out jeep, truck, or tank is beyond your financial reach or free space in your garage, consider adding a Rokon as your bug-out vehicle. For those who have the scratch, it could also serve as a secondary ride mounted on your truck bed or on a trailer hitch. It's available in street legal or strictly off-road versions and is highly customizable from dealer options. Dual-sport bikes fit the higher speed, on-road/on-trail route scenario very well (see RECOIL Issue 10, and OFFGRID Issue 7 or turn to "(No) Easy Rider, our feature on motorbike techniques, elsewhere in this issue). Still, when SHTF, Rokon riders say the low and stable two-wheel-drive difference is unbelievable if you have to leave the urban landscape and go beyond established trails, all the while towing a trailer or dragging big-game behind you.

In-The-Dirt Testing

In a series of real-world tests, we were able to validate the Rokon's billy-goat-meets-Big-Foot qualities by joining a small group of hardcore riders on a 200-mile journey deep within the Ocala National Forest. There the U.S. Forest Service Rangers receive training on the usage of the Rokon for taking chainsaws and other gear deep within trails that are too narrow for ATVs. Rangers favor the low-pressure Rokon tires (3.5 pounds psi) and spark arrestor mufflers in the deep sugar sand, inclines, and muddy crossings. The tubeless tires are said to leave less pressure than a human footprint, passing easily between narrow trees on handlebar-width trails. The bikes also can perform search-and-recovery efforts, even towing out other vehicles with a ball hitch if needed.

"These Rokons are not about speed," said one of the riders, a retired U.S. Army brigadier general who once demo'd the Rokons for the Pentagon. "These are about torque. These are about getting from Point A to Point B when there is little or no path before you and you must absolutely arrive. They are unstoppable. They will go where a dirt bike, quad, or ATV will not pass."

Rokons feel very different from traditional dirt and street bikes or ATVs and require a shift in thinking. All Rokon controls are accomplished by the hands. The unsprung, folding front or rear foot pegs serve only to support the rider and passenger's sturdy boots while riding, allowing the riders to place one or both feet on the ground to steady the bike on slow maneuvers and obstacles.

The tractor-like tires and high (14-inch) ground clearance allowed seesaw, teeter-totter log crossings by

shifting weight fore and aft. Compared to high-riding dirt bikes, the Rokon's low-seat position inspired confidence while traversing slopes.

Although one novice rider laid his bike down about three times in deep shifting sands, the rider was never thrown and was faulted more than the bike. These were not bunny slopes, and the fact that a beginner could negotiate these hills is a tribute to the bike's low center of gravity and pure torque.

Orientation commences with powerful front and rear hydraulic disc brake levers, with the left hand braking the rear and the throttle hand controlling the front. Both brakes are mounted high to keep them free from mud and water. The left hand also controls a black engine emergency "kill" button that shuts off the engine if the bike goes down, plus headlight switch. Above all, we insist on opting for the "Brush Buster" optional handguards to protect the grips and hands from impacts with trees, rocks, or any other obstacles.

Getting Hands On

On the lower right-hand side, fuel management is controlled by the fuel tank shutoff valve, for storing or transporting the Rokon. Close by and beneath the choke, an engine fuel valve is opened for riding and closed for storing the motorcycle. The fuel tank cap air valve may be closed to air intake in the event the Rokon is floated sideways — during our test, this was followed by an immediate and sure start. Some early model bikes attending were equipped with snorkels for exceeding the recommended maximum operating depth of 24 inches.

With the engine in neutral, and using the three-position (anti-theft) ignition key switched to on, the Rokon is started either from a steady pull on the right-side starter rope or from an optional key electrical starter.

What sets the Rokon apart from other motorcycles is the sealed three-range transmission that appears as a straight shaft inline horizontal plunger on the lower right side of the bike, with a black ball end. Shifting is not done on the move, but from a dead stop and only then at idle speed or when the engine is off. Grasping the plunger ball and pulling outward all the way brings the bike into first gear. If needed, gently rock the bike until the gears synch. The shift pattern from the inside to the outside is as follows: third, neutral, second, neutral, first. There's no reverse. To turn the bike in tight quarters, it may be pivoted 180 degrees on its kickstand.

The Rokon may be started in gear, with one hand lightly on the brake lever and without revving the engine. From any gear, the Rokon may be run from a dead standstill to the top speed range of its gear. When coupled with the automatic torque converter, it has extremely broad capabilities from steep grade climbing to routine routes. The torque converter provides a large overlap of speed and torque between gears, making frequent gear changes unnecessary and eliminating the need to shift on the move. In the event a dangerous encounter occurs, the Rokon may be brought to an abrupt stop, still in gear at idle speed, and hands switched to sidearm or

△ Testing the Rokon's flotation at lakeside. With carb side up, the Rokon creates a splash, but comes up and starts.

< Auto-Grab suspension has 8 inches of travel, and the aluminum wheel holds 2.6 gallons of water or fuel.

< With the front wheel chain guards removed, proper chain tensioning and lubrication is accomplished with simple wrenches.

Front suspension soaks up the drop

long-gun without downshifting or going to neutral. Even in third, one twist of the throttle later, and you are gone.

The torque converter is designed especially for Rokon and provides smooth automatic clutching and ratio changing in response to throttle control and terrain requirements, all without loss of engine revs or power, as the front and rear-driven pulleys transfer power through the gears to the front or rear chain drives.

We crawled and drove up tree trunks and ditches in first, floated through sand in second, and hauled down logging roads in third, although some expert riders never left third and managed the responsive throttle beautifully.

For many years, riders had only an adjustable seat spring for one or two riders and low-pressure tires to absorb vibrations while covering terrain. More recently Rokon offers a new Auto-Grab front suspension, allowing for 8 inches of shock travel via a swing-arm pivoted at the bottom of the front fork. In order to maintain proper chain tension as the suspension moves, a second chain was added up front on a dual idler sprocket, adding a slight amount of weight and improving traction. Rokon's Geoff Richardson said the front spring was developed at the insistence of the Jordanian military for ease of negotiating asphalt that's pockmarked with mortar rounds. Jordan now imports its own Rokons and assembles them in a plant, where the King of Jordan maintains a Rokon museum.

Maintenance on most items is accomplished with a simple set of wrenches and lube, with many parts available from local hardware stores. Checking for front and rear chain tension and lubrication is standard operating procedure.

Kit Up

A cult-like following of Rokon rebuilders is constantly searching for Rokons to restore and to rally with in remote locations the nation over, while squeezing out an additional 5 to 10 mph. During our ride, accessories were basic, ranging from tomahawks and handheld GPS units to ammo cans that went unopened. To equip and customize a modern Rokon, the company makes it simple for new owners by providing an itemized accessory menu, with a rumored Prepper Edition in all black arriving some day.

Meanwhile, for bugging out and keeping a low profile, we highly recommend accessories, including:
› Trail Maintenance Kit, (fuel filter, air filter, spark plug and wrench, two connecting chain links, two half links and chain, chain breaker, low-pressure gauge, pump, tubeless repair kit, and drive belt in leather pouch
› Camouflage upgrade
› Carrier ramp plus ratchet straps to secure Rokon to trailer hitch or truck

Off Grid Tip

Company president Tom Blais pounded the Chilean Andes with his. The U.S. Special Forces covered sands with it in Desert Storm. And U.S. Border Patrol agents use theirs to pursue narrow foot paths. Rokon motorcycles are relied upon by the military and law enforcement agencies all over the world, from Fort Bragg to Brunei.

So, we were thrilled at the chance to join the ranks of those who've tested these all-terrain vehicles. Here are some lessons learned from a recent hardcore training session:
› Starting in neutral is best.
› Carry maps, a GPS unit or two, plus plenty of fuel in reserve.
› Keep a few basic tools with you to tighten up any loose fittings, and always keep your chain properly tensioned and lubricated.
› Practice your bug-out skills by creeping through the woods or your given landscape, walking the bike if necessary. Work less on speed and more on negotiating obstacles.
› If you're unable to avoid traveling on or across roads, keep your head on a swivel, scanning and assessing 360 degrees when traveling and stopping, watching first from the woods and listening before crossing.

- Gun boot, saddle style; keeps the width of the bike down and is safer than carrying a rifle across the handlebars on narrow, wooded trails.
- Tow bar kit chain, trailer hitch, and hard bar
- Brush Busters (handguards)
- Tachometer/hour meter
- Game Carrier, which replaces the rear seat to transport backpacks, cargo, rigging saddle bags, and large objects
- Single Track Trailer, a long linear carrier that increases carrying capacity
- GPS/cell phone holders
- Fuel siphon pump
- Waterproof 12-volt plug for recharging cellular phones, lap tops, and powering low-pressure air pump for tires
- Tactical carry system (two ammo cans) on saddle bag position
- Stihl chainsaw, machete, axe, rope, spare fuel, trail maps, tent, pack

The Rokon Trail-Breaker has come a long way from its origins in 1958, one year after some young Americans first carried the M-14 into Vietnam. Just as a new generation of fighters has rediscovered the worth and staying power of the old battle rifle, so too are new generations of "urban bug-out planners" realizing the potential of the Rokon ride.

Our deep wilderness ride ended with one broken mirror, but we're not courting bad luck. As this author tells his firearms students, "Leave luck to the unprepared." Rock on, Rokon.

Rokon Lineup

Rokon offers three similar models with slight variations in color, available suspension, wheel, and motor-gearing options. Each model is available with 50 factory accessories, from a one-bolt add-on sidecar to a 2,000-watt generator.

ROKON www.rokon.com

	Trail-Breaker	Ranger	Scout
	The flagship bike is the complete package with Auto-Grab front wheel suspension, 12-inch aluminum drums, and the high-output 208cc 7hp Kohler engine.	The middle-of-the-pack model, appealing to those wanting the 160cc 5hp Honda engine and solid non-drum heavy-spoke wheels.	Basically the same as the Trail-Breaker, only without the drum wheels and the front suspension for a lighter or more traditional feel.
Drive System	Full-time all-wheel drive	Full-time all-wheel drive	Full-time all-wheel drive
Engine	7hp Kohler, one-cylinder, four-stroke	5hp Honda, one-cylinder, four-stroke	7hp Kohler, one-cylinder, four-stroke
Piston Displacement	208cc Kohler	160cc Honda	208cc Kohler
Power Transmission	Auto torque converter into a three-gear range selector		
Fuel Tank	2.69 gallon	2.69 gallon	2.69 gallon
Grade Capability	60-percent	60-percent	60-percent
Wheels	12-inch aluminum sealed drum	12-inch steel spoke	12-inch steel spoke
Tires	8x12x25 tubeless	8x12x25 tubeless	8x12x25 tubeless
Wheelbase	51 inches	51 inches	51 inches
Ground Clearance	14 inches	14 inches	14 inches
Height Over Seat	32 inches	32 inches	31 inches
Height Over Handlebars	41 inches	41 inches	41 inches
Width	30 inches	30 inches	30 inches
Length	79 inches	79 inches	79 inches
Weight	218 pounds (dry weight)	218 pounds (dry weight)	218 pounds (dry weight)
Fordable Water Depth	24 inches	24 inches	24 inches
Base Price	$7,350	$6,975	$6,500

Extreme

Apocalypse Wow!

When Survival Goes to the Fittest, this Rig Will Definitely Make Road Warriors Out of its Occupants

By John Schwartze
Photography By Henry Z. De Kuyper

ver the years we've seen Hollywood conjure up countless interpretations of how vehicles would take shape in preparation for, or in reaction to, doomsday. But if things go haywire in real life, would you really want to be driving Mel Gibson's blown Interceptor or the rocket-launching Landmaster from Damnation Alley? Style is great on the silver screen, but in the event of a catastrophe, practicality is where the cream rises to the top.

In previous issues of RECOIL we've shown you what's possible in accessorizing a fairly new ride, but the buck doesn't stop there. Jim DeLozier has taken what many consider an old dog and outfitted it with all the trappings hell on Earth might necessitate. These older trucks are pretty damn resilient and given their versatility, affordability, and abundance, here's a perfect example of how one was transformed to stay one step ahead if every man must fend for himself.

Start thinking backwards from Armageddon and ask yourself what a vehicle would need. Are we talking civil unrest? Disease outbreak? Widespread power outages? The answer is all of the above, because in a true SHTF ordeal, a domino effect is likely. As a security consultant and father of two, DeLozier was not only thinking of how to bug out, but how his brood could survive for an indefinite period of time with limited resources if their only shelter was this truck. Jim carefully thought about how every single aspect

MAKE:
Chevrolet
MODEL:
C70
YEAR:
1980
ENGINE:
366ci V-8
DRIVETRAIN:
4WD
PHONE:
(888) 755-7769
EMAIL:
info@survivortruck.com

EXTREME • APOCALYPSE WOW!

of this truck would fare in austere conditions.

Jim's quest for the ultimate survivor vehicle began with deciding what kind of utilitarian platform would best suit his vision. He felt that a ¾-ton or 1-ton truck didn't have the capacity he was looking for and wouldn't be feasible as a daily driver in terms of mileage. He figured if he was going to go bigger, using it as a daily driver wouldn't be practical anyway. Since the largest vehicle he could own without a commercial license couldn't exceed 26,000 pounds, he began to narrow his search to a commercial/military-grade chassis that could support a high payload.

Then there was the question of whether a modern vehicle or an older one would make more sense. The absence of electronics in these older vehicles helps protect against electromagnetic pulse damage and solar flares. Eventually Jim decided on a 1980 Chevy C70, which was previously used as a commercial drilling rig. Jim picked up this truck for about $10,000 on trade.

When he found it, the chassis had already been upgraded to four-wheel drive, was reinforced with a double frame, had a 10-inch frame lift, and had the factory 366 tall-block engine. These motors can run on gas or propane, or both at once, so the mixture can be modified depending on barometric pressure and altitude. Jim felt having a vehicle that could run on propane would give him an advantage because it has a longer shelf life than gas or diesel, can legally be stored in larger quantities, and tanks in people's yards can be found all over the country if fuel scavenging becomes necessary. He also dressed up the engine with a custom kit from Carburetion & Turbo Systems with an

1 LOWER LIGHTS
MAKE: Lightforce
MODEL: 170 Striker combo-beam
URL: www.lightforce.com

2 UPPER LIGHTS
MAKE: Lightforce
MODEL: 210 Genesis (two spot / two flood)
URL: www.lightforce.com

3 SIDE LIGHTS
MAKE: Lightforce
MODEL: 170 Striker with infrared filter
URL: www.lightforce.com

4 LIGHT BAR
MAKE: Bulldog Lighting
MODEL: 50-inch Bone LED combo beam light bar
MSRP: $1,096
URL: www.bulldog-lighting.com

5 WINCH
MAKE: Mile Marker
MODEL: SEC15 — 15,000-pound electric winch
MSRP: $699
URL: www.milemarker.com

6 AIR CONDITIONER / HEATER
MAKE: Dometic Corp.
MODEL: 10K Class A
MSRP: $7,999
URL: www.dometic.com

7 CAMO NETS
MAKE: SAAB / Barracuda US
MODEL: Thermo-regulated 360-degree camouflage netting system — desert tan
MSRP: $11,256
URL: www.saabgroup.com/northamerica

1 TANK
MAKE: Manchester Tank
MODEL: 77-gallon propane tank
URL: www.mantank.com

2 WHEELS
MAKE: Titan International
MODEL: Military 10x20 wheels
MSRP: $3,990
URL: www.titan-intl.com

3 TIRES
MAKE: Michelin
MODEL: XZL 16:00 R20
MSRP: $1,995
URL: www.rallequip.com

4 RUN-FLAT TIRE INSERTS
(not visible)
MAKE: Hutchinson
MODEL: Mine-resistant run-flat system
URL: www.hutchinsoninc.com

5 GENERATOR
MAKE: Coleman
MODEL: 6250 12/110/220 gas and propane generator with Briggs & Stratton engine

6 COMPRESSOR
MAKE: Oasis
MODEL: 12V air compressor and supplemental 6-gallon tank
MSRP: $1,800
URL: www.oasismfg.com

7 SIDE LIGHT BAR
MAKE: Bulldog Lighting
MODEL: 20-inch Bones LED combo beam light bar
MSRP: $506
URL: www.bulldog-lighting.com

8 LEVELING SYSTEM
MAKE: Equalizer Systems
MODEL: Hydraulic ram automatic leveling system
URL: eqsystems.us

9 COMPARTMENT CONTENTS
MAKE: Pelican
MODEL: EMT case with full medical kit and remote area lighting system
URL: www.pelican.com

10 COMPARTMENT CONTENTS
MAKE: Chinook Medical Kit
MODEL: EMPK – Level 4
MSRP: $750
URL: www.chinookmed.com

MAKE: Aqua Sun International
MODEL: Responder "S" solar/battery/12v water purification system – reverse osmosis and UV
URL: www.aqua-sun-intl.com

MAKE: PowerEnz
MODEL: LFP-40 – mobile solar generator 72 watt foldable solar panel and battery pack
URL: www.powerenz.com

MAKE: Marvac Electronics
MODEL: electrician's tool kit
URL: www.marvac.com

MAKE: Snap-on
MODEL: mechanic's tool kit
URL: www.snapon.com

11 COMPARTMENT CONTENTS
MAKE: Miller Welding
MODEL: Multimatic 200
MSRP: $1,965
URL: www.millerwelds.com

MAKE: IDS Solar Technologies
MODEL: Rescue 3,000-watt Pure Sine Wave Solar Generator
URL: www.idssolartech.com

MAKE: 5.11
MODEL: RUSH MOAB backpack
MSRP: $110
URL: www.511tactical.com

MAKE: Broco
MODEL: Mini Breaching Saw Kit
URL: www.broco-rankin.com

12 STEPS / HANDRAIL
MAKE: Torklift International
MODEL: GlowStep 8-inch tread depth step
MSRP: $900
URL: www.torklift.com

MSD ignition to assist in the timing advance for effective propane use.

Jim keeps extra electrical components onboard such as backup HEI, control modules for the timing advance, and other such parts that can be replaced quickly in case of a remote EMP attack. To further accessorize the truck, Jim sold people on his vision, had parts and services donated, and eventually it snowballed into what you see here, which is a prototype and still a work in progress.

Jim enlisted Tilling Consulting in San Clemente, California, to handle much of the design by mocking it up in SolidWorks to optimize their use of space. Danny Delamater up at Delson Products in Santa Fe Springs, California, was responsible for a lot of the custom touches throughout the truck, and most of the welding was handled by Marty Klett, Mike Phillips, and Duncan Jones. Ashley Tilling at Tilling Consulting also assisted in the design and engineering.

A custom pop-up camper created by Four Wheel Campers with a cab-over portion may look pretty milquetoast to the unsuspecting eye, but it houses the survivalist heart of the truck. Encased in a ballistic-reinforced active faraday cage within the camper and serviced by a positive-pressure, nuclear/biological/chemical air filtration system is what Jim calls the command center. It is essentially a safe room housing all the communications, surveillance, computers, night vision, ground radar, and thermal imaging equipment and can hold six people belted into jump seats. It's all kept at a comfortable temperature by a custom heater and Class A air-conditioning system.

Want more specifics on the tech gear? OK, you asked for it. Three thermal cameras that can be mounted in front (wide, medium, and narrow) can monitor the driving area ahead for heat signatures in case driving needs to be done with only the front infrared lights activated while wearing night vision equipment. Surveillance cameras can be mounted on each side as well as a long-range camera that faces forward. A pan/tilt/zoom can be affixed to a masthead above the vehicle for a 360-degree view, along with a laser/thermal combo camera.

A CB radio, ham radio with repeater, and private encrypted two-way radio with repeater will also keep Jim in the know if standard communications become limited. Chem suits and SCBA kits are kept onboard to drive through hazardous areas, and Jim intends to run the air filtration system directly into the cab. Though the camper itself is not airtight, the positive pressure system makes it acceptable. A ground radar system monitors the surroundings for objects, movement, aircraft, combatants, and animals.

OK, but what about the actual surviving abroad part, like having water? Seven tanks capable of holding a combined 150 gallons of water were added and run through a solar-powered water purification system. It can be used for drinking water or can be plumbed into a portable shower system that can be set up within the camper. The water supply can be recycled for an indefinite period of time. Water could also be pumped in from another source when it's time to replenish. The system can be powered electronically or with a hand pump. And yes, there's a toilet that goes into a separate septic tank.

Yeah, but this thing's so heavy, what if it gets stuck? No problem. A 24-ton capacity hydraulic leveling system can help this beast out of spots if and when it gets stuck. Dual 15,000-pound winches can also be employed if need be. You may also be wondering about ordinance Jim may encounter — he was too. Those 53-inch military tires were fitted with mine-resistant run-flat inserts, and there are plans for explosion-resistant paneling to protect the undercarriage.

The entire truck is also Rhino lined, which quiets the vehicle. And if that wasn't enough, its texture allows it to become embedded with dirt over time to add to its camo-colored aesthetics. Jim also keeps extra paint onboard to switch up the vehicle's color to match different surroundings. No, it's not an armored car per se, but this is not a war fighter, it's a long-term escape vehicle meant to take the abuse any gauntlets along the way could throw at it.

But what's powering this monstrosity? A lot of things. Dual alternators and a 12-volt belt-driven generator run off the engine, along with four separate battery banks all charged from the same system with separate high-amp isolators to charge multiple systems independently. Add to that a solar panel on the roof, a standalone 3,000-watt solar generator, and deployable

COMMAND CENTER

AR500 armor plate, ¾-inch ballistic fiberglass by Pacific Bulletproof covered by ¾-inch cabinet-grade plywood for attachment of desired items. Thor-Shield EMP protection. Custom made by Delson Products.

URL:
www.thorshield.com, www.pacificbulletproof.com, www.delsonproducts.com

1 AIR FILTRATION SYSTEM

MAKE:
American Safe Rooms

MODEL:
12-volt NBC (Nuclear, Biological, Chemical environment) air filtration system with auxiliary hand pump for power failures

URL:
www.americansaferoom.com

2 RUGGEDIZED PC

with RAM mounts, docking station, 4G wireless internet, remote camera management

3 ELECTRONICS

MAKE:
Wamar Technologies

MODEL:
C4ISR Tactical Video Monitoring System, multi-mode wireless connectivity, ROIP radio over IP, thermal imaging, laser camera, pan/tilt/zoom (PTZ) cameras, ground radar, video recording

MSRP:
not for commercial sale

URL:
www.wamartech.com

MAKE:
Motorola

MODEL:
Two-way radios kit

URL:
www.motorola.com

MAKE:
Yaesu

MODEL:
Ham radio kit

URL:
www.yaesu.com

1 CAMPER

MAKE:
Four Wheel Campers

MODEL:
modified/custom Keystone model with queen size bed, bench seat that converts into double bed, sink and shower with hot and cold water, toilet, air conditioner, heater, two-burner stove, refrigerator, food storage, television with DVD player and satellite, dual 12-volt batteries, solar panel on roof, shorepower hookup.

VALUE:
$45,000

URL:
www.fourwheelcampers.com

GUN INVENTORY

(1) Springfield Armory M1A rifle

(2) POF P416 f/a 10.5-inch barrel 5.56x45mm gas piston carbine with EOTech HHS-II sights (EXPS2-2 sight and G33 3x magnifier with switch to side mount) and YHM suppressor

(2) POF P416 f/a 14.5-inch barrel 5.56x45mm gas piston carbine with Aimpoint Micro T1 with high mount and Aimpoint 3x Magnifier with twist-mount base for interoperability with PVS-14 Gen III+ NV and YHM suppressor

(2) POF P308-FA 16.5-inch barrel 7.62x51mm gas piston carbine with NightForce NXS 2.5-10x24 rifle scope and YHM suppressor

(4) POF P308 20-inch barrel 7.62x51mm gas piston rifle with NightForce NXS 5.5-22x50 rifle scope with MLR reticle and YHM suppressor

(1) FN A3G 24-inch barrel .308 Win bolt-action rifle with McMillan A3 stock and NightForce NXS 5.5-22x50 rifle scope with MLR reticle with SureFire suppressor

(1) Blaser .300 WinMag bolt-action rifle with Schmidt & Bender 3-27x56 PMII Hi-Power rifle scope with SureFire suppressor

(4) Springfield Armory XD-45 pistols

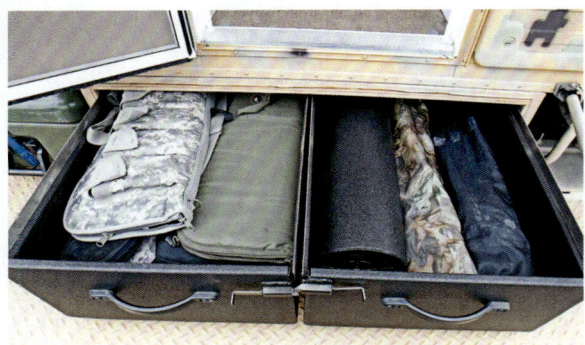

solar generator and you've pretty much got all your power sources covered. Three gas tanks and two 77-gallon propane tanks also power the vehicle, while a 110/240-volt gas/propane generator on the side can power various other items stored on the vehicle. Fully fueled, the truck is capable of a 3,000-plus-mile range, depending on payload.

Surely you'd need to protect a vehicle like this, right? Of course! Aside from the surveillance measures, motion, vibration, window break sensors, audible alarm, and remote access via 4G wireless help keep the truck secure from intruders. Thermo-regulated camo nets can also be deployed to completely cover the vehicle. Jim also keeps guns onboard with anywhere from 10,000 to 30,000 rounds of ammo. Sub-cache canisters are also part of the truck's inventory so that they can be buried anywhere he sees fit in case he needs to come back later and dig up supplies.

Speaking of supplies, Jim has pretty much checked off everything you'd find on a survivalist's holiday list. An industrial breaching saw, industrial chainsaw, a full medical kit including oxygen and transfusion apparatus, 12-volt air compressor, portable welder, fire-suppression system, bow and arrows, glass breakers, 1,800 MREs and additional sea rations, remote-area lighting, air/electric/fuel line reels, body armor, and a variety of outdoor clothing are just some of the things residing in compartments throughout the truck.

So what's next for this behemoth? At present, Jim plans on outfitting it with spare tires, an overdrive system, a navigation system, thicker insulation in the camper to reduce heat signatures/light emission, and even building a production vehicle for global sales on a new chassis from Freightliner, Mercedes, Ford, Fuso, and more. Not each will be alike of course. Additions in one place can create deficits in others, which Jim discovered through trial and error.

You've probably been wondering what this truck cost to build. At present, Jim has over half a million dollars invested. Now, before you go pour yourself four fingers of that bourbon we recommended on page 138 to handle the initial shock of that investment, remember this is a prototype for which most of the parts and services were donated based on sharing the owner's vision. No, this wasn't built after winning some big Powerball jackpot.

The idea behind producing Survivor Trucks is to ultimately create a modular vehicle to satisfy the demands of the end user, as no one vehicle can satisfy every demand. Who knows, you may start seeing multiple Survivor Trucks out roaming the countryside. Sure, you could go cheaper and cut corners, but is it any surprise that a vehicle outfitted with this much stuff would be so costly? What are the lives of you and your family worth when it comes to nationwide upheaval? Like the old saying goes — better to have it and not need it than need it and not have it.

Hagglunds Bv206

We Ride Along in the World's Most Elite and Versatile Tracked Vehicle

By Mike Landers
Photography By Scott Majors

This beast can tackle some brutal landscapes. A mountainous plateau bombarded by a relentless blizzard? Check. A backcountry path pockmarked by boulders and felled trees? No biggie. Dirt roads and asphalt make this ride laugh. The Hagglunds Bandvagen 206 — or Bv206, as it is more commonly known — is a multipurpose, tracked small unit support vehicle (SUSV) capable of handling extreme terrain and offering accessibility to some of the world's most remote locations.

The Bv206 can climb boulders, ford streams, and conquer snow.

Built as a successor to the Bv202, made by Volvo, the Hagglunds Bv206 met the Swedish government's need for an all-purpose vehicle with more power and lower maintenance issues than its Volvo counterpart. While the Volvo Bv202 tracks were iron and easily rusted out, the Hagglunds Bv206 features a track made of reinforced nylon, with some of the newer models using Kevlar tracks.

The Bv206 is suited for a variety of conditions, and spanning harsh winter environments is just the tip of the proverbial iceberg for the

Ideal Uses for the Hagglunds Bv206

TRANSPORTATION
The Hagglunds Bv206 all-terrain vehicle is excellent for transporting personnel or cargo because of its load capacity (up to 4,400 pounds). The six-passenger Bv206 Cargo model can transport bulky, heavy equipment over the toughest terrains. The rear compartment can load up to three European-style wooden pallets.

SEARCH, RESCUE, AND RECOVERY
The Hagglunds Bv206 can travel up to 34 mph and can respond immediately from a fixed location, obviating the need for trailer transport. Capable of transporting up to four patients on stretchers, the Bv206 is a serious high-tech emergency response vehicle: It can be equipped with state-of-the-art navigation equipment, including radar, thermal imaging, GPS positioning with satellite photo overlays, night vision, gyro-stabilized optics, and much more.

TOURING
The Bv206 can transport up to 17 passengers comfortably. The vehicles are routinely retrofitted with such comforts as bucket seats, onboard DVD player, plasma screen TVs, high-quality audio entertainment systems, refrigerators, microwave ovens, and sleeping facilities, as well as other luxury options.

diverse capabilities of this vehicle. In addition to excelling in extreme snow, the Bv206 can also ford streams, scale rock surfaces, swim deep water, and maneuver through mud, muck, and post-disaster/combat debris. The unit is even fully amphibious without extra preparation. Hydrostatic, articulated steering allows for a surprisingly tight turning radius, and the 2-ton payload makes the vehicle absolutely invaluable during personnel or cargo transport.

That said, the vehicle is easily the most sought after in the world when it comes to the Snowcat/Bearcat market. RECOIL Magazine had the pleasure of receiving an afternoon lecture and ride-along from Art Seely, who is president and CEO of Safety One Training International and a licensed dealer/expert of the Hagglunds Bv206.

One of the first certified rescue paramedics in the United States and a world-renowned trainer with more than 25 years of experience in snow survival and snowcat operations training, Mr. Seely had much to share regarding the development and implementation of this unique vehicle across the world.

"I got called to do some consulting work on the design changes and this led to the production of Bv206 models with six-cylinder petrol and five-cylinder diesel Mercedes engines," he says. "The first off the lines had a

Photo courtesy of Safety One International, Inc

six-cylinder Ford Capri engine, and then production shifted to include the five-cylinder Mercedes, and the final sequence yielded a very nice six-cylinder 3L engine. This is the same engine you'll find in a 2007 Mercedes 300SD Sedan."

Given the vehicle's rugged construction and speed capabilities, the Bv206 is only on par with itself when it comes to deployment potential and use. "During my time with SWAT, I drove an M114 and there's just no comparison. These things will go anywhere," says Art.

Because of the versatility of the Hagglunds and the fact that the parent company has now become a part of BAE Global Combat Systems, these original models are becoming increasingly rare and extremely tough to find. Even more intriguing, the models in production under BAE differ from these original models, making them that much more sought after. "You have to have a State Department permit to purchase or deal them as they are classified as 'implements of war.' Then you have to have a ATFE Class 1, Class 2, Class 3 Form 6, and a Special Occupational License," Art explains. "Then you have to have a license from the government of Norway. On the off chance the cargo docks ship the Hagglunds via Binghamton, England, you also have to have a special permit from them, too!" Consequences of trying to purchase or secure these vehicles without proper authorization make doing so unadvisable. "I know of a guy who spent three years in prison in England, and

two former military officers from another country who went to prison, for trying to acquire Hagglunds without all the proper permits," Art cautions. "It's a very sensitive item."

For reference, the model we rode in was a Mercedes five-cylinder, with cab and rear heaters, a comm system to communicate between the two units, a built-in fire extinguisher system, and a commander's seat in the cab — allowing one to "pop the top" and ride with a torso out of the roof for maximum visibility. The articulated steering and track system offered a surprisingly nimble ride, given the terrain we scaled and the vehicle's weight.

Simply put, the Hagglunds Bv206 is unparalleled in its field, and one incredible piece of equipment. It's definitely worth checking out in person.

HAGGLUNDS BANDVAGEN 206

ENGINE OPTIONS:
- Industrial Ford V-6 gasoline (136 horsepower)
- Mercedes-Benz five-cylinder turbo diesel (125 horsepower)
- Mercedes-Benz six-cylinder turbo diesel (136 horsepower)

Transmission: Daimler-Benz W 4A 040 (comparable to an Allison 432)

Gear Ratios: High 1.28:1, Low 2.11:1

Track: Reinforced nylon (some use Kevlar)

Electrical: 24 volt

Turning Radius: 26 feet

Height: 7 feet 9 inches

Length: 22 feet 6 inches

Width: 6 feet 1 inches

Seating Capacity: Six in front, 11 in rear car

Payload: 4,400 pounds

Gross: 13,940 pounds

Cargo Space: 283 cubic feet

Maximum Speed: 34 mph (gas); 31 mph (diesel); 2 mph in water

Gradeability: 31 degrees hard surface / 17 degrees deep snow

Fuel Capacity: Two 20-gallon tanks, which can be shifted automatically or manually

Body Material: Fiberglass reinforced plastic with PVC foam insulation (can be upgraded)

Original Base Cost During Production: $388,000

Current Retail Cost: $900,000-plus

Miscellaneous Parts Costs:
- Differentials - $28,000
- Engines - $30,000
- Transfer Case - $22,000
- Custom Transmission - Price varies
- Track Replacement - $16,000 to $20,000

Unidentified Fighting Object

Putting the K.I.S.S. Principle to Work in No Country for Off-the-Lot Vehicles

By John Schwartze
Photography By Straight 8

We know what you're thinking. Is this Ivan "Ironman" Stewart's tactical vehicle or some addition to Area 51's security fleet? We're going to keep you guessing for the moment and speak to a belief that often gets reiterated in the pages of RECOIL...ounces equal pounds and pounds equal pain. So when it comes to dreaming up your bug-out/survival vehicle blueprints, while it may seem like a good idea to pile on every single piece of cool gear you can dream of (after all, you might need it), it may actually interfere with mobility more than you think.

Would you believe this actually started life as a 1975 Chevy ½-ton pickup? We certainly had a hard time wrapping our heads around that, but when its owner/builder John Kanicsar started telling us what the vehicle was used for, we couldn't help but be intrigued by the ingenuity of it all. Sparse on bling, yes, but the Southern Arizona desert where it spends most of its time doesn't really care about cool paintjobs and expensive gear. Its 9,500 square miles are desolate, difficult to traverse, and a major thoroughfare for illegal activity. So when you've got both the elements and the criminal component to contend with, you quickly begin to understand that less is more when you need a vehicle robust enough to handle it. Breaking down in the middle of nowhere is something you want to avoid at all costs.

The "Multipurpose Off-road Tactical Vehicle," or MOTiV as it's called, is the culmination of Hunter Offroad owner John Kanicsar's fabricator background, experience working in law enforcement, and four-wheeling knowledge. After participating in some search-and-rescue operations, he saw how law enforcement vehicles and 4x4 driving methods weren't as practical as they could be. John knew he could create something with high clearance for climbing, high mobility, and high payload, all while still being street legal. So he showed up at the next big search with something he'd built. From then on, he's been developing vehicles as well as teaching recovery tactics, search-and-rescue, and off-road driving techniques to everyone from police to Special Forces around the country.

The MOTiV is actually the third vehicle of its type that Kanicsar has

1975 CHEVY CUSTOMIZED
4X4
½-TON PICKUP
350 V-8
TH350 AUTOMATIC
WWW.HUNTEROFFROAD.COM

---

1 BALLISTIC ARMOR
MAKE: Custom
MODEL: Levell IIIA

2 ROLL CAGE
MAKE: Custom
MODEL: 2-inch, 120-wall tubing
URL: www.hunteroffroad.com

3 COMBO LIGHT
MAKE: Rigid Industries
MODEL: 10-inch E Series white/IR light prototype
URL: www.rigidindustries.com

4 COMBO LIGHT
MAKE: Rigid Industries
MODEL: R-46 LED light
URL: www.rigidindustries.com

5 TIRES
MAKE: Pro Comp
MODEL: Xterrain 37x14x16
URL: www.procompusa.com

6 WHEELS
MAKE: Eagle
MODEL: Aluminum 16x8
URL: www.aewheel.com

EXTREME • UNIDENTIFIED FIGHTING OBJECT

1 LED LIGHT BAR	
MAKE:	Rigid Industries
MODEL:	E2 20-inch combo
URL:	www.rigidindustries.com
2 INFRARED LIGHT	
MAKE:	Rigid Industries
MODEL:	E2 10-inch combo
URL:	www.rigidindustries.com
3 WINCH	
MAKE:	Warn
MODEL:	9,500-pound high-speed winch with high-strength synthetic line
URL:	www.warn.com
4 RED AND BLUE LIGHTS	
MAKE:	Code 3
MODEL:	Single Head LED X Series
URL:	www.code3pse.com
5 LED LIGHT	
MAKE:	Rigid Industries
MODEL:	Dually Diffused Single
URL:	www.rigidindustries.com
6 BACKPACK	
MAKE:	Grey Ghost Gear
MODEL:	Legacy Three-Day Pack
URL:	www.greyghostgear.com
7 VEHICLE BLOW-OUT KIT	
MAKE:	Delta
MODEL:	Steel Side Storage Box
URL:	www.deltastorage.com
8 BACKPACK	
MAKE:	Grey Ghost Gear
MODEL:	Predator Patrol 45 PLCE
URL:	www.greyghostgear.com

built — and it's still an evolving platform. John is usually the guy behind the wheel when the truck is tapped to go out into the field, so he's the perfect person to know what needs to be modified and how. Why an old Chevy pickup and not some brand-new 4x4 or UTV? The biggest answer is simplicity. There are aspects of one that you can't really get on the other. John wanted the flexibility and durability of a UTV, but something that can carry the weight and has the speed of a full-size truck.

Drawing from his experience, John wanted a platform with solid ½-ton axles, an automatic transmission, and a reliable powerplant. That good ol' Chevy 350 is still moving this rig around and sports a Holley Truck Avenger carb, mechanical fuel pump, and RV cam for torque at lower rpm. The absence of electronics on the engine is deliberate, because no one wants to be pinning down problems with a voltmeter out in the desert. It's all connected to the venerable TH350 trans with an NP-203 transfer case. The rear is a locking 12-bolt, while the front differential is a 10-bolt with an open carrier.

Most of the original Chevy frame and body is gone. The cage is made out of 2-inch, 120-wall tubing, and ABS plastic panels throughout keep things light while concealing Level IIIA ballistic soft armor panels behind them that can be pulled out and used as shields if necessary. John wanted a suspension that'd handle a substantial weight change and kept the leaf springs since they tend to be more dependable and predictable, have good flexibility, and behave under high speeds

1 RED AND BLUE LIGHTS
MAKE:
Code 3
MODEL:
Dual Head LED X Series
URL:
www.code3pse.com

2 RIFLE
MAKE:
Grey Ghost Precision
MODEL:
.308 with Vortex Optic
URL:
www.greyghostprecision.com
www.vortexoptics.com

3 RIFLE
MAKE:
Grey Ghost Precision
MODEL:
.223/5.56 Light Rifle with Vortex Optic
URL:
www.greyghostprecision.com
www.vortexoptics.com

4 RIFLE LOCK
MAKE:
Blac-Rac
MODEL:
1070
URL:
www.blac-rac.com

5 HARNESSES
MAKE:
RCI
MODEL:
Four-point
URL:
www.rciracing.com

better than coils under varying weight demands of crew or cargo. The rear springs were moved inboard about 5 inches for improved left/right articulation and off-road travel, while maintaining weight capacity.

Interior appointments are pretty meager, and you may notice the floor is actually open mesh. The idea there is to let debris fall out easier, allow better airflow, keep the heat down, and enable the driver to see through the floor if he gets hung up on something — rather than require someone to get out and guide him. Aftermarket seats with four-point harnesses and Blac-Rac rifle locks keep everyone and their weapons safely strapped in. Ammo cans hide a variety of comm equipment. Rigid Industries light bars and IR lights allow the truck to keep things illuminated or operate in no-light conditions. And in case you're still wondering how this is still street legal, it was retitled as special construction to be in compliance since it doesn't have much of its original garb.

Since the MOTiV gets some serious use and abuse, improvements will continue to be made. From locating lost kids to assisting in high-risk special operations support, John's unique knowledge and creation has undoubtedly saved lives — and that's what it's all about. John is spending more time teaching some of his hard-earned lessons in the field working as a vehicle instructor and plans to branch out into the civilian market so there may be MOTiVs popping up at agencies and driveways near you.

Two-Track Mind

One Commie's Trash is Another Man's Treasure

By John Schwartze
Photography By Rob Curtis

Let's face it, who hasn't fantasized about having their very own tank without being subject to the usual prerequisite of military service or stealing one from a National Guard armory? Schwarzenegger's YouTube charity videos might make you think he's the only one with the money and connections to be able to personally own and operate some decommissioned iron, but there's hope for those of us who've felt that same indescribable yearning that could only be satisfied by having tracked armor. Dead Air Armament founder Mike Pappas is living proof that the average civilian can realize that dream as well — assuming your local laws permit such a thing. If not,

perhaps it's time to move or write to your congressman.

After looking at different options for surplus military vehicles on the market, Mike found this OT-90 the most conducive to his needs. It holds 11 people, can float, and (at 12 tons) is light enough to be hauled on the back of a big-rig trailer as a "wide load." The history of this particular tank is a little unclear. It was a Russian BMP-1 converted to an OT-90 by the Czechs, and although bullet strikes are visible, he's not sure if Slobodan Milošević may have had it terrorizing the Balkans.

For those of you already calling us out on our nomenclature, you're right, the OT-90 is an infantry fighting vehicle (IFV) as opposed to a tank. As a variation of the BMP-1, the OT-90's original 73mm turret was removed at some point prior to sale for a lighter version that held a 14.5mm KPVT to work coax with a PKP rifle. Mike wasn't interested in the original guns, which he could've only taken possession of if they were cut up. Since trying to find 14.5mm ammo isn't very easy, and cut-up guns are essentially junk anyway, Mike passed in favor of retrofitting the turret for an M2 and 1919.

Mike wasn't interested in the original guns, which he could've only taken possession of if they were cut up. Since trying to find 14.5mm ammo isn't very easy, and cut-up guns are essentially junk anyway, Mike passed in favor of retrofitting the turret for an M2 and 1919.

A friend of Mike who is a military vehicle broker, and had also imported a BMP-1 for Oakley, helped him with the transaction and necessary paperwork. The broker did a Form 6 and Mike filled out an end-use certificate along with some export paperwork required by the DoD and ATF, but as he puts it, the whole process "wasn't that big a deal." He took possession about a year after the money changed hands and paperwork was filed. The whole ball of wax, including importing fees, only came to about $60,000. The process would be a bit easier if one were to buy something stateside like an old M60 Patton. Since it's essentially a big gun with wheels, purchasing a domestic tank would be more of a straight transaction, although we're sure the turret would have to be inert.

Firing this thing up took some work. Mike had to call the exporter to help him identify switches that were written in Cyrillic. Although it took some back and forth, he got it off the trailer and spent the ensuing months labeling the controls in English. The startup is a little complex until you get the hang of the procedure. The UDT-20 19L V-6 engine is multi-fuel capable, and runs on the same things you'd put in an M35A2 truck. On a full tank it has a range of roughly 400 miles.

Inside, the IFV is surprisingly spacious. Mike plans on replacing the HF radio with a modern version, in addition to instaliing a 2M/440. Other than that, it really only needs some cosmetic touches here and there. Mike decided to leave the troop weapon portholes on each

side cradled for AKs as they were originally intended. Larger portholes in front for Vz.59s are also going to be left as-is, since Mike already has one and plans to get another.

No, the OT-90 is not street legal. Mike lives in a rural area that enables him to use an off-road vehicle license to cruise it around. If you've never driven a tracked veicle before, as Mike hadn't, the driving controls are not overly complicated, but he suggests being mechanically inclined if you plan to purchase a used tank or IFV. Trying to find someone who can work on them is a pretty tall order. Parts are available online, but Mike says the market for communist-block armor is very competitive. Apparently militants buy these up for their local conflict and, after it's over, sell whatever they can't afford to maintain.

If you're serious about buying something like this, Mike also suggests finding a vetted broker in your own state who can import a vehicle. In the event you can't find one who you feel comfortable with, contact Mike through his company so he can turn you on to some reliable sources. It'd also make sense to ensure you have somewhere you can actually drive it. If you don't live on or near lots of accessible undeveloped land, don't have adequate storage, and don't have neighbors who aren't threatened by the sight of a war implement, this really isn't for you.

While you might have the desire, but not the means to own a tank, at least you know that having a military vehicle of this ilk is not impossible. Do your homework and don't make an impulse buy. You might get excited about finding a cheap WWII-era Tiger tank online, but at around 60 tons, it's impractical for anything other than sitting still or leasing it to museums. It'd make quite a conversation piece though if you have the aptitude to support this sort of possession. You could create license plate holders that say "My other car is an IFV" and actually mean it.

If you're serious about buying something like this, Mike also suggests finding a vetted broker in your own state who can import a vehicle.

1982 OT-90 JPJ

ENGINE:
19L UDT-20 V-6
DRIVETRAIN:
Five-speed manual
LENGTH:
23.39 feet
WIDTH:
9.65 feet
HEIGHT:
6.91 feet
WEIGHT - EMPTY:
27,577 pounds (approx.)
WEIGHT - COMBAT:
29,762 pounds (approx.)
MAX SPEED - ROAD:
40 mph
MAX SPEED - OFF-ROAD:
28 mph
MAX SPEED - WATER:
8 mph
CREW:
3: driver/gunner/commander
FIGHTING COMPARTMENT:
8 fully armed troops
ENGINE BHP:
300 bhp
FUEL TYPE:
Diesel
TANK CAPACITY:
15.89 cubic feet (main) + 2 x 6.36 cubic feet (aux)

3x CREW
8x FIGHTING COMPARTMENT
2x WEIGHT (COMBAT)

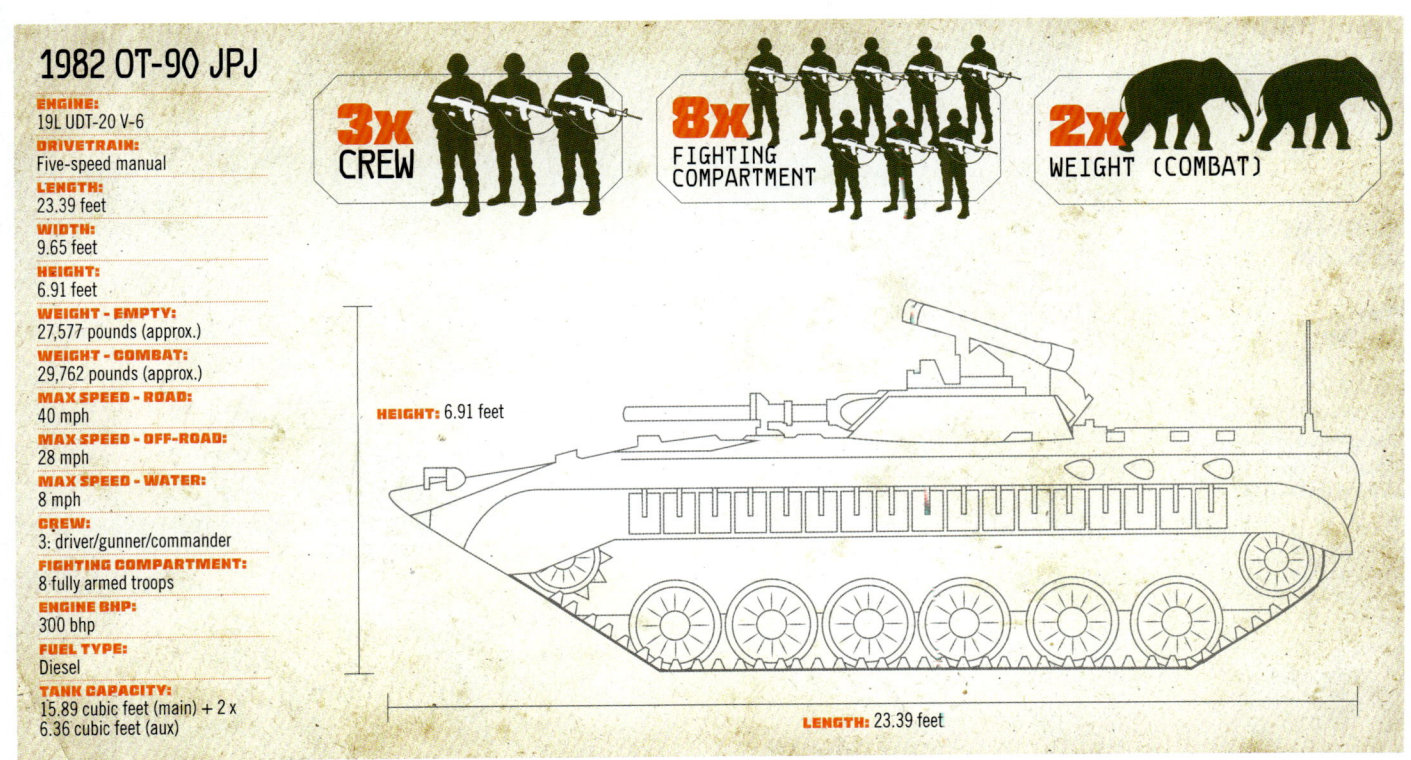

HEIGHT: 6.91 feet
LENGTH: 23.39 feet

EXTREME • TWO-TRACK MIND

The Millennial Falcon

She May Not Look Like Much, But She's Got it Where it Counts

By John Schwartze
Photography By Kenda Lenseigne

DRAGON WAGON

CAB:
MK48

CHASSIS:
1994 M932A2

ENGINE:
Cummins 6CTA 8.3L

TRANSMISSION:
Allison five-speed

OVERALL LENGTH:
32 feet

WIDTH:
96 inches

HEIGHT:
12½ feet

URL:
slicknessindustries.com

Millenials are often looked at as a bunch of undisciplined commitment-phobes. Talk-show panels discuss their unconventional proclivities like a bunch of jabbering scientists hypothesizing about Dolly the cloned sheep. Although this age group might be lambasted for defying norms that many people regard as the zenith of human existence, sometimes you've got to wonder if they've got things more figured out than you'd care to admit. Nicholas Bauer is one such member of this generation who isn't putting an image-driven lifestyle ahead of pragmatism. Unlike many who now live hand to mouth for the sake of keeping up appearances, he's too busy building cool sh*t and enjoying the wanderlust it affords him.

"As a millennial, rising home prices have far exceeded both income growth and inflation during this modern period, in the Phoenix, Arizona, area. I realized that financing a home is a serious 30-year fixed commitment that I don't want. I wanted a home that I could build with cash and no financing, one that can adapt to the modern American economic times by moving anywhere, over any terrain, when required. I enjoy living a completely debt-free lifestyle, even with a limited budget," Bauer says. Did an image of your most recent credit card statement just come to mind? Contain your reluctant jealousy and read on.

Nick's an automotive engineer by trade and has done everything from designing Local Motors' Rally Fighters (covered in RECOIL Issue 14), to serving as head of manufacturing at Thor Trucks, to working as a mechanical engineer at Nikola — two companies quickly giving Tesla a run for its money in the electric semi-truck space. That said, it's clear he's got the acumen to design and build damn near anything on his own. While some retiring baby boomers are selling off everything and traveling the country in an expensive RV, Nick went about it in reverse. The vehicle you see here is affectionately referred to as the Dragon Wagon.

At first blush it looks like some sort of bastardized HEMTT, because it came to Nick as a work in progress, started by the previous owner. While the cab is from an Oshkosh MK48, the running gear is actually from a BMY M932A2 6x6 truck, which consists of a Cummins 6CTA 8.3L motor and Allison five-speed with selectable, low-range, six-wheel drive. Since it's a civilian motor, parts are much easier to get. In the front camper section, the engine cover is custom and stylized to access the engine just like it is on a HEMTT.

"It's extremely nimble due to its tractor truck wheelbase, the shortest of all the M900 series 5-tons at only 2½ feet longer (2.58 to be exact), than a Ford Excursion. It's also very light, weighing in at just under 26,000 pounds and thus is fully street legal in the USA without the need for a CDL if not used for non-commercial purposes and as a private residence," Nick says. "It has a top speed of 65 mph and a reliable cruising speed of 55 mph, it gets a confirmed 8 mpg on the highway at 55 mph, 3 mpg off-road, and can hold 110 gallons of diesel for a range of 800 miles on road or 330 miles off-road."

The splicing of two different truck DNAs understandably led to some Frakensteining to make them get along. The front frame was extended and boxed in with ½-inch plate to make it more resilient in case it needs to be picked up by a wrecker. "The steering is custom, with a 180-degree in-and-out steering shaft that adapts the forward control MK48 cab to the 5-ton tractor box. The steering arm is push/pull and hydraulically assisted with a ram on the passenger side," Nick says. Making it livable came about by adding a 1987 Fleetwood Prowler camper. Although a box of this era may not have been his first choice, the Craigslist find was cheap, practical, and had a low ceiling height that'd be proportional to the size of the cab.

Some of the more mechanically inclined reading this may be asking how he grafted living quarters to frame. "The camper sits atop a pivoting subframe, which allows the camper to move independently of the Dragon Wagon's frame," Nick

Home, sweet self-reliant home.

The Dragon Wagon's forward control steering box linkage is a work of art, and not inconsiderable ingenuity.

says. "I designed and prototyped this on another, smaller expedition vehicle I own. The original design is based on the three-point camper pivot engineered by Mercedes-Benz on the Unimog 404 series. Without the pivoting subframe, the camper would be ripped apart when the Dragon Wagon's frame flexes."

"After lifting the camper in the air, I cut the fifth-wheel tongue and suspension off. My pivoting subframe had alignment tabs that allowed me to perfectly center it in place underneath the Prowler's frame. It was then lowered and driven to an area where it could be welded to the subframe pivots I constructed," Nick says. The rear frame was too short for the camper, so Nick cut the horns off and water-jetted about another 5 feet of frame section that he welded on to support the rear camper pivot and tow hooks for anything he wants to pull with it.

The camper has 300 watts of solar from Renogy 100-watt 12-volt monocrystalline panels, 200ah worth of energy storage in 12-volt SLA batteries, a Xantrex PROWatt 2000 for the inverter, and a Xantrex C40 charge controller. "The current setup is more than enough to run my laptop, LED lights inside, and water pump for the shower," Nick says. The cab was upgraded with a GPS speedometer and VDO gauges to replace unreliable military units for all engine temps as well as rearview and passenger-side cameras with a 4-inch monitor for all the blind spots.

"Future camper mods include 1kW worth of solar and 20 kWh worth of storage using Nissan Leaf cells in between the area of the cab and camper. I wish to build a self-sufficient home and 48V DC power supply large enough to do DC arc and MIG welding with a modern inverter and split A/C for cooling using nothing but the sun for power. The goal is to be completely self-sufficient without the need to spend money on any consumables," Nick says.

Although it won't do anything in less than 12 parsecs, we're impressed by both the engineering to make it livable and highway compatible, as well as the practical repurposing of a remaindered military vehicle for a nomadic lifestyle unhindered by debt. Could Nick be pioneering a new genre of "mobile homes" that'd appeal to an entire generation that major automakers can't seem to successfully engage? Since he is in fact offering to build other similar vehicles for those who can come to an appropriate negotiation, we're wondering if Nick's going to be the next Elon Musk. He's definitely someone we'll keep an eye on and anxiously await his next project. If he starts dating Amber Heard, we'll be first in line to buy stock in any IPO that he's pulling the strings on.

Isolating the camper shell from the frame took a lot of work, but it means the toughest terrain can be tackled without things coming apart at the seams.

In 2010, a standoff with police in Hoonah, Alaska, on the northeast shore of Chichagof Island led to a shootout that resulted in two officers being killed and the suspect barricading himself inside a house. Alaska State Trooper Rodney Dial responded to the call that day and came to a sobering realization — local law enforcement needed an armored vehicle. Alas, not one could be found in the entire state. After the situation came to an end, his search began for a platform that could be used to respond to similar confrontations in the future.

Rodney took it upon himself to research this category of vehicles and quickly discovered how cost prohibitive it'd be to get a modern one

Cars Against Humanity

People Suck. That's Why Having Your Own Personal APC Makes Sense When Things Go Haywire

By John Schwartze
Photography By Jesse D. Ranke

with all the bells and whistles better-funded departments had. That led to scouring forums and websites dedicated to surplus military vehicles that could be purchased for considerably less. After poking around the interweb for a while, Rodney found this six-wheeled beast owned by a militia member in the Midwest who had a brush with the law and was forced to sell it. Upon dropping around $22,000 for the vehicle itself, and then about another $5,000 having it shipped to Alaska, he was now the proud owner of a 1956 Alvis Saracen FV603 Mark V.

To provide a little background, the Saracen FV600 series was an armored personnel carrier (APC) produced by British manufacturer Alvis from the early '50s up to the mid '70s. Many of them are still in use today throughout the globe. This model of APC was often seen during the Troubles in Northern Ireland, and you may have also recognized a few of them in Stallone's *Judge Dredd* movie. The Mark V is an up-armored variant of the FV603 model and, according to Rodney, can withstand a 20-pound landmine as well as .50-caliber armor-piercing rounds. The factory ballistic glass is around 6 inches thick. The vehicle can hold 10 people including the driver and gunner, but it isn't amphibious.

After taking delivery of the vehicle, it quickly became a maintenance nightmare. The startup procedure required checking dozens of fluid levels, and the amount of oil it leaked rivaled the Exxon Valdez. The recurring mechanical issues, coupled with the fact that parts had to be shipped over from Europe, consistently sidelined it. The original Rolls-Royce powertrain with its fluid flywheel system was only getting a top speed of about 40 mph — when it ran.

Some additional research, and the good fortune of being located near one of the best diesel mechanics in the state, led to swapping out the drivetrain with a Navistar DT 466 six-cylinder diesel engine with an Allison automatic transmission, which was sourced from a dump truck. With the addition of a handmade gas tank, K&N custom intake, and specially made exhaust system, the performance was dramatically improved. Top speed is now about 70 mph, and mileage is up to a surprising average of 15 mpg (not bad for 11 tons).

Rodney also installed a new bumper system, reinforced deck plating on the sides, custom front armor, interior gun mounts, a ladder for the turret, additional lighting, and a police radio, among other touches. Although Rodney has retired from active duty and is currently mayor of Ketchikan, the vehicle is still available to local law enforcement if needed. Operating it is similar to driving a heavy truck, although visibility is understandably limited.

Like any heavy-duty commercial vehicle, it uses air brakes. Currently, the vehicle is only two-wheel drive but can be made 4WD — at the moment Rodney has it disconnected. The independent center wheels serve as backup to keep the vehicle stable and driving in case the others are destroyed and function on a hydraulic system that can be raised to make tighter turns. Rodney tells us it has a better turning radius than his pickup.

You might be asking yourself how it's possible to own one of these

The owner fabricated a one-piece removable front cowling with extra armor and ballistic glass.

Among the touches on the interior are a tank control panel from an M1A1 Abrams as well as an air defense control unit from a Canadian tank (mostly for the coolness factor).

The interior also sports small arms gun locks, survival gear, and can hold 10 passengers.

unless your golfing buddies work for the State Department. It's actually easier than you might think. Rodney tells us no special permitting was required to purchase it because it was shipped over as "demilitarized," meaning the grenade launchers and guns are disabled. The main armament was originally a Browning .30 cal, but Rodney replaced the barrel with one from a 20mm Vulcan cannon, which is merely for looks. Rodney does have a .50-cal BMG that he could use in the periscope-equipped turret if needed.

"People interested in purchasing a vehicle like this should search the military forums online," Rodney says. "There's a few different companies that sell military surplus vehicles. It's not easy to find one like this for sale in the country, but you can definitely find one in Europe and import it. Sometimes they have similar ones on eBay under the military vehicles section. If you buy one, you have to do one of two things: Understand that it's something you can just drive on a limited basis because they break down periodically, or you're going to have to modernize it with a current drivetrain and other components."

As was the case with Rodney, owning one will require finding a specialized mechanic who knows how (and is willing) to service it, upgrade it, and can possibly fabricate parts. Given the inflated weight, if you get it stuck somewhere you better have the number for a big-rig tow truck company saved on your phone.

To comply with the formalities for street legality, Rodney had to get it inspected, pay for a surety bond, and register it as a special-use vehicle. Believe it or not, it's insured through a well-known insurance provider and only costs him about $400 annually. "People need to make sure they get a vehicle like this titled so they can register it," Rodney says. "Every state is different on what they'll allow and consider 'special use,' but I registered it in a similar manner as companies that take old amphibious WWII vehicles and use them for tourists."

If you're part of the thin blue line and having trouble convincing the tribal elders why they should appropriate funds to acquire a vehicle like this, be sure and remind them about the situation that prompted Rodney to purchase his. If that doesn't work, try mentioning Shawn Nelson, who stole an M60A3 Patton tank from a National Guard armory in 1995 and went on a rampage in San Diego, California. You could also relay the "killdozer" case of Marvin Heemeyer, who rigged up his D355A bulldozer with extra armor before deciding to go out and demolish several buildings in Granby, Colorado, in reaction to his ongoing disputes with city officials.

Rodney's vehicle might've already looked familiar to you, as it's also been featured on an episode of *Doomsday Preppers*. If you're looking to get one for a SHTF situation, it's perfectly legal (and we think commendable) for private citizens to procure a Saracen and vehicles of the same ilk. See the sidebar for used military vehicle resources. Just like having an AR, though, you're bound to get resistance from the local yokels who want to undermine your ability to own it on the grounds that it's impractical, threatening, and that you "don't need it." We're sure you've heard all these arguments before. Anyone who thinks the worst examples of human nature only exist in third-world countries is clearly well on their way to Mensa membership. Think we're immune to a failed state? Go repeat remedial world history. Go directly to remedial world history. Do not pass "Go." Do not collect $200.

At this point Rodney estimates he has about $120,000 of his own money sunk into the Saracen, but has it out on the road regularly and might even be spotted in a local drive-thru. Something about a politician who owns an APC makes us want to reach deep into our pockets to help him with his future campaign endeavors. Hopefully, his next step is running for Congress.

1956 ALVIS SARACEN FV603 MARK V

MOTOR: DT 466 six-cylinder diesel
TRANSMISSION: Allison automatic
LENGTH: Approx. 15 feet
WIDTH: Approx. 8 feet
HEIGHT: Approx. 9 feet, 5 inches
WEIGHT: Approx. 22,000 pounds
TOP SPEED: Approx. 70 mph

» MILITARY VEHICLE RESOURCES

http://hmvf.co.uk
https://tanks-alot.co.uk/military-vehcles-for-sale
www.usmilitaryvehicles.com
www.milweb.net

Snakpak

A Pilot Converted This Aircraft Provisioning Truck into His One-of-a-Kind Home on Wheels

By Patrick McCarthy
Photography By Zack Podell

"In spring of 2021, I camped out at Shadow Mountain. I parked with the deck facing the Tetons and raised the box up. Every morning, I would conjure up two shots of espresso, sit out in my swing chair, and listen to the wind through the aspen trees, thinking about how lucky I am to be alive." — Mark Pankey

When COVID-19 hit, it drastically affected the work environment for many Americans. Some began working remotely, while others were forced into reduced hours or lost their jobs entirely. Mark Pankey had been working as a first officer (copilot) for Southwest Airlines since 2016. Prior to that job, he spent 20 years in the U.S. Air Force, most of which was as a fighter pilot flying F-16s. After transitioning to civilian life, Pankey felt a lingering desire for independence and adventure in the great outdoors. Strangely, COVID presented the opportunity he had been waiting for — a sudden reduction in demand for flights caused Southwest to seek volunteers who were willing to take up to five years off with partial pay.

Pankey accepted the offer and used this sabbatical to tackle a project he had daydreamed about for years: building a DIY off-grid home on a commercial truck chassis.

The seed for this idea was planted after Pankey's first year flying for Southwest. Like many pilots, he commuted to the nearest major city (Denver) before work and spent much of his time between flights in hotels. In order to save some money, he bought a Ford Econoline cargo van and converted it into a "crash pad" he could sleep comfortably in. It worked but wasn't ideal. Pankey recalls, "I was leaning toward something a little bigger that I could stay in much longer — possibly full time. I wanted to be able to live completely off-grid and be totally self-sustaining." He discussed this plan with one of his pilot friends, and that friend soon sent him a screenshot of a Ford F-650 box truck that was up for auction. In an almost-poetic twist, it was a retired provisioning truck that had been used to load snacks and beverages into Southwest Airlines flights. As a result, this unusual vehicle included a built-in hydraulic scissor lift that raises the box and deck roughly 20 feet in the air.

After bidding against only one other person, Pankey won the auction in April 2020 for a mere $3,300. Two days later, he flew to Seattle-Tacoma airport to pick it up ... wearing his full work uniform. A supervisor in a fluorescent vest was baffled to see a Southwest pilot picking up a

EXTREME • SNAKPAK | **275**

Pankey put a new roof on the box that's 2 feet higher on one side and 10 inches higher on the other. This provided room for side windows and a queen-sized loft bed.

An ECM Synchronika espresso machine and V-Titan 64 grinder sit atop the custom live-edge kitchen countertop.

A Nature's Head composting toilet and Aston Orbitus frameless shower provide all the comfort of a proper bathroom. There's a second exterior shower head for rinsing off on the back deck.

This corner contains Pankey's gun safe as well as the Icom 7300 ham radio and Victron Energy solar power system.

Southwest provisioning truck, but eventually handed over the keys and paperwork.

Back home in Colorado, Pankey's neighbors dubbed the truck Snak-Pak due to the Southwest slogan emblazoned on the sides of the box, so he decided to leave the lettering in place. However, its flat fiberglass roof was replaced with a single-slant metal roof and a support structure Pankey custom-fabricated. Logs were milled to create a rear wall with a rustic cabin look, and skis and snowboards were cut up to fill gaps around the new taller roof. Water runs through a gutter into a rain-harvesting filtration system; there's also a 55-gallon freshwater tank on-board. At the front of the box, Pankey converted the 9x8-foot deck into a comfy patio, complete with custom-made French doors, artificial turf, a removable table, tiki torches, and a Traeger 575 smoker.

Pankey gutted the interior of the box and lined it with closed-cell foam

insulation, then added stained and sealed aspen wood flooring, rough cedar plank walls and ceiling, and a natural flagstone entryway. A shoe and coat rack near the entrance is flanked by a spacious kitchen with a live-edge wood countertop and shelves. The kitchen contains a deep sink, Webasto diesel/kerosene stove, 6.9-cubic-foot fridge/freezer, and high-end espresso machine. Opposite this area, there's a frameless all-glass shower and composting toilet. A large loft area contains a queen-sized Tempurpedic bed beneath the remote-controlled skylight. The truck is equipped with an Espar Hydronic M12 heater/boiler, Isotemp 4-gallon water heater, radiant heated flooring, a Dwarf 3kw tiny wood stove, and a DC mini split air conditioner. Other highlights include a gun safe, mini bar with humidor, JVC/Rockford Fosgate sound system, movie projector with pull-down screen, CB and ham radios, and a sophisticated power system with three 375W roof-mounted solar panels, two 300Ah lithium batteries, and a Champion 4500 generator.

Pankey says he did 99.9 percent of the work on this truck himself, and it certainly wasn't easy. "I worked on this project from 5 a.m. to midnight (on average) every day for a total of seven months and lost about 20 pounds … I sold and gave away pretty much everything I owned minus all my fun

There's a Traeger smoker, artificial turf, and a seating area on the front patio. This area is level with the floor of the box when it's fully raised.

2000 FORD F-650 AIRCRAFT PROVISIONING TRUCK

DRIVETRAIN: Cummins 5.9L 24-valve diesel with Allison 643 4-speed automatic transmission

BUILD TIME: 7 months for initial build, upgrades are ongoing

BUILD COST: $3,300 for truck / $40,000 total

OWNER & BUILDER: Lt. Col. Mark "Spanky" Pankey, USAF, Ret.

INSTAGRAM ACCOUNTS: @snakpak20 / @spanky301

stuff — mountain bike, skis, kayak, a few guns, fishing gear, camera equipment, etc." He estimates total cost for the project was roughly $40,000. But after living in SnakPak and traveling the western U.S. for the last two years, he says it was all worth it. "This entire journey has been the most incredible time of my life. You really learn who you are when you do something you've never done before and challenge yourself to be uncomfortable in the unknown. I would not change a thing if I had to do it all over."

Center: Basking in the Northern Lights at a campsite in Montana. Photo by Anna Wilbur (@thescenicroutewest).

Right: SnakPak carries a mountain bike and Sur Ron e-bike on-board for shorter outings. The F-650 is also set up to tow Pankey's Toyota Tacoma via a heavy-duty trailer hitch and tow bar.

What Da Hell Ahh You?

Meet the Predator 6.6 — an RV That's Actually Meant to Travel on Something Other Than Paved Roads

By John Schwartze
Photography By Eddie Sanderson

It's funny to see the amount of coin some people drop on RVs that are about as robust as Gersh Kuntzman's rifle skills. If you own a Silver Crown, Prevost, or Goss motorhome, you may think you have the Hearst Castle on wheels, but the joke's on you. Virtually all modern RVs are two-wheel drive and have the ride height of a lowered Monte Carlo, so where can you go? You're relegated to RV parks, stacked up alongside a bunch of other glampers in what looks like a cross between a bus yard and a mobile home park.

While that may suit some people's idea of a sound investment and "getting away from it all" just fine, others prefer enjoying a remote camping or hunting trip on God's green splendor. If only there were a durable off-road vehicle capable of venturing out to the middle of nowhere.

That was exactly Hunter RMV founder Keith Storey's impetus for creating the Predator 6.6. You may recognize the foundation for this vehicle if you spent any time as a ground pounder. With a history of refurbishing and selling military equipment, Keith already had exposure to plenty of capable platforms. So the light bulb moment came — why not combine the luxury of a high-end trailer with the resilience of a military chassis? His first experiment along those lines was to use an M939 6x6 as the foundation for his personal rig. Its ability to meet the demands of remote treks and the interest it generated began the domino effect.

When it came to executing the idea as a business venture, Keith's next task was building an RV on what he considers the Cadillac of military vehicles — a Stewart & Stevenson LMTV chassis. Why? They're resilient, the taxpayers already picked up the tab, and, like other discarded military vehicles, they're routinely auctioned off with very low mileage. Another reason is they're all-wheel drive and powered by Caterpillar engines and Allison transmissions, two names known for longevity and being able to climb like a mountain goat.

Ticking off another important box, the Predator 6.6 is multi-fuel capable, giving it the ability to run on kerosene,

With great ground clearance, the Predator 6.6 can reach remote destinations with ease. Try that with a new Prevost. Actually, no … don't try it.

While the exterior may be intimidating, the interior has all the appointments you'd expect from a high-end RV.

Jet A, and various non-domestic diesel types. (Many trucks have emission controls that will not run outside the continental U.S. because the engine is too sensitive to the sulfur levels in the fuels.) To top it off, each vehicle has a central tire inflation system inside the cab, allowing the driver to regulate tire pressure to better handle softer terrain.

Every Predator 6.6 has about 1,000 hours of labor and fabrication invested in it. Once an appropriate chassis is sourced, it goes through a meticulous inspection and replacement of seals, belts, hoses, fluids, and other components prior to starting the build. The 4x4 version is fitted with a 19x8-foot Forest River box, with a slide-out living area, full A/C and heat, and a 5.5kW LP or full diesel generator, just to name a few features. A 6x6 version is also available with a longer box made by Total Composites out of Germany.

When it comes to playing around with options, you have quite a bit of bandwidth to build it the way you want. You can specify the water and fuel tank capacities; add a full solar array; throw in under-floor heating; upgrade with high-speed gearing; choose fixed, bunk, or retractable beds; select a bath or shower stall — the list goes on.

You can expect a year's warranty on the box and 90 days on the vehicle itself. Even if it can't be fixed locally, Hunter RMV can fly out one of their techs to your location.

What Storey created is definitely one of those forehead-smacking ideas of, "Why didn't anyone do this sooner?" Although it may appear slightly intimidating, with great ground clearance and a very easy-to-drive, quiet ride, it'll take you in comfort and safety with four to six of your buddies to places other rigs just can't get to. Out the door, you're looking at spending $200,000 to $300,000, depending on your options.

We live in a society where there's a misconception that the more you spend, the better you'll get. Compared to many of the land yachts you see out there, the value of which typically sinks faster than Enron stock, the Predator 6.6 answers a lot of the expectations you'd have from a return-on-your-investment standpoint. Rental and leasing options aren't currently available, but may be at some point down the road. If you're a true four-seasons outdoor person, this may be the vehicle you've been waiting for and never knew existed. The Predator 6.6 has certainly redefined recreational travel.

HUNTER RMV PREDATOR 6.6

ENGINE: Caterpillar 6.6L six-cylinder turbocharged diesel
TRANSMISSION: 7-speed Allison automatic
LENGTH: 27 feet, 6 inches
WIDTH: 96 inches
HEIGHT: 13 feet, 2 inches
WHEELBASE: 153.5 inches
GROUND CLEARANCE: 22 inches
HORSEPOWER: 225
TORQUE: 637 lb-ft
PAYLOAD: 5,000 pounds
CURB WEIGHT: 17,214 pounds
TIRES: 395/85/R20 Goodyear MV/T
BRAKES: Air actuated
TOWING LOAD: 10,362 pounds
PAYLOAD CAPACITY: 6,000 pounds
RANGE: 400+ miles
PRICE: Starting at around $200,000
URL: hunterrmv.com

Work Horse

With Roots in the Austrian Military, the Pinzgauer is a Proven Off-Road Beast

By David H. Martin

Sturdy and agile as the Alpine mountain horse she was named after (and not the cattle breed that shares its name), the Pinzgauer was born and bred in the European Alps during the early 1970s, then proved worldwide militarily from desert to jungle rivers for decades. These early generation Pinzgauers — now old enough to be exempt from certain U.S. non-EPA import equipment requirements — were gradually decommissioned and released from service by Swiss and Austrian military forces, driving demand throughout the United States and the world.

Today, a vast yet scattered network exists among thousands of knowledgeable off-road Pinz enthusiasts, gathering everywhere from the Colorado Rockies to the Hawaiian Islands. Though on rare occasions you might find a street-legal Pinz tucked nicely into an average parking space, Pinz owners universally own a second vehicle for daily or long-distance driving and preserve the Pinz for hunting, special touring, or work as ranch vehicles. Increasingly, the demand is ratcheting up among savvy preppers looking for a relatively affordable world-class vehicle designed to remain decidedly low-tech, field-maintainable, and (perhaps most important to survivalists) resilient. On that fateful day when all other land transportation grinds to a panicked halt, Pinz drivers claim they'll keep on rolling — along with 11 of their closest amigos.

So when a well-used, low-profile 1975 model was discovered recently, we here at *OG* jumped at the chance to introduce this high-mobility all-terrain vehicle to our readers. During the process, we discovered some tips that will help our readers select and plan their own bug-out vehicle layout.

Go Hard or Go Soft

We located this Pinz parked on a southwest Florida ranch, the site of a private shooting resort. A breeze blew openly through the rolled-up canvas canopy roof and sides that marked the Pinz as a 710M model. This model was the four-wheel-drive version, but there are many six-wheel-drive 712 models available, which can sometimes be found with snowcat-style tracks. Pinz owners told us the six-wheel version provides a nicer road ride, but the four-wheelers are more nimble in tight quarters. The Pinz is available in the rare 710K van model with a sheetmetal roof and hard-panel sides, which is more ideal as a bug-out vehicle considering a soft top is a security risk and vulnerable to cold weather.

Depending on condition, a Pinz 710M four-wheel soft top might range from $8,000 to $14,000. The 712 six-wheeler could cost anywhere from $12,000 to $20,000, says Dan Fanning of the 35-member Rocky Mountain Pinzgauers, one of the largest Pinz clubs in the United States. Other vehicles currently located online can command higher prices with add-ons and customizations.

No Smashing Pumpkins

The torque-friendly Pinz was known for its ability to keep going in high water experienced during summer monsoons, owing in part to the momentum maintained by shift-on-the-fly capabilities. This kept a ranch owner's family high and dry with 360-degree visibility for wildlife and livestock viewing. The Pinz punched through creeks, easily plunging down steep embankments and up far sides.

This could be in part because of its complete absence of front and rear center axle "pumpkins" common on 4x4 trucks. On other vehicles, these can leave you high-centered, meaning one or some of your tires aren't touching terra firma because the underbelly is caught up on steep trails or boulders. Without pumpkins, a Pinz is far less likely to get high-centered. One look fore and aft reveals

Optional trailers feature locking hubs to prevent roll away on slopes. They can hold a week's worth of supplies, leaving more room for loved ones and your survival group inside the vehicle.

amazing 45-degree approach and departure angles, with almost 15-inch ground clearance in a narrow and nimble radius that appears no larger than a Jeep.

To create the amazing clearance and space, Austrian Steyer-Daimley-Puch engineers placed the forward-mounted motor in a slightly offset angle, situated beneath a removable cowling between driver and shotgun seat. The 2.5L aluminum four-cylinder inline block is air cooled by an enormous fan, making 92 horses at 133 lb-ft of torque at 2,000 rpm, drawing upon dual, two-barrel Solex36 NDIX carbs, similar to the Volkswagen engines of the early 1970s. (This engine was consistently produced from 1971 through 1987, while later and even current models went to a turbodiesel VW engine.)

The Pinz features a five-speed manual transmission with a short driveshaft fitted into a two-speed transfer case just forward of the rear axle, effectively providing the driver with 10 forward speeds and two speeds in reverse. They're all closely meshed and geared low, starting with a 5.33:1 first gear ratio and no overdrive. This allows the Pinz to cruise at 60 mph, making about 15 to 16 mpg on a 20-gallon fuel tank for a max range of about 300 miles, although off-road usage in low range will seriously reduce that. A floor shift lever took us through the five speeds, while a shorter high and low-range control lever was close at hand.

Advanced for its time and still solid by today's standards, the hydraulic shift-on-the-fly levers allow for four-wheel drive and the locking of front and rear differentials.

This Austrian workhorse can climb mountains, brave high water, and endure blizzard conditions. Photos courtesy of the Rocky Mountain Pinzgauers.

Owners speak of the famous Pinz "backbone" as a massively overbuilt housing containing the drivetrain and forming a support system for the chassis. The suspension is a swing-axle type, with portal units taking power directly from the differentials to the wheels. The differentials may be locked. Dual rear coil-springs provide a secure and sure-footed connection on uneven or rain-rutted inclines. Power steering isn't included, preventing over-steerage and eliminating one more thing to go wrong. Six-wheel-drive models make use of leaf springs.

The hydraulic transmission was "revolutionary for its time" because it allowed the driver to shift into four-wheel drive without exiting the vehicle to lock out external hubs, Pinz enthusiasts say. Pointing out the three levers located centrally on the dash at the driver's right hand, one owner said the first lever enables the driver to engage the forward two wheels on the fly without losing momentum on steep grades. The second and third levers enable the driver to lock out the front and rear locking differentials for the ultimate in troop or utility transport, respectively.

An external dual-battery compartment provides easy maintenance access via a 24-volt system. The access is consistent with the design philosophy, complemented by a series of circuit breakers and no electrical fuses, including an ignition system sealed against water. Electronics consist largely of the coil, a generator, and spark plugs.

The driver and passenger compartments are separated by a removable series of heavy-gauge wire fence-like panels that don't impede visibility or airflow. Cabin

circulation is improved thanks to multiple fans. The rear compartment bench seats are accessible through a rear swing-out half-door. The rear backs of the bench seats may be folded down to provide a flatbed for transporting pallet-sized equipment. In keeping with its military heritage, the spartan interior is devoid of any nonfunctional frills.

The Pinz's open-door policy makes entering, exiting, and protecting your ride pretty easy — even with a 16-inch Colt AR and SureFire suppressor in hand. Though it also leaves your cargo unsecured and you more exposed to the elements.

Worldwide Application

The Rocky Mountain Pinzgauers have assisted authorities during snowstorms by serving as medical transports and emergency search vehicles, Fanning says. But for fun, the group stages "treffens" or gatherings throughout Colorado and even in out-of-state detours like Moab, where owners navigate rocky passes, climb slabs of granite, and punch through snow.

Having acquired his first Pinz 20 years ago, Robert Rainek of the Milwaukee-based North American Pinzgauers said he originally had no idea how dependable and bombproof the Pinz were until he attended some off-road demos in Leadville, Colorado, where the Pinz ran side by side with Jeeps, Hummers, and Land Rovers. He now has 50 and is constantly impressed with the level of maintenance the surplus Pinzs arrive with when they are located, traded, or resold.

"Now the preppers aren't looking for something too fancy," Rainek said. "Just something sort of low key. Many people are amazed that the vehicles were so advanced, even by today's standards. These saw extensive use from North Africa to the Middle East, Australia, and throughout Europe."

Rainek said potential buyers were concerned about the engines overheating in the desert. Fanbelts were undone on test models and the engine still did not overheat, he said. And these have higher ground clearance than military Humvees, he said, due to the portal axles, even with the standard military tires, while many opt for Super Swampers and other upgrades. We have long looked to the Swiss and to Austria for excellent weapons system engineering and innovation, and like a true world-class weapon, the Pinz has proven itself around the world — from tropical terrain to snow-capped mountains.

If you're looking for a conversation starter, the Pinz draws a crowd. If you're looking to get away from the crowd, you might not find anything more sure-footed except the Alpine horse. But then you won't be able to bring a dozen of your closest friends, shouting in your best Austrian accent, "Get to da Pinzgauer!"

1975 PINZGAUER 710M (SOFT TOP)

ENGINE: 2.5L four-cylinder, air-cooled aluminum block

HORSEPOWER: 92 at 4,000 rpm, with 132 lb-ft of torque at 2,000 rpm.

TRANSMISSION: Five-speed transfer case, with two-speed high and low range for 10 forward speeds and two reverse speeds

WHEEL BASE: 86.6 inches

FUEL CAPACITY: 13 feet, 2 inches

WHEELBASE: 86.6 inches

FUEL CAPACITY: 20 gallons

APPROACH ANGLE: 45 degrees

DEPARTURE ANGLE: 45 degrees

RAMP BREAKOVER: 152 degrees

SEATS: (driver, front passenger, 10 in rear)

Upgrades:

Can you acquire something old, indestructible, and somewhat unique without the risk of being labeled a member of "a cultlike following?" Pinzgauer owners don't seem to mind, and increasingly these drivers are launching vehicle clubs, social media pages, and regional rallies, driving the desire for more modifications. The most popular upgrades for a Pinzgauer are:

› Ignition system: An improved aftermarket distributor cap and fully water-shielded wiring consistent with mil-spec protection can ensure starting capabilities in the harshest conditions. It's all compatible with the stock 24-volt dual battery system.

› Winch: Capable of being placed fore and/or aft on the Pinz, a winch can be used to assist with ascents, descents, or recovering stuck vehicles.

› Step assists: This improves one's safety while entering and exiting the high-riding vehicle. The looped steps are aftermarket single steps to be placed forward of the cab. The center-step assists fit centrally near the hub of the stock wheels and are said to not interfere with mobility or traction.

› Weapon storage: No bug-out vehicle is complete without weapon retention systems.

› Other considerations: The no-brainer is a tire upgrade, but there are other options, including but not limited to a toolkit (including winch gloves, tall jack, and tow strap), tire pump and repair kit, and extra fluids.

RECOIL OFFGRID

PRESENTS

DIY SURVIVAL

BEST HACKS FOR WORST-CASE SCENARIOS

ORDER TODAY AT
GUNDIGESTSTORE.COM
OR CALL **920.471.4522**